I FOUND
MY FRIENDS

Also by Nick Soulsby

Dark Slivers:
Seeing Nirvana in the Shards of Incesticide

I FOUND MY FRIENDS

The Oral History of

NIRVANA

NICK SOULSBY

THOMAS DUNNE BOOKS
St. Martin's Griffin
New York

CONTENTS

Acknowledgments   **xi**
Preface   **xv**

1.0   **First Fruit**   **1**
February to December 1987

2.0   **The First Album: Nirvana in Studio**   **17**
January 1988

3.0   **The Lost Drummer**   **25**
February to May 1988

4.0   **Becoming a Seattle Band**   **35**
April to June 1988

5.0   **Sub Pop and *Bleach***   **49**
June 1988 to January 1989

6.0 **First Tour, First Lessons**   **72**
February to July 1989

7.0 **Still Broke: Second Tour**   **94**
September to October 1989

8.0 **Young Band in New Land: Europe**   **107**
October to December 1989

9.0 **Home Soil**   **116**
January to February 1990

10.0 **Nobody Knows We're New Wave**   **133**
March to May 1990

11.0 **Intermission**   **150**
June to September 1990

12.0 **New Blood**   **168**
October to December 1990

13.0 **Corporate-Rock Whores**   **179**
January to July 1991

14.0 **Takeoff**   **198**
August to December 1991

15.0 **Falling Apart in Asia/Pacific**   **216**
January to February 1992

16.0 **Festival Season**   **233**
June to September 1992

17.0 **Politics, Pressure, and South America** 255
October 1992 to January 1993

18.0 *In Utero* 270
February to September 1993

19.0 **Creaking: The *In Utero* Tour** 285
October 1993 to January 1994

20.0 **One More Solo? The Curtain Falls** 302
February to April 1994

Timeline 319
Index 335

ACKNOWLEDGMENTS

Thank you to the following bands, musicians, and individuals for their support throughout this work—I always wanted to say more and more about each of you!

24-7 Spyz (Forrest), 3 Merry Widows (Charles Shipman, Alice Spencer, Sean Garcia, Marc Enger), Nirvana/Under Sin (Aaron Burckhard), Adam Kasper, Alex Kostelnik, Amorphous Head (Joe Goldring), André Stella, Jux County (Andrew Monley), Anxiety Prophets (Josh Kriz), Arm (Danielle Mommertz, Stephan Mahler, Marcus Grapmayer), Bad Mutha Goose (Tim Kerr), Barb Schillinger, Bayou Pigs (David Yammer), Becca Jones-Starr, Bhang Revival (Lori Joseph), Bible Stud (Glen Logan), Biquini Cavadão (Bruno Castro Gouveia), Björn Again (Rod Stephen), Black Ice (Duke Harner, Tony Poukkula), Blank Frank and the Tattooed Gods (Bill Walker), Blood Circus (Geoff Robinson), Bruce Pavitt, Butthole Surfers (Paul Leary), Calamity Jane (Lisa Koenig), Calamity Jane/Sister Skelter (Gilly Ann Hanner), Captain America (Andy Bollen, Gordon Keen), Carl Chalker (the Twist), Cat Butt (James Burdyshaw), Caustic Soda (Renée Denenfeld), Nirvana (Chad Channing), Charmin' Children

(JB Meijers), Cheater Slicks (Dana Hatch), Chemical People (Dave Naz), Chemistry Set (Scott Vanderpool), Chokebore (Troy von Balthazar), Claw Hammer (Jon Wahl), Cliffs of Dooneen (Lex Lianos, Flynn), Coffin Break (Peter Litwin), Come (Chris Brokaw, Thalia Zedek), Conrad Uno, Cordelia's Dad (Peter Irvine, Tim Eriksen), Cows (Kevin Rutmanis), Crash Worship, Crow (Peter Fenton), Crunchbird (Jaime Robert Johnson), Cynthia Bergen, Cypress Hill (B-Real), D.O.A. (Joe Keithley), Dangermouse (George Smith), Nirvana/Helltrout/Mico de Noche (Dave Foster), David Von Ohlerking, Death of Samantha (Doug Gillard), Defalla (Castor Daudt, Edu K), Dickless (Lisa Smith), Distorted Pony (Ted Carroll), Dominic Davi, Dr. Sin (Ivan Busic), Eleventh Dream Day (Janet Beveridge Bean, Rick Rizzo), Enas Barkho, Fitz of Depression (Ryan von Bargen), Flor de Mal (Marcello Cunsolo), Gillian G. Gaar, Girl Trouble (Bon von Wheelie), Gobblehoof (Tim Aaron), God Bullies (Mike Hard), Grinch (Billy Alletzhauser), Grind (Ben Munat, David Triebwasser, Pete Krebs), Gumball (Don Fleming), Half Japanese (Jad Fair), Haywire (Vadim Rubin), Heavy into Jeff (Robin Peringer), Hell's Kitchen (David Chavez), Helltrout (Jason Morales), Herd of Turtles (Shawn Lawlor), Hitting Birth (Daniel Riddle), Hole (Eric Erlandson, Jill Emery), Holy Rollers (Joseph Aronstamn), I Own the Sky (Joseph Hayden), Industrial Pirata (Elias Ziede), Inspector Luv and the Ride Me Babies (Ty Willman), Skin Yard (Jack Endino), Jacob's Mouse (Hugo Boothby, Jebb Boothby, Sam Marsh), Jardal Sebba, Jello Biafra, Jesse Harrison, Jim Merlis, JJ Gonson, Jonathan Burnside, Happy Dogs (Jose Soria), Kai Kln (Neil Franklin, Scott Anderson), Kaptain "Scott Gear" Skillit Weasel, Kevin Kerslake, Kill Sybil (Larry Schemel), King Krab (Nathan Hill), Knife Dance (Tom Dark), Leaving Trains (Falling James), Lisa Sullivan, Lonely Moans (J. M. Dobie, Shambie Singer), Loop (Robert Hampson), Los Brujos (Gabriel Guerrisi), Love Battery (Kevin Whitworth), Machine (John Purkey, Ryan Loiselle), Yellow Snow (Brian Naubert and Pat Watson), Sleeper Cell (Bobby Delcour), Hell Smells (Maria Mabra), Meat Puppets (Cris Kirkwood), Medelicious (Henry Szankiewicz), Hole (Melissa Auf der Maur), Mexican Pets (Patrick Clafferty), Midway Still (Paul Thomson), Monkeyshines (Tom Trusnovic), Mousetrap (Craig Crawford), Mudhoney (Steve Turner), My Name (Abe Brennan), Napalm Sunday (Ed Farnsworth), Nardwuar, New Radiant Storm King (Peyton Pinkerton, Matt Hunter), Nubbin (Timo Ellis), Nunbait (Shaun Butcher), Oily Bloodmen (Seth Perry), Pansy Division (Jon Ginoli), Paradogs (Eric Jeevers), Paul Harries, Helltrout/Landsat Blister (Paul Kimball), Pele (Ian Prowse), Pirata Industrial (Elias Ziede), Kill Rock Stars (Portia Sabin), Power of Dreams (Keith Walker), Psychlodds (Ryan Aigner), Rat at Rat R (John Myers, Victor Poison-Tete), Rawhead Rex (Eric Moore), Rhino Humpers (Brian Coloff), Roger Nusic, S.G.M. (Cole Peterson, Rich Credo), Saucer (Beau Fredericks, Fred Stuben, Scott Harbine), Screaming Trees (Mark Pickerel), Second Child (Damien Binder), Seven Year Bitch (Valerie Agnew), Shawna at Cosmic Primitive, Shonen Knife (Naoko Yamano), Sister Double Happiness (Gary Floyd, Lynn Truell), Sister Skelter (Chris Quinn), Slaughter Shack (Colin Burns, Dana Ong), Nisqually Delta Podunk Nightmare/Lush/Witchypoo/Kill Rock Stars (Slim Moon), Sons of Ishmael (Tim Freeborn, Mike Canzi, Paul Morris, Glenn Poirier, Chris Black), Soylent Green (Bruce Purkey), Sprinkler (Steve Birch), Steel Pole Bath Tub (Mike Morasky), Stone by Stone (Chris Desjardins), Strange Places (Xavier Ramirez), Sun City Girls (Alan Bishop), Surgery (John Leamy), Swallow (Chris Pugh, Rod Moody), Swaziland White Band (Lloyd Walsh, John Farrell, Dennis Fallon), Sweet Lickin' Honey Babes (Jim Roy), Tad (Tad, Josh Sinder, Kurt Danielson), Teenage Fanclub (Gerard Love), Television Personalities (Dan Treacy), Terry Lee Hale, the Bags (Crispin Wood), the Bombshells (Siobhan Duvall), the Boredoms (Yamantaka Eye), Buzzcocks (Steve Diggle), the Cateran (Cam Fraser, Murdo MacLeod), the Derelicts (Duane Lance

Bodenheimer), the Didjits (Rick Sims), the Doughboys (John Kastner), the Dwarves (Blag Dahlia), the Fluid (Matt Bischoff), the Gits (Steve Moriarty), the Guttersnipes (Andrew Rice, Mark Hurst, Michael McManus, Paul Brockhoff), the Jesus Lizard (David Yow), the Thrown Ups (John Leighton Beezer), the Wongs (Kevin Rose), Thinking Fellers Union Local 282 (Anne Eickelberg and Mark Davies), Thornucopia (Jed Brewer), Tracy Marander, Treacherous Jaywalkers (Josh Haden), Treehouse (Ronna Myles-Era, Damon Romero), Tumbleweed (Richard Lewis), Unrest (Mark Robinson), Unwound (Justin Trosper), Vampire Lezbos (David Whiting), Vegas Voodoo (Kevin Franke, Marc Bartholomew), Victim's Family (Tim Solyan), Volcano Suns (Peter Prescott), Vomit Launch (Lindsey Thrasher), Wool (Al Bloch, Franz Stahl), and Youri Lenquette.

PREFACE

BLAG DAHLIA, The Dwarves: The '90s were such a special time, full of warmth and good cheer—and Nirvana really helped that along by crying all the time, doing dope, and fucking ugly chicks . . . helping to bring flannel and heroin to the unwashed masses . . .

Kurt Cobain's demise was not a media event, or a breaking news story. Among the community of musicians to whom he was a well-liked friend, it was a death in the family. While speaking of those times means celebrating achievement and fun, for many of the people who tell this story it also means remembrance of pain. Death should never feel like a nothing; to most of the comrades sharing their memories with us, it still doesn't—and that's good. Nirvana was a bunch of normal guys sharing a musical life with thousands of other talented and dedicated individuals, and this is the story of the life they all shared.

Nirvana's tale is inseparable from that of the life and death of Kurt Cobain. His story, however, is not just the story of a normal man. It's about a guy who became part of the less than 1 percent of humanity who rise to the top of the creative professions; the one boy among Aberdeen, Washington's 18,000 residents to become a global legend. His death, at the peak of his fame, only increased his exceptionalism.

VICTOR POISON-TETE, Rat at Rat R: Why do and/or should we love Kurt Cobain and Nirvana? They will not be given the opportunity to disappoint us. No future song entitled "Smells Like the Interior of a New Lexus." No duets with a current octogenarian to broaden the audience demographic. No holiday specials or a department-store clothing line (pre-washed grunge apparel), sugary soda downloads, halftime wardrobe malfunctions, or attempts to build an alternative marketing strategy that actually works, only to turn around and appear on lamestream media shows that flash signs prompting you to clap or laugh. And Nirvana will never attempt to bring sexy back, buy a basketball team, or act as judge on a talent show.

This book came about while browsing the *Nirvana Live Guide,* a truly astounding website listing details of as many of Nirvana's performances as are known, and being fascinated by all the rarely mentioned bands. Many of them have vanished, leaving only names on old fliers but, by chance, live on through association with one of the world's most celebrated groups. Nirvana never felt it was above the many bands they befriended; they always felt they were part of the community who tell this tale rather than of the celebrity world they joined. This book is about the magic of everyday people doing something remarkable because they had the guts to ignore the naysayers and go for it. For the many people who were good enough to lend their time and energies, I hope you feel happy reading the result and it reminds you of your great times. It's been an honor to learn of your worlds—thank you.

For Nirvana fans, I hope it makes the fiction of the superstar feel closer to the reality of everyday life and gives you that sneaking feeling that you could be extraordinary too.

And Dad? Thanks for letting me sit by the bedside at the hospital with you and finish this—and for so much more besides.

I FOUND
MY FRIENDS

1.0

First Fruit
February to December 1987

One evening in April 1987, a sweaty-palmed and fidgety trio of young men purporting to be a band named Skid Row (and decidedly not the more famous hair-metal band) lined up at the doors of the Community World Theater, Tacoma—a ramshackle punk venue in a small town in Washington. There was no reason to notice them; they were nothing special. Just two house parties into their life as a band, with their first performance only a month earlier, this show was the big test. Their scrawny, fragile, and shy front man, at twenty years of age, wasn't even old enough to drink.

Sandwiched on a four-band bill, Skid Row's performance passed without incident or laurels.

BRIAN NAUBERT, Yellow Snow: A combination of having to tear down after our set, deal with our gear, and all the beer we drank—forty-ouncers of Old English, if I'm not mistaken—I'm sorry to admit it but I don't remember being impressed by anyone that night. We were a little bit shy and defensive because even though the punk scene welcomed us, we were not one of them. Yellow Snow was appreciated for having its own sound. Something that would be considered "indie" these days.

PAT WATSON, Yellow Snow: They were older than we were, I was sixteen, seventeen, high school—they seemed to be pushing past twenty. We were nervous because we were one of the young bands age-wise . . . We might have bailed, so I don't remember if I saw them. But while we were playing our set—it was someone's birthday in the band. so we played the Beatles' birthday song and some guy yelled out, "The Beatles suck!" Really loud. And then Kurt Cobain said, "Shut the fuck up, man! The fucking Beatles rule!" Everybody laughed and that guy didn't heckle us again.

BRUCE PURKEY, Soylent Green: They were unique. Honestly, I wasn't sure what to make of them at first—noisy, a bit chaotic, unpolished. They could've easily, at first blush, been one of those bands you see a couple of times then fades away, never to be seen again.

AARON BURCKHARD, Nirvana: I lived right across the alley from Dale Crover's house; I was 'round there all the time, at Melvins practice every day. So, Krist Novoselic brought Kurt 'round—first time we'd met—and the very next day they asked me if I wanted to play drums. They knew I was a drummer, they needed someone and I said, "Of course! Yes!" But I didn't have drums, so we drove up to a friend in Westport and he set us up with some drums, and that same night we were in Kurt's living room set up playing. That was late '86; we were a band for two or three months before we played our first show.

The soon-to-be Nirvana boys probably sorely underappreciated they had grown up just as a wave of musicians came through the remote Aberdeen, Washington, area. The community of musicians was small enough too that they all knew one another, even if the absence of outlets except parties and practices affected everyone.

TONY POUKKULA, Black Ice: That area cultivated a lot of talent . . . It was like there were layers of bands, so the band in front of us in school was Crystal Image, and part of that turned into Metal

Church—those guys were a year or two ahead of me and it was full of camaraderie, to the point they'd let us come watch them practice or they'd swing by our pad . . . Kurt used to come watch us too; he'd come watch just standing on our front porch—we had a big window, it was a beauty salon—he'd stand there and watch through the window . . . Dale Crover and I used to jam all the time—we used to live less than a mile from each other, so I'd go down there and we'd play Iron Maiden . . . Krist and Rob Novoselic were in there too—they lived just up from me, so I went over to their house and we listened to, when Metallica first came out, [a] Cliff Burton bass solo and we were all like, "That's *bass*?!" . . . We saw those guys at school—Krist towered over everybody; you knew when he walked in the room it was Krist. Nice guy, pretty intelligent. But Kurt was super-quiet . . . He was just one of those guys who would walk by and you just wouldn't notice him right off the bat. One day in school he passed up a note to the girl behind me; she passed it to me and it said, "Will you teach me to play guitar?" I told him, "Yeah, no problem." But it never happened.

DUKE HARNER, Black Ice: Since we were so young and there weren't any venues for young bands to play at, ours and other young bands mostly had small get-togethers at their practice rooms . . . As for the radio stations and newspapers, you had to be a big name or be playing at one of the top local clubs to even get any kind of mention; neither source did anything for the young bands on the Harbor. At the time we were growing up, there weren't any underage clubs or venues, so it was practice, practice, practice! . . . My cousin is married to Mike Dillard [the Melvins' original drummer] and asked if I cared if they came by . . . so they stopped in for about an hour. They didn't look too impressed but sat there and bullshitted us and had a few questions about amps and PA stuff. Later, I asked my cousin what they thought, and she said they weren't too into it: "No Ramones, no Sex Pistols, no Police, no Clash . . . no thanks!"

Nirvana's first public performance in March 1987, in the small town of Raymond, had relied on their friend's willingness to make the connections for them.

RYAN AIGNER, Psychlodds: I was at these rehearsals two or three times a week, so I was just listening over and over again to them doing their set. Probably after the fifth or sixth time this discussion starts up . . . I'm telling him, "Kurt, this doesn't sound that bad, you may not like it but it sounds OK," and he's like, "Yeah, I dunno . . ." He was pretty insecure about the whole thing. One time we had this discussion and I said, "I could picture this on the radio," and it was a real insult to him because our radio station locally had a bad reputation because they just played schlock rock. So I'm like, "No, that's not what I'm saying!" This is pre-'91, before anyone ever thought that there would be an alternative status-quo mainstream—it was insulting to insinuate that could ever happen, and I'd just done that. "How dare you say something like that! I wouldn't want that!" That's where the thing comes—"You don't believe me?" He replies, "No, no one would want to listen." I say, "I'll prove it to you . . ."

TONY POUKKULA: In the Raymond days, at that house, we'd party every night, doesn't matter what night it was! We'd have musicians in, didn't matter who you were, you could just come on down and play—not even necessarily bands, but play, we just wanted to hear. That house was very isolated, even if there was a fight out in the driveway it didn't affect anybody, very secluded.

RYAN AIGNER: I worked with a band called Black Ice. They were a very successful cover band that did shows locally . . . these guys seemed so skilled and so talented, so good technically . . . Tony Poukkula rented the house where the first Nirvana show went down—that's why it happened, because I'd worked with Black Ice. He was their guitar player.

TONY POUKKULA: I talked to Ryan and he was saying, "Hey, I've got these guys—Kurt, Krist, and Aaron—they've got a band together, they're coming up with some cool stuff, would you mind them coming by and jamming sometime?" It was Ryan's suggestion, and I just said, "Yeah, we're going all the time, just tell me when you want." It was pretty quick after that.

RYAN AIGNER: They didn't have the wherewithal, they didn't have the place, they didn't have the van, they didn't have the money, they didn't have the job . . . I was a carpet-layer so I had all these things at my disposal and I was thinking in terms of networking—that's how my mind worked. So I put these pieces together and casually said, "What are you guys doing Friday? Let's do this thing . . ." Initially there was a kneejerk "Nah, we better not" . . . I just finessed and kept it up—there wasn't a lot of pressure, they could go try it out and it'd be fun and they could try it out . . . It didn't take a lot of effort on their part, put it that way. It's about a forty-five-minute drive, so we pile in and start playing.

TONY POUKKULA: Ryan's good. He'll have made sure they had their act together before they came down. To me it was just going to be the regular thing: a jam session. I had my guitar warmed up by the time they were setting up . . . I didn't actually know the song. You'll hear me say "I don't know it!" That's why you hear the whammy bar going nuts, plus I was probably "on my way" . . . After Ryan told me, "Hey, they don't really jam with people," I was like, "Cool, I'll go grab a beer," so I sat my guitar down and went into the kitchen and after a little bit Jeff opened his jacket and pulled his collar out and showed me he had that recorder going. I said, "Right on, they actually sound pretty good. They've got some cool stuff." . . . They were really rough, but back then you can tell they were just trying to be themselves—coming up with some melody lines—it was different, definitely, to what we were used to. I was just having fun. Krist was standing on the coffee table with duct tape on his nipples and I was just sitting there laughing.

RYAN AIGNER: We weren't hated, but we weren't liked . . . . when you grow up in a conservative culture and you try to be liberal or avant-garde or artsy, then you get a kind of rejection—a feeling of "You're not welcome here." That's hard to take, growing up. The things you've heard, the negative things, about how Nirvana felt about Grays Harbor County, we didn't make that all up. We really wanted to be accepted by our peers and we really weren't until much later. It wasn't because we didn't try to do shows down here. It's what the Raymond show was—they went down, did their thing, and the crowd stood in the kitchen and went "Wow, what the hell is this?" I was in the room, Shelli [Dilley], Tracy [Marander] . . . about four of us who would have been at the rehearsal if they'd been back in Aberdeen while the Raymond crowd looked through from the kitchen thinking, What the hell is that? and not running into the room like they did in 1991, '92, '93—not pogoing like they did at the Coliseum. We didn't forget that. Standing on the stage at the Coliseum in '92, I was a youth-group advisor for our church and looking out in the crowd I saw kids from my youth group looking up at me onstage and I'm looking out thinking, You were the guys who didn't think they were good enough for the radio—there's 16,000 people pogoing to "Teen Spirit"—I tried to tell you this in '88.

Kurt Cobain, Krist Novoselic—Cobain's best friend and a gregarious foil to his band-mate's quieter presence—and Aaron Burckhard were not the new Beatles. In this first incarnation they were blaring out a diverse vibe ranging from hard rock to psychedelic covers to sludgy punk—they weren't quite sure what they wanted to be, and that showed in other aspects of their behavior onstage.

SLIM MOON, Nisqually Delta Podunk Nightmare: Kurt was definitely showing his "performer" side already. To the best of my recollection, although he seemed nervous, he was dressed very outrageously, sort of a send-up of a glam outfit, and he did a memorable "solo" by squatting down and messing with all the controls on his effects pedals.

For some, however, there was an immediate connection.

JOHN PURKEY, Machine: I was in a band called Noxious Fumes—we did a lot of shows at the Tropicana, and Krist Novoselic would travel with the Melvins to the Tropicana . . . I met Krist when he roadied for them. So, years later, one of those random nights where I went to the Community World Theater—didn't know who was playing—Skid Row was onstage . . . It was maybe a couple dozen people—maybe twenty-five people or so . . . I walked in and was like, Wow, that's Krist . . . His band's cool . . . Right on! Krist is on bass . . . So I sat down and watched them play and totally loved it. The emotion, what I was hearing—I really liked. Kurt's voice really blew me away from the start, hands-down—it's a certain sound in his voice. After the show I approached Kurt and I asked him if they had a tape, a demo. He said they were going to record.

Recording was still some way off for this young band. April 1987 was a fresh start for Kurt Cobain in which he gained something that proved crucial to his artistic flourishing: a real home at 114½ Pear Street in Olympia. His parents' split in 1976 had torn him from the one he had known for eight years—the longest he'd been at a single address in his whole life. From age fifteen, his living arrangements had further imploded and for the next half a decade he didn't stay even a year at any address. At seventeen, eighteen, and again at nineteen he hovered on the border of homelessness and in the ultimate regression slept at the hospital in which he'd been born.

With nowhere lower to go, he climbed. It wasn't through pluck or courage, though. Cobain had a benefactor: his girlfriend, Tracy.

RYAN AIGNER: Tracy Marander was really involved with the scene and had become a big advocate of the Melvins early on—that's how she met Kurt. She was one of the few Olympia people buying into the little music scene that was happening down in Grays Harbor, which was pretty important because she validated what he was doing from a position of having this much vaster exposure to the music and artists going on around Olympia and the Evergreen State College, yet she was saying, *You guys are kind of cool* . . . Tracy went to every Nirvana show. She was very supportive . . . Krist had [his girlfriend] Shelli. She worked. He worked too, but he could quit working and not work for two-three weeks or a month; he was a painter so he'd work the summer months but then not work because it poured down with rain, so Shelli had this constant job that was always making sure the rent was paid and food was on the table. But when he was away from Shelli, he might or he might not have money in his pocket. Kurt was the same way, he had jobs when he absolutely had to—but he had Tracy Marander, and both Shelli and Tracy worked at this cafeteria for Boeing, worked graveyard shift there, but when either one of those guys didn't have their girlfriend around to support them, they might not have money in their pocket . . .

Nirvana's next show in May nearly stopped before it started due to a simple case of youthful high spirits—possibly the *whole* case of spirits.

SLIM MOON: Krist was very drunk, and yes he was a jolly drunk but also sometimes very annoying. I remember parties where he set off fire extinguishers, broke furniture while dancing on tables . . . His inebriation didn't affect the music, or at least I don't remember it being affected, but I do think that Kurt was less theatrical at that show.

This was a band sufficiently practiced that they could still go onstage when one-third of the band turned up blitzed . . . Yet not so focused that the band members made a point of not arriving blitzed.

This was the closing event of the Greater Evergreen Students' Community Co-operation Organization (GESCCO), Nirvana's introduction to the unusually fertile musical environment of Olympia arising significantly from the presence of the Evergreen State College.

SLIM MOON: GESCCO came about because some college students figured out that they could get funds from the college for a "student organization" that they could use to rent a warehouse space and put on rock shows and art-gallery stuff. It was closing because the college had figured out that rock shows created an insurance liability. GESCCO was a big empty warehouse; it might once have been an auto garage.

GEORGE SMITH, Dangermouse: It came with money from Evergreen State College to cross-pollinate the college cultural scene with the Olympia cultural scene—it was definitely a planned endeavor to engage the two communities . . . when it started there was a seminar where they invited everybody to come down and they had a big group discussion with somebody moderating and a circle of chairs and everyone could have their say about what GESCCO should be . . . music dominated the scheduling, while the powers behind it were always trying to get more visual arts or theatrical arts, but it never really panned out. As much as anything bands are more organized; if you're touring, you might book a show two months in advance, so the schedule would fill up with music . . .

Although small, Nirvana's April show had won them an early supporter.

SLIM MOON: I was not a regular organizer at GESCCO. I just ended up putting on that show because word had gone around that GESCCO was closing very suddenly, and I thought it'd be good to have a "last show." The bands that played were mostly picked because they were willing to play on short notice, although I definitely asked Skid Row because I had enjoyed their show at CWT . . . The audience was punk rockers and college students. Mostly friends, people in the music scene in Olympia. I bet half the audience were in bands of their own . . . For some larger shows like the Melvins, the organizers had brought in stage risers, but for the show you are talking about, we just set up a little PA in one corner.

This show went well enough that the band were invited onto the college radio station, KAOS in Olympia. The band's musical home at this period of time was usually Tacoma.

JOHN PURKEY: What happens is a lot of musicians come from here and they move—you'll hear that a lot. There's a lot of bands . . . who are from Tacoma or were in Tacoma or had connections then move down the road. Someone like the Melvins, they never lived in Seattle. Pretty much their original stomping grounds were Tacoma and Olympia and being from Montesano, then they split, started touring, and ended up moving to L.A. . . . There was a house that Noxious Fumes and Girl Trouble lived at, it was called the Hell House, and it was pretty much the only place that punk bands played in Tacoma. There was one bar called the Bed Rock—they did a couple shows, but it was pretty much nothing. But the Hell House was basically the party house in 1983–85. They would have touring bands play there— Soul Asylum played there, a lot of different bands.

Krist Novoselic moved to Tacoma in 1987 and it was here, at the Community World Theater, that one of the residents of the Hell House, Jim May, would host five of their seven real shows between April 1987 and April 1988.

The Community Theater was a hub for bands; in a brief eighteen months the venue staged an astonishing 130 shows for all-ages audiences.

BRUCE PURKEY: Unless you were in a big city, and Tacoma is still relatively small, there was very little, if any, punk-rock community back in the early '80s. Most schools had a small group of three or four friends who were into punk. Punk was not cool in any way. You might as well have been the biggest nerd in the school. That's how people looked at you. So when you discovered another person into punk/underground music, you immediately felt a kinship . . . The Hell House on Fifty-Sixth Street was a hub of house-party shows and welcomed any local band . . . It wasn't until after some of the major venues like the Gorilla Gardens in Seattle closed that a real community of bands started actually growing and playing in Tacoma. Of course, the Community World Theater made it easier for a Tacoma band to find a place to play. Mid-to-late '80s you started to see a few bands becoming Tacoma fixtures: Soylent Green, He Sluts, Inspector Luv and the Ride Me Babies, Silent Treatment, Subvert, AMQA . . . The Community World Theater was a rare thing. Run by Jim May, one of us. He didn't make anything on the venture, I'm sure. It was probably a huge headache, and I would guess it lost him money, but for a brief moment the kids had their own place to play. Sure, it was a former porn theater with no heat and a shitty PA, but it was ours. It is no accident that the Community World Theater is remember fondly by most everyone who ever played there, or saw a show there. It was as if, for a moment, the punks actually ran things . . . It was how things felt for a few months right after Nirvana broke huge—essentially killing hair metal—it felt important, like we were finally noticed, finally being heard. Of course, it was short-lived and quickly coopted.

TIM FREEBORN, Sons of Ishmael: Compared to many of the places we played that summer—a barn in rural El Paso, a boxing club (the ring was being disassembled as we arrived), a garage, a couple of living rooms, a ramshackle VFW hall, a roller rink, a pizza joint—it seemed like a palace, the very Fillmore.

MIKE CANZI, Sons of Ishmael: I'm pretty sure that it was decrepit; most of the venues we played in were. I'd be willing to bet that there was red carpet in the lobby and that it was covered in cigarette burns and wads of blackened bubble gum, and that the smells of urine and mildew were an almost physical presence.

CHRIS BLACK, Sons of Ishmael: They had removed several rows of seats at the front in order to create a space suitable for moshing. However, I also recall most people sat in the seats that were still there and watched the show . . . Later, when I knew there would be no sleep for me in the lobby of a haunted theater I, of course, headed out to the van.

PAUL MORRIS, Sons of Ishmael: This venue stood out, and the fact that it was rumored to be haunted made it doubly noteworthy. It is also unusual that we would sleep overnight in the venue as well, but for our promoter, Jim, this was normal . . . I think he lived in the projection room.

GLENN POIRIER, Sons of Ishmael: I recall trying to sleep in the lobby on a blue vinyl bench by the popcorn machine in full view of the street outside the front doors. The theater was reputed to be haunted; I pity the ghost that had to endure that flatulent night air!

Nirvana returned in June, under the name Pen Cap Chew.

RYAN LOISELLE, Machine: We'd seen Pen Cap Chew at the CWT, and Skid Row. We'd go there every weekend, it didn't matter who was playing—it was our church.

DAVE CHAVEZ, Hell's Kitchen: Hell's Kitchen was a side band I started . . . I had to quit when Verbal Abuse went on tour . . . We only played together seven months. The show in question was the biggest highlight playing live, that and recording the HK demo . . . I just remember they were a loose garage band with cool vocals . . . Kurt wore a lot of clothes and was hella hot . . . They looked like they sounded, so to speak.

Cobain would still do this later in life, compensating for his skinny frame by layering clothes to conceal his body.

BRUCE PURKEY: The music stuck with me much greater the second time. The first time, it seemed looser, more chaotic, noisier. I'm not sure if that's just my ear hearing it better on a second go-round, or if they actually were a more cohesive band. I'm guessing it was a combination of the two. Like other "noisy" bands—Sonic Youth, U-Men (another vastly underrated early Northwest band) it often takes a few spins of the record to start seeing the shapes amid the seeming chaos.

By August, the band had morphed again, into Bliss. Yet having played to a mere twenty-five people in April, the audience this time around had swelled only to perhaps forty.

PAUL MORRIS: We rolled into Tacoma (famous for its poor bridge design) suffering from head colds that I believe we picked up from Youth of Today in San Francisco at the Maximum Rocknroll house.

TIM FREEBORN: We were pleased to sell out the Community World Theater. The first row, anyway . . . Big Black were playing their final show in Seattle, so I assume that several Tacomans who might have attended our show drove up to Seattle.

MIKE CANZI: I'm not being sarcastic here, but I think there was someone in the audience wearing a red-and-black lumber jacket.

For Bliss, this show was no more or less successful a musical happening than the performances in April, May, or June.

TIM FREEBORN: Their songs were pretty sludgy and unmemorable, to my tired, ravaged ears.

MIKE CANZI: I have no memories whatsoever of Bliss's music. We heard a lot of bands that summer, but only three stood out in a positive way: Nomeansno, False Prophets, and Porn Orchard.

PAUL MORRIS: Like Tim, at this time I was suffering from the burnout of seeing too many bands in such a short time . . . Musically and visually I was not impressed and I did not care for them.

GLENN POIRIER: Bliss didn't stand out at all to me . . . they were a young band finding their way . . . I liked the Magnet Men that played that night more.

CHRIS BLACK: I do remember a lot of plaid, and long songs—two maybe three minutes in length some of them . . . mumbly stage banter, lots of looking down at the floor, and long, slow-tempo songs . . . I recall thinking that either speedy hardcore hadn't yet arrived in this neck of the woods, or that they were already past it.

TIM FREEBORN: Aside from the promoter—the affable and, at that time, broken-footed Jim May—I can name no one that we met that night . . . I do remember chatting with Jim May at a greasy spoon after the show about a local scenester with an exotic STD, which produced pyramidal growths on his forearm.

These weren't stunningly professional shows. They were more like exotic sleepovers with no commercial prospects.

DAVE CHAVEZ: I just remember people chanting, "We brought our sleeping bags and we're not going home!"

TIM FREEBORN: I remember chatting with the Magnet Men, who turned their earnings over to us . . . The fact that it was a bag of coins did not lessen my appreciation of either the gesture or the cash.

BRUCE PURKEY: I have a photo of George and me from the same show with Slim Moon playing in the background. So much future fame behind us, but for all of us it was just another night with fifty or sixty of our friends in this cavernous, freezing old movie theater, sitting in the shitty seats once occupied by old pervs, now occupied by young punks, but we loved it. It was ours and we made it something special, if only for a little while. Of course, at the time, we complained about the cold, complained about the small crowds, no money, whatever . . .

Although Bliss was too shy to engage with the audience and too preoccupied trying to perform their intricate early compositions to rock out, they still displayed a degree of ambitiousness . . .

TIM FREEBORN: Bliss kind of sent out . . . mixed signals; maybe a joke? After all, the guitarist was wearing satin pants and platform shoes (and what kind of looked like a Lynyrd Skynyrd–style hairpiece).

PAUL MORRIS: When I saw these guys get up there with platform shoes and silky flare pants, my skepticism went way up . . . Beyond the clothing there was nothing memorable about the stagecraft.

The clothing was as far as the stagecraft went, but it still represented a band figuring out how to stand out.

Then it all ground to a halt. Burckhard was dismissed and the band disappeared for nearly five months.

AARON BURCKHARD: I was drunk and I got Kurt's car impounded— that's why he fired me!

RYAN AIGNER: I remember when they lost Aaron. He was a liability because he was a little older and he had an interest in girls and drinking that at times superseded the interests of the band, and that became the biggest drawback . . . he was one of these guys who didn't feel the need to go get the Black Flag tattoo. What Kurt and Krist were looking for was one hundred percent dedication—they expected you to morph into one hundred percent of what they were doing. I'm not sure what it would have taken to convince them of that total commitment.

The band's uncertain status was all-pervasive, and with only six shows all year it wasn't clear if it was anything more than a hobby. Similarly, their diverse early sound made it unclear if these were Melvins clones, a New Wave act, or a hard-rock/punk-fusion outfit. The most telling sign was that they couldn't even settle on a name. Cobain knew that a name was crucial in creating connections to a musical legacy.

JACK ENDINO, Skin Yard: Kurt used "Kurdt" a few times as a subtle tip of the hat to the only other famous musician to ever emerge from Aberdeen, Washington, prior to Nirvana: local legend, guitarist Kurdt Vanderhoof, cofounder of the Northwest-based band Metal Church (with several major-label records in the '80s) . . . Metal Church was huge here, and if not for Nirvana, Vanderhoof would probably still be the *only* successful musician to have ever emerged from Aberdeen. You can bet every kid who grew up in tiny Aberdeen in the '80s knew who he was.

Summing up 1987: little had changed. Cobain started a band, as he had in two previous years, but the public results amounted to two house parties, a college show, and three run-throughs in Tacoma—leaving perhaps one hundred witnesses. They could feel encouraged that they'd made it onto radio . . . Yet not one person interviewed mentioned having heard it. Nirvana didn't exist. A nameless hobby band from a tiny Northwest town got on the road . . . But there were no guarantees the road led anywhere.

2.0

The First Album: Nirvana in Studio
January 1988

Cobain and Novoselic wanted to greet the New Year by making progress, so they booked time at Reciprocal Recording in Seattle for January 23 under the name Ted Ed Fred. The timing would become a trend; 1992 would be the only year they didn't record in January. Some people hit the gym, Nirvana made music. Before the recording, they first had to return to Aberdeen, where they hammered out three practices at the home of Melvins drummer Dale Crover, who was temporarily substituting as drummer.

JOHN PURKEY: At a Community World Theater show that Dave Foster played at, Kurt finally had made me a copy of the first demo tape. I'd heard it from Jim May, who ran the Community World Theater, and Kurt had given him a copy to get a show there and then I heard it and was like, Oh my God, I've got to get a copy of it . . . I had a dream and I told Kurt about it. We were walking back, we walked up to his car, he got the tape, the other side was Montage of Heck, and he gives it to me and we're walking back and I said, "Kurt, I had the weirdest dream, I was in the Coliseum watching you guys play in front of thousands of people . . ." I don't remember what his response was—it wasn't like, *Whoa, really?!* It was more like, *Whoa, cool.* I remember the dream to this day; being in there with thousands of people watching those guys play—in my mind the music was that good.

CHRIS QUINN, Sister Skelter: The first time I ever met Kurt was at a party in Olympia, late '87. Dale from the Melvins was there—I asked how he was doing. He explained, "Oh, I'm doing this thing with this guy," and he points over and there's this scrawny-looking rocker guy with a jean jacket—he had this Scratch Acid thing he had painted on the back of the jacket—I loved them, so I thought, Whoa, Dale Crover, Scratch Acid . . . I wanna know what this is! I said hi to him that night, talked about his jacket, Scratch Acid, the whole thing intrigued me.

RYAN AIGNER: I watched "Hairspray Queen" be composed—Kurt had the vision, he had the parts and the pieces, so much so that he physically showed Krist how to play the bass line—I was physically in the room. It's a weird bass line, with those slides up and down the neck . . . When Dale came in, Dale was given the early demos and he got the fundamental idea of things . . . The fact that Kurt was able to find three drummers in one town willing to play in the band and with the style of music shows that there was a lot of activity and a lot of talent in those days.

Producer Jack Endino accepted the booking because Crover's presence reassured him it'd be an interesting band. Others reacted the same way.

RYAN LOISELLE: It's 1988, John Purkey played in a badass band, Subvert, and we became really good friends. So he comes into high school with this Nirvana cassette, back when there were cassettes: "Man, you've got to hear this! My friend Kurt!" Their first demo with Dale. I felt if Dale was playing drums, then, hell, all right! We played it and knew this is really good, love this . . . they're really good, but the reason they were good was because Dale was playing drums . . . But the other reason was that they're original and crazy, the recording was awesome . . . Whatever that demo was, it was the best album.

Nirvana's ability to go around making friends was critical—the underground thrived on people knowing people.

PETER LITWIN, Coffin Break: My standout memory is just what a nice bunch of guys they were. I mostly just knew them back then, from playing some gigs together. Remember, they didn't live in Seattle at first. I remember Kurt as being a quiet, kind of shy pothead. Krist was supercool and has always been a really friendly guy.

DAMON ROMERO, Lush: We played a house party with them at our bass player's house, the Caddyshack, before the Community World Theater show in March . . . I'd heard their demo tape that Slim had a copy of (I was a DJ at KAOS for a brief time. Kurt gave me the Nirvana cassette demo to play on air. He also gave me his four-track of solo stuff that I played a few times), so seeing those songs live for the first time was amazing. It was a packed house, over capacity, people still out in the front yard—people were going nuts! They hadn't heard these songs before, but they all loved it—they were awesome. In general, people in the Northwest are kinda subdued, they don't go crazy all the time, but when Nirvana played people went ape shit. I was blown away: *Holy shit, these guys are on a whole 'nother level!* . . . We all knew that punk rock was stuck in the past, people were trying to bring different influences to it, Nirvana were really able to bring the heavy rock sound and the punk rock simplicity together really perfectly. Those songs were amazing—that first set they had. I don't think this is true, but the sort of mythology that was going around at the time was that the first twelve Nirvana songs were the first twelve songs

Kurt had ever written. It's not true; he had demoed, he had done other stuff . . . but that was the mystique. It kinda made sense: here's this kid out of Aberdeen, he's a brilliant songwriter . . . Nirvana really did play a lot when they were in Olympia—they'd play parties, they made themselves very accessible, they just had some magic combination that everyone loved them—K Records loved them, the more slick Seattle people liked them.

Reciprocal Studios had definite advantages for bands just starting out, including price—Nirvana barely scraped together the $152 required.

JAIME ROBERT JOHNSON, Crunchbird: The first time I went over there to record, it was affordable, comfortable, and very unpretentious. I was someone with hardly any resources to generate income in those times, so that was a very important consideration.

PAUL KIMBALL, Lansdat Blister and **Helltrout:** Reciprocal, it was *the* place to track heavy music at the time. Jack Endino pulled folks in with all the great work he was doing for Sub Pop bands, and Chris [Hanzek] wound up doing lots of the stuff that Jack couldn't do. We didn't know either of them before we recorded there, but we knew we wanted some of that Reciprocal magic.

Nirvana would come to work with Endino more than with any other producer—an indication of how his approach and attitude set musicians at ease.

DUANE LANCE BODENHEIMER, The Derelicts: Most of our stuff was engineered by Jack Endino—super nice guy. Really easy to work with, put up with our crap . . . No attitude at all—very knowledgeable in his profession . . . Straightforward, precise, does everything timely . . . One time I recall I said I wanted to practice first, I didn't want him to record it, I wanted to practice first. He said, "All right, cool," so I did it—and of course he recorded it and it was a great take. He just laughed—"This is it, this is the take." He knows what he's doing. He makes you feel comfortable.

JAIME ROBERT JOHNSON: I was a pretty squirrelly guy back when I met Jack. I didn't have the ability to sit still because I was so intense . . . I wanted to be in a constant state of constant creativity, whether it was working out a song by humming the chords to myself, writing poetry on the nearest piece of paper . . . what I liked about him was the fact he was an opposite to me in a good way, and the first thing I learned from him was how to listen to other people and how to actually hear what they were trying to communicate . . . If I mentioned any bands like King Crimson or brought up an artist like Frank Zappa or Ornette Coleman, he didn't judge and I didn't have to explain what I was talking about to him . . . When Jack said it, he said it with the authority of his expertise and (excellent) taste in music. Also, Jack knew how to do things with a guitar that I wanted to learn to do, and if you catch him in an unfettered moment, he is more than glad to share his expertise . . . The other thing that Jack has is this ability to tell me the unvarnished truth.

JOHN PURKEY: When you're in the studio with him, basically . . . he knows when he hears a mistake and he's not going to let any mistake slip by. He's not going to be all, "Oh, how do you feel about that?" If he hears something, he'll just say "OK, let's do that again." He's a really nice, really mellow guy.

The session created a decent-enough effort on limited time.

JACK ENDINO: None of them were recorded or mixed with any time spent due to budget; plus, I had only been working as a recording engineer for three years at that point. The songs with Dale drumming were all mixed in a total of two hours . . . ten songs on the original demo . . . do the math. It would have been nice to remix them with some care taken . . . I never liked the way it sounded . . .

Unfortunately, the band had only limited money, which meant they couldn't finish the last song they attempted—"Pen Cap Chew"—or record two other songs that they had prepared—"Annorexorcist" and "Erectum."

JACK ENDINO: The multitrack master tape ran out just at the start of the second chorus, and the band didn't want to buy another reel, so more correctly the song is "permanently incomplete," not "unfinished." You can't finish it when a third of the song is missing. I did the fade ending for the hell of it, just so they could listen to what was there less jarringly.

That same night, back at the Community World Theater again, the band ran through all the songs they'd taped, still veering between sounds and styles.

DAVID WHITING, Vampire Lezbos: I felt like they were just another new band playing rock 'n' roll while periodically trying to throw in some musical elements of punk . . . usually the quick, faster, yelly stuff.

JOHN PURKEY: I specifically remember when those guys played with Dale—it was just that one show, right after they recorded the demo—it was one of the most intense Nirvana shows I ever saw. I think the level of intensity with Dale helped form some of those songs—he's a really original drummer, he has his own style. I think Kurt wrote some of those songs along the lines he thought Dale could play. So when Chad [Channing] joined, he was more of a 4/4 basic drummer and that could have influenced what Kurt wrote—he would have written stuff Chad could play. And Sub Pop turned down the first album, so Kurt just wanted to be part of Sub Pop . . . He may have changed the sound, but I think it was more to do with the drummers he was with. He was a drummer, he played a little bit, so that could have easily been something he kept in mind, depending on who he was playing with.

Cobain's most underrated talent lay in assimilating sounds that were swirling through the underground and stamping them with his own approach.

1988 had started well. Most significantly, Jack Endino would become the band's newest champion.

JOHN PURKEY: He was one of a handful of people who gave a shit about early Nirvana; Jack was there. He was instantly a fan—the early stuff was that good . . . Literally, I'd be standing next to Jack at most of the shows—two or three shows where I'd be hanging out with him . . . right after Nirvana had recorded their first demo with Dale I heard it. I had conversations with Jack about it and how amazing it was and then I'd see him at the shows and we'd hang out and talk.

Endino's appreciation made a lasting difference to the future of the band. He passed the tape into the hands of Bruce Pavitt and Jonathan Poneman at Seattle's upstart label Sub Pop while the band themselves continued to pass out copies to anyone who would take the time to listen.

ABE BRENNAN, My Name: We got into Nirvana before they put anything out via demo tapes that our friend John Purkey had—he was friends with Kurt; these were the recordings that Dale Crover . . . played drums on, some of which ended up on *Bleach* (and maybe *Incesticide*; I can't remember—fucking pot! I'm telling you! I'm glad I quit!) . . . We dug the Nirvana stuff right away and started going to their shows—really small stuff back then; we'd go see them play parties at K Dorm at the Evergreen State College in Olympia, stuff like that . . .

BRUCE PURKEY: It wasn't until the fall of '88, when I got a cassette copy of their early demo from my brother that I fell in love with them. I played that tape to death in my dorm room . . . At the time, the dorms were filled with the sounds of Rush, the Cult, Love and Rockets, and the Cure. I tried to play Nirvana and tell everyone how amazing it was, but was mostly met with comments like, "They have horrible production values." . . . . All the while I was in Bellingham, my brother was telling me stories about his band and Nirvana, but neither of us really possibly expected that Nirvana would gain any sort of widespread success.

3.0

The Lost Drummer
February to May 1988

Nirvana's first recording was in the can, but they were still little more than a no-name garage band with barely a half dozen shows under their belt. This was to change rapidly in the short time their third drummer, Dave Foster, occupied the drum stool. He is the mystery man of the Nirvana story.

SLIM MOON: He was during the time Nirvana was still based in Aberdeen, and I doubt there were any better drummers in Aberdeen, other than Dale Crover.

RYAN AIGNER: If anybody thinks that Dave doesn't have the chops then they have obviously never listened to Helltrout or Psycho-Samaritan—any of the projects he's worked with . . . If you want to find the most prejudiced people in the world, talk to a bunch of punk rockers, because if you're not "in," if you don't have the tattoo and the clothespin or whatever, if you're not part of the club, then they're worried about it. They want you to be a bona fide member and they want you to be one hundred percent. It was pretty obvious Dave wasn't and was never going to be—it had nothing to do with his ability to play the drums. I think they didn't know who else to bring on. Most of the bands 'round here are musicians playing with each other not because we've all been the best of friends but because they're the only other musicians we know. There weren't a lot of other options—Dave was the logical decision, he was the right age, he had the chops, he could do it!

Foster's tenure started with a seemingly unimportant house party, yet this wasn't just someone's home, the Caddyshack was a very well-connected residence. It was this rapid introduction to key individuals in other bands and labels that would allow Nirvana to progress at pace.

SCOTT VANDERPOOL, Chemistry Set: I went to high school in Bellevue [an east Seattle suburb] with Ron "Nine" Rudzitis [later of Love Battery] and Scott Boggan . . . I quit to go to the Evergreen State College and was promptly drafted into the Young Pioneers with Brian Learned [who had been in the Silly Killers in Seattle and would later end up in Chemistry Set] . . . Chris Pugh [who would go on to start Swallow, Creep, and SABA] and Brad Sweek [who would go on to be a major junkie who got clean and helped tons of Seattle music people get off that shit] . . . It was there I met Bruce Pavitt and Calvin Johnson . . . We were the Kings of Oly back then. Room Nine got a new drummer and went on to be quite popular in the pre-grunge years in Seattle where the Young Pioneers shared bills with them at places like the Metropolis [where the future Mrs. Chris Cornell, Susan Silver, worked the concession counter] . . . Chemistry Set played our first show at the Rainbow Tavern, directly behind the notorious Room Nine house, where I lived along with photographer Charles Peterson and artist Ed Fotheringham.

This intertwining of personalities was a constant feature, and Nirvana was regularly playing for fellow musicians, plus the label bosses, journalists, and photographers who made up the Seattle scene—though it didn't mean luxurious circumstances.

SCOTT VANDERPOOL: A totally beat two-bedroom house with Visqueen plastic for a roof. Painted the moldy walls with paint-store mistake colors . . . this dump happened to be on the tenth green of a private golf club, so we called it the Caddyshack . . . When I moved back to Seattle, Chris Pugh stayed and Mike McDowell, lead singer of Noxious Fumes from Tacoma, moved in . . . I'm pretty sure that's who was there when Nirvana played . . . I was fairly bummed when the landlord, a former Thurston County commissioner (who once told the religious zealot that called him regularly to complain that the Young Pioneers' satanic music was killing her daughter to quit complaining because we usually got paid when we played and she was getting it for free) finally told 'em all to get out because he was building a luxury golf-course home there. So they had a party and totally destroyed the place . . . And no one told me!

CHRIS PUGH, Swallow: That place was great—bands on tour would stay there, lots of bands played there. Olympia was so small and such a tight-knit scene, if there were ten bands in town then you knew everyone and every member . . . I was friends with Bruce [Pavitt]; we'd worked at a place called Muzak that provided music services to restaurants and businesses—we'd go out to lunch, see each other. I gave him a cassette of my band and since we were friends already it wasn't a sophisticated contract or anything—he just said, "Yeah, we could put this out for you."

The Caddyshack was another element splicing Cobain and company into the wider music scene of the Northwest.

March 19, 1988, was the first Nirvana performance.

JOHN PURKEY: I got this phone call, I answer the phone, it's Kurt: "John, I found a band name, I wanted to know what you think . . . Nirvana." "Man, it's perfect, great." "That's the new name of the band . . ." Kurt went to Buddhist meetings in Olympia; Nichiren Shoshu Buddhism. In 1980 my mom became a Buddhist; I was really interested . . . I became a Buddhist and was off and on through the '80s, I'm sure I told Kurt one time . . . he went to a couple of meetings in Olympia . . . I believe the name Nirvana could have been inspired by Buddhism . . .

The show that night was the first time Nirvana took the stage.

DAVID WHITING: When I phoned the Community World Theater in Tacoma saying we were coming over . . . we were offered headline position to an already "in-process" show. After all, this was the month of our first LP release, which was a big thing at the time, for the area and for us, and we had played the CWT in the past. When we got there, we used our "headline clout" to ask to play middle slot so that we could push onward to Seattle for a late-night show. Typical headline-band maneuvering.

LARRY SCHEMEL, Kill Sybil: The Nirvana Community World show had Dave Foster on drums. I never met him and my only memory of him was his massive drum kit and how great of a drummer he was, very hard-hitting drummer . . .

Yet while it marked the beginning of Nirvana, the show was when the band said an unwitting farewell to the Community World Theater, which closed before a planned July 3 return. Instead, over the year to come, the fledgling band would perform across the state of Washington. In Nirvana's first year, half of the bands they played with had been Tacoma-based, yet on March 19, their co-performers were Lush, from Olympia, and Vampire Lezbos.

DAVE WHITING: Born on the conservative-cowboy-laden plains of eastern Washington, in the Orwellian year of 1984 . . . We spent five years of our initial history in Spokane . . .

Of the bands Nirvana played with during Foster's stint, not one had its roots in Tacoma.

DAVE WHITING: Needless to say, I don't remember much from that night, or the actual band. We of course met, talked superficially, and courteously listened to each other while mulling about, all the while waiting to push onwards to Seattle . . . I was fairly oblivious of the music from that night and was not stricken with any sort of awe of having heard something great. My head was more into what we came to do that night, so anything less than extraordinary would not have registered with me . . . No succinct memories except the vague ones mentioned earlier. What a downer, eh?

Even later, in May, it was still the case that Nirvana were playing second fiddle or lower to numerous other bands.

SHAWN LAWLOR, Herd of Turtles: I don't remember their show much. People were moshing from the get-go and really into their sound . . . It was a big crowd. I remember Nirvana played earlier than we did—so yes, I joke about being able to claim that Nirvana opened for my band—we played right before the Young Fresh Fellows, who headlined the show . . .

And this wasn't unusual. Neither was the Olympia house party.

RONNA MYLES-ERA, Treehouse: This was a fun, crazy, and productive time in Olympia. There were a lot of bands and there were shows pretty much every weekend. In Olympia you didn't need a club to play at, just someone willing to let you play in their house, and there were plenty of those. House shows were the best . . . House shows were a really big part of the music scene, and that made it easier to play because even if there were only fifteen people, it felt like a full house and you just gave it your all. And if you didn't get invited to play a show, you just put on your own . . . Our practice space was in the basement of our house, and Steve [Helbert], Damon [Romero], and I all lived there. Our house was called the Tree House.

Nirvana readily embraced the house-party ethos of the local music community. At least a third of their shows from 1987 to 1988 were house parties or college dorms.

SLIM MOON: I think that some of the house-party shows have been lost to the ages and aren't on any lists. At that point Lush was hopeful of putting out an album, or going on a tour, but we never did . . . Locally (meaning Olympia and Aberdeen and Tacoma), everybody knew that Nirvana were special. We knew we weren't nearly as good as them. And they drew more local fans than we did. We always played before them, even at parties.

The community within which Nirvana's members lived and socialized throughout the majority of their career was one of living in shared band houses in Olympia, playing one another's shows, sharing parties, and living life on the cheap.

LISA KOENIG, Calamity Jane: The good ol' Alamo . . . there was the Witch House, the Glass House, the Caddyshack—and the first place I ever lived after moving out of my parents' house was the Mansion, or, I think it was called the White House too; it was so cool it had two names. There were twelve of us living there, so our rent was only $50 a month. And we still couldn't afford coffee! What losers we were! None of us really had jobs, we just jammed and made money wherever we could . . . Then Tim Tafoya brought home scabies one day and the whole house broke out itching. It sucked the big one 'cause we kept passing it around and it seemed like it took forever to get rid of. I think we can rename that one the Scaby House.

While building their reputation within the band-house crowd in Olympia, it was Dave Foster, an old friend from Aberdeen, who held them together on drums. Yet there has been precious little true assessment of Foster's time in the band.

DAMON ROMERO: I thought he was a solid drummer, good with the band. He rocked hard, he hit hard—I remember once having a conversation with Kurt and Krist where they were sort of complaining, but not about his drumming. It was just that they didn't think he was committed, that he didn't really want to leave Aberdeen. They wanted to be a band that worked and played and recorded and toured and they just got the sense he wasn't on board with that. He just wanted to play in a rock band and drink beer and be a good drummer.

Later biographies dwelled on various differences, and Cobain's journals fueled the fire with a letter claiming Foster was from "a totally different culture." Yet crucially, what stands out in this unsent venting is that it's one of the rare occasions when Cobain acknowledged how good one of his early drummers was.

PAUL KIMBALL: He was a great drummer to work with, really fun and funny a lot of the time . . . just a super-sweet soul.

RYAN AIGNER: He's a funny guy, a crossover. You've got these worlds in every community: there's the mainstream . . . People that are musicians, number one, they're not part of the mainstream. They interact with the mainstream, but they've taken this passion for music, they've honed it, and they've become proactive and learned how to play an instrument. Now, you take that same guy that's a musician and you put him into an aesthetic like punk rock—now he's another step or two removed from the mainstream socially acceptable thing. Dave, he worked in the middle there: short haircut, he didn't wear the punk-rock weirdo clothes, he didn't give a flying crap about that, he was just a damn good musician and he just wanted to play and he really thought the music of Nirvana was good. I did too. When I said to Kurt that it was good enough to hear on the radio, that's what Dave heard. Kurt was so worried about whether or not it was Black Flag enough, Dave and I didn't care—it just sounded good and it was original and Dave didn't want to play Judas Priest covers the rest of his life. He wasn't going to get the Black Flag tattoo, he was just going to keep on being Dave.

Others remember little beyond the heft of Foster's equipment.

SHAWN LAWLOR: Equipment-wise I don't remember what they had, except the drums being what I perceived as *too* big. The toms were probably 18 to 20 and 22 [inches].

SLIM MOON: He had a really good *large* drum set. By large, I mean each piece was large, not that it had a lot of pieces. He tried to have a more "heavy" style than Aaron . . .

And some remember both his drums and his talent.

JASON MORALES, Helltrout: We were at another keg party and we met this other strange crazy redneck dude who happened to be partying there that night—we started talking to him and he pointed out he had played drums in Nirvana. "No way! I just saw those guys, they're great—why don't you come over to our place and play with us?" We hooked up with him the next morning; he was strolling 'round with a wicked hangover but he remembered us. We were waiting three, four hours, and he showed up with this gigantic drum kit—big double bass drum, everything huge, very Bonham-esque. He set it up and the first song . . . by the time we'd finished, we were like, *Holy shit this is awesome*. That's the birth of Helltrout right there.

While it was the Crover demo that kick-started Sub Pop's interest, it was Dave Foster holding the beat down when the label's owners saw them in April and when Nirvana received a spot on a Sub Pop Sunday show that month.

CHRIS QUINN: He gets short shrift in history [but] he was an incredible drummer—this was a guy able to play stuff that Dale Crover had played on, he was great . . . He was always cool when I talked to him, but a real Aberdeen guy, and he didn't have the same aspirations or the artistic inclinations that Kurt and Krist did. He just wanted to be a kickass drummer, and he was. A lot of the stuff said about him was just Kurt's personal stuff . . . That guy filled Dale's shoes, and that's no joke—they looked really good with him. I don't think he was as creative as Dale, but he could play those parts, do a lot of what Dale did. That's not to say I don't understand why they got rid of him and got Chad—Chad helped them do more of the poppy stuff. But Dave, being the type of drummer he was, for the time it was and what they were playing, he was amazing. I think the guy deserves more credit. He did help Nirvana bridge that gap.

The final piece soon fell into place. Nirvana fell into line with the sound Sub Pop was peddling and, on Foster's watch, the first songs showing off this alignment— "Blew" and "Big Cheese"—emerged.

SLIM MOON: I think that Kurt was very influenced by what he was listening to in those days. When I first met him, he was listening to a lot of stuff on Touch and Go, such as Scratch Acid and Big Black, and those influences plus Devo and the Melvins inform the earlier stuff. He *did* start listening to more Sub Pop bands, along with stuff that he was being introduced to through the Olympia scene, and that started to show in the newer songs. I think Dinosaur [who were not yet called Dinosaur Jr. at that time] also influenced him a bit at that time, and he became less shy about his "classic rock" influences from his earlier teens. He once played me the first song he ever wrote, and I thought it sounded like vintage Aerosmith.

By June, Nirvana already had three more songs—"Mr. Moustache," "Sifting," and "Blandest"—mining the hard-rock/punk amalgam known as grunge.

CHRIS PUGH: When I saw them play, I was a fan almost immediately. I felt that though their playing wasn't fantastic, their songs were great, so it was evident even in the early days that they got better fast, rehearsed a lot . . . by the fourth or fifth time they were really good. The crowds would erupt, people would dance! Their songs and Kurt's singing was very compelling. A lot of bands when they first start they're going to be rough—what got Nirvana to make the jump to great was Kurt's singing, his sense of melody; he was able to capture great hooks and still be a punk rocker—but it's the melody that set them apart.

But Foster wasn't there to see it.

AARON BURCKHARD: Kurt and Krist would pick me up to come practice with them and just not tell Dave!

JASON MORALES: The way they kicked him out was pretty lame— they didn't tell him anything, just advertised a show in the paper and he called them to ask about it and they said, "Well, you're not, but we are . . ."

Regardless, Dave Foster's brief spell with the band saw real change. He was there when it counted and Cobain wouldn't lose his desire to have a hard-hitting drummer someday . . .

4.0

Becoming a Seattle Band
April to June 1988

Punk wrapped itself in the banner of rebellion, ostensibly against the "old dinosaurs" of '70s rock; generational conflict was explicitly part of the template for the US underground in the '80s. Frozen out by bars either unable to let in teens or simply not fond of punk, the underground was built around any locale in which underage kids could tear through songs. This was the world Nirvana inhabited, and they shared these same challenges and conflicts throughout their early years.

ALAN BISHOP, Sun City Girls: The original scene (at least in Austin) was made up of college art and RTF students with "weirdos" thrown in. The places you played, for the most part, were places where kids could not get into the shows . . . What was known as hardcore was largely based on [a] Do It Yourself ethic that realized that we all needed to find places where shows were all-ages and kids could come see for themselves that *they* could start bands, start fanzines, do something on their own . . . It was about showing that there was another choice on the table where self-expression lived and *everyone* could participate if they wanted. If you weren't interested, no worries. If you were, come on . . .

CRAIG CRAWFORD, Mousetrap: The music scene in Omaha at the time was very DIY . . . almost all of the shows were held in rented halls. Since bars in the States require one to be twenty-one years of age to enter, you would have to play independent venues that didn't serve alcohol. The Cog Factory on Leavenworth Street served this purpose, and the names of bands that came out of that place is long and legendary . . . The Lifticket was located in a lower-working-class neighborhood called Benson, and while the owner was very accommodating to bands, depending on the night the clientele could be a little rough. Later, there was the Capitol Bar downtown, and that became pretty much our main venue from '91 to '95.

JOSH KRIZ, Anxiety Prophets: The Zoo, ah the Zoo . . . miss that place. As you walked in, there was a tall Plexiglas wall that divided the two lower halves of the venue [the over-21 section, and the stage and dance floor area that was all-ages]. There was an upper level that was also all-ages that had a banister that allowed concertgoers to look over the railing and see the action below. The walls were all painted in zebra and animal-print paint jobs (the Zoo, right?). The common denominator was black . . . lots and lots of black paint—probably about 70 percent was painted black. It allowed smoking back in the day, and there was a thick smoky haze inside.

In Seattle the Teen Dance Ordinance of 1985 generated a clear divide between venues that were friendly to those under twenty-one and those with closed doors.

JAMES BURDYSHAW, Cat Butt: Made it nearly impossible to put on an all-ages show in a legitimate club. The ordinance would insist if your place was under-21, you had to pay hefty fees for insurance and to meet fire codes. It was a move by the city to close clubs that were havens for teen runaways to do what they wanted and not tell their parents anything . . . Every time Seattle opened all-ages or eighteen-plus nightclubs, they would be shut down quick. The Underground in the University District was where the *Sub Pop 200* record-release party was held, and that place lasted maybe six months tops.

TY WILLMAN, Inspector Luv and the Ride Me Babies: Squid Row, that's going way back. It was the first club you'd play in Seattle, or one of the first, when you came to town. Very small place on Capitol Hill. They just opened up to letting a lot of bands play there even though it was only there a short space of time. The OK Hotel was the best all-ages venue.

BEAU FREDERICKS, Saucer: There were a lot of house parties, and all-ages venues would come and go. The Show Off Gallery (all-ages) and the Up & Up Tavern (over-21) were the main places at the time. They were very friendly places, and all you needed to do was say you were in a band and they would give you a show . . .

SCOTT VANDERPOOL: All-ages shows were big early in the punk/alternative days in Seattle, largely because all the established local bar venues (a) didn't think they could sell any beer to bands with a young audience and (b) fucking hated the music. (Still the case when I got a gig running sound at the Fabulous Rainbow Tavern in the U-District; the guy who owned the PA didn't want to be anywhere near the place when Jon Poneman–booked bands played!)

A number of all-ages events shuffled out of the city into neighboring towns—the Community World Theater being one example of the opportunities that arose.

SLIM MOON: It did mean more big shows in Tacoma and Bremerton, but Olympia is too far away from Seattle. In fact, it probably hurt Oly because it meant that some bands decided to skip the Northwest entirely if they couldn't get a show in Seattle. Olympia did have a better all-ages scene than Seattle, which might be partially attributed to the Teen Dance Ordinance. But I should point out that I lived and went to shows in Seattle in 1983 to 1985, and also drove from Oly to Seattle to see shows from 1986 to 2006, and even though the TDO existed, there was never a time that all-age shows weren't happening in Seattle. People either found ways to get around it, or they ignored it and took their chances of getting busted . . .

GLEN LOGAN, Bible Stud: These all-ages fans were/are incredibly dedicated and supportive. Years earlier the Lake Hills Roller Rink shows filled this gap on the east side. There were/are unique challenges faced by bands and promoters who wanted to play to the all-ages crowd and for the all-ages crowd who wanted to attend these shows. For example, a bar owner who doesn't mind what band's fans he or she sells booze to may be more open to having bands at their club. The bands are the honey that attract the bees who buy the booze. There is potentially more monetary risk where the built-in liquor sales are absent. This can lead to less all-ages opportunities for bands and fans alike.

NATHAN HILL, King Krab: Ellensburg was small and boring, so the only entertainment was music, crime, and drugs . . . Highway 18 to Olympia was a nightmare and was also a three-hour drive . . . Calvin Johnson went to elementary school here with Mark Lanegan. Through that connection I met the band Dangermouse, Slim Moon, and Dylan Carlson . . . Slim Moon's Lush had played in Ellensburg earlier and I thought they were great. I called him to book another show and they couldn't play so he suggested I call his friend Kurt Cobain. I did: they showed up and blew us all away. Well, all twenty of us . . . The Hal Holmes Center was the only place we could put on shows ourselves, and it sucked. Me and another guy put on all the shows because we wanted our bands to play somewhere, anywhere. We would try to bring in an out-of-town band, but we couldn't pay anything more than gas money. It was very punk-rock, and I remember it fondly . . . We always let the out-of-town band headline unless they didn't want to. We thought any band was better than we were! They were loud and heavy and blew us away. None of us realized that we could be that way—they were inspiring and a really nice bunch of guys . . .

Nirvana's relatively strong focus on younger fans, on college audiences, was in part an outgrowth of the scene's firm ideological commitment to all-ages shows.

SCOTT VANDERPOOL: All-ages shows were almost required to be cool in Olympia, Calvin Johnson would flat-out refuse to play to a 21-plus for years. The Tropicana wouldn't have dreamed of getting a liquor license . . .

GEORGE SMITH: Again, the Tropicana, it was an incredibly important place in Olympia music—it was always in danger of getting shut down. All-ages clubs over here are always living week-to-week in danger of getting shut down because they attract a weird-looking bunch of people and I think it makes people nervous. To be sure, there are attendant minor crimes—vandalism, empties littering the street—I don't think that it's necessarily worse than other sorts of venues, but they get targeted. The Tropicana was always getting shut down and having flare-ups with the law. Reko/Muse was another club that was in town a year or two after GESSCO—another all-ages venue that had a short run. It was definitely one of the places to play, one of the short-lived places . . . We didn't really consider taverns to be the same—the lifeblood of the scene was all-ages shows. A badge of honor was to keep playing all-ages rather than bar shows so that the kids could go. When you're twenty-two, twenty-three, you still remember it was so lame there had been good shows you couldn't go to. It was nice not to arbitrarily omit 50 percent of the audience. By twenty-four, twenty-five I guess you start to feel it's nice not having all these kids running around!

By the time they started playing Seattle, Cobain and Novoselic were twenty-one and twenty-two, respectively, but had to be discreet regarding the youngster who would soon join them on drums: Chad Channing.

DAMON ROMERO: The laws in Washington State are really tricky. To play in a bar under the age of twenty-one is a real hassle. I did it, but you can't just go in the club, not until it's time to play, or you had to stay in a really dingy area in the corner of the bar—it wasn't much fun. You were just relegated to some little corner at the side of the stage or had to stay outside. There were a couple of actual punk-rock venues in Seattle, one was an old cinema that had been converted—well, the seats were ripped out, so it was basically a concrete box—that was Gorilla Gardens Rock Theater. There was another place called the Gray Door . . . Unfortunately, as teenagers, we never made it down to the Tropicana—but we spoke about it, just never made the trip.

While these difficulties didn't limit the ability to get shows, it restricted the free movement of band members and made it harder to draw enthusiastic teens. Sub Pop would work to ensure Nirvana played all-ages shows. For example, they secured Nirvana a December 1 slot below two punk legends.

PETER LITWIN: Jonathan Poneman actually called me and asked me if I could get them onto the gig. We had a fairly well established all-ages following at this point and Jonathan thought they needed to do more all-ages shows . . . I should mention that Jonathan gave Coffin Break our first bar show in Seattle—he was always supportive of us, so I was more than happy to do him a favor. Plus, I loved Nirvana . . . I never knew Kurt was a big Coffin Break fan till many years later.

JOE KEITHLEY, D.O.A.: Seattle was one of the worst places to find an all-ages show—the city councilors were absolutely draconian and puritan about not wanting kids near alcohol . . . In L.A. what they would do is check your ID and if you didn't have ID then they'd take a sharpie and put a big X on your left and then your right hand, so if you were trying to reach for a beer the bartender would see your X . . . in the Northwest they just wouldn't let you in unless you had these completely separate shows with no alcohol. The promoter invited us down either at the end of a tour back from California or maybe just for the weekend, but the singer from Coffin Break said we needed to go do some fliers, so we walked to Kinko's and when we got back Nirvana had finished and were taking the cymbals off the stand so I had no clue who they were.

The generational divide was written indelibly into the emerging music.

CHRIS BLACK: I recall that Bliss and the other bands were slow and sludgy, and that they had long hair.

ROD MOODY, Swallow: We were the fourth band on the official label . . . all featured big, loud, ugly guitars, screaming vocals, and relentless rhythm sections. None were very subtle but all had their distinct personalities and influences. Green River had Stooges and (later) glam. Soundgarden had psych elements mixed into their Sabbath/Zep foundation. Blood Circus was straight-up biker rock, and Swallow brought in some pop elements. We were all a little different musically, but we had a common ground as well. That was the heavy. And we all had long hair.

Punk spat at its counterculture precursors by dispensing with hippie/rock-god hair, then hardcore took it to the extreme with Marine Corps–esque skinheads. A few more years and the next wave of youngsters again wanted to stand out alongside their immediate elders, which they did by re-embracing hard rock and long hair.

MIKE MORASKY, Steel Pole Bath Tub: Funny, of all things, I do remember Nirvana's long hair and thinking that it was cool, like they were a heavy Southern rock band or something. Even though we were referencing some of the same music sources, they were coming at the heaviness from a very different direction . . . we were art punks and players; they were a pop band.

Of course, the mainstream believed that unwashed natural "grunge" hair was just a reaction to hair metal's bouffant hairdos; most people missed entirely that it was also a reaction to the dominant hairstyles of the punk scene too.

TIM KERR, Bad Mutha Goose: You have to realize that up until the early '90s, the majority of the rest of the US looked at all of this like we were from Mars. It was this little uprising that they had no idea what was going on . . . You would have the random knuckleheads come in to "fuck with the weirdo faggots." Same thing happened with skating. In Austin it was the frats, kickers, or jocks that came in to shows looking to fight.

The "Seattle look" was so prominent that as early as 1989 it was worth parodying.

SHAMBIE SINGER, Lonely Moans: All those dudes—all the Sub Pop bands—had longer hair than us, which shook around a lot more than our shorter hair. That made an impression . . . we did a photo shoot for Sub Pop promo stuff at one point. A woman named Paula Huston took the photos. And we borrowed long-hair wigs from the Hampshire College Theatre Department for the photo shoot. I think Paula got the wigs for us through a friend. I recall we thought it was kinda funny to do that. Sorta mocking all the long-haired head wagging that was going on in Seattle at the time. But also sorta interested to fit in aesthetically.

The Northwest accepted both punk and the hard rock their precursors had lashed out at.

DANIEL RIDDLE, Hitting Birth: When the same kids that spat on us in school yelling, "Whip it good, Devo" and "Fucking punk faggot" were now showing up to our little punk-rock shows, slam dancing with the same violence and disrespect shown to us punks in the school-yards and on the streets, with no respect for the culture [or] the etiquette of the punk-rock dance, no respect for women, the venues, or the musicians . . . we all knew it was *over*. Punk bands were now fucking weightlifters, Nazis, military strategists, and preachers. Kids like us needed to go deeper underground. The total *un*-coolness of '70s rock and long hair was perfect camouflage . . . Coopting the discarded, dismissed sounds and styles of the '70s that had already been trashed and labeled worthless was one of many suitable social responses for our desire to continue our rebellion.

DAVID WHITING: We tended to be perceived as "has-beens" and "old-schools" when we perhaps perceived these newer rock hybrids as even more so the "has-beens," emulating styles, fashion, and sounds from an even earlier bygone time.

JOE KEITHLEY: Punk rock really weakened after about 1986—it wasn't the same movement it had been, although there were still a lot of good people and good bands, but it didn't have the same impact it had had on society between 1977 and 1983. It started to wane, it got tougher to go to shows, there was more violence with skinheads . . . Things need to move along, or we'd still be dressing in greaser jackets and singing doo-wop songs.

This generation had an issue with the '80s manifestation of hard rock, not the '70s originals.

SLIM MOON: The Pacific Northwest was a weird place where a rock influence was always there in the punk and indie music . . . At a time when, in most of the country, punk bands were very against hard rock, Seattle punk bands still loved AC/DC and Kiss and Aerosmith. All over the country, punk was giving way to all kinds of indie sounds—the rise of college radio had a lot to do with this—but the Northwest particularly contributed with "heavy" sounds, partially because the Northwest underground had never fully rejected hard rock the way much of the underground had.

While straddling the generational lines, Nirvana simultaneously stood with their feet on either side of a geographic divide.

SLIM MOON: In the period from the late '80s to the early '90s, the Seattle scene and the Olympia scene wasn't really very friendly; there was a lot of competition, and if you were in Seattle you heard a lot of jokes at Olympia's expense, and if you were in Olympia, we told jokes about Seattle bands. Seattle thought Oly bands couldn't play our instruments and were naïve. Olympia thought Seattle bands were drunks and heroin addicts without any convictions or creativity.

It was only when Nirvana had sponsors within the Seattle scene—Jack Endino and Sub Pop—that they made it there.

DUKE HARNER, Black Ice: Krist, I first met him in high school. He's a really nice guy, intelligent, quirky sense of humor and of course tall! We used to have a couple of classes together and were usually goofing off in them . . . he worked at Sears during the same time my girlfriend worked there. I'd go to have lunch with her and would run into him while I waited for her to take her break. He and I would talk about what we was doing musically and at that time, he would usually be headed to Seattle to see if he and Kurt could find somewhere to play. He said they would drive around during the day, trying to convince bars to let them play there and then sleep in their van and do it all over again. I told him it sounded exhausting, but he thought it sounded like fun!

GEORGE SMITH: Tacoma and Olympia definitely had more of a connection than those two and Seattle—distances though may play a part in that, Seattle is fifty miles north from Olympia, twenty-five miles north from Tacoma . . . for an Olympia band it definitely felt tougher to break into Seattle. It was more competitive; there's five times as many people as Tacoma. Olympia's a lot smaller than that. There was more drive to get to a status level there—and more opportunity. Most of our shows we got were through bands ahead of us in the pecking order, benefactors, who would help us out . . .

Even firmly established Northwest bands could encounter difficulty trying to break into Seattle; friendly connections would be vital to Nirvana.

DAVID WHITING: Trying to get a Seattle show was much more laborious, as there always seemed to be an attitude against the smaller cities and the bands that came from them. The big-city/little-city syndrome has continued to this day . . . it became much easier to skip Seattle than to try and line up a show which involved multiple contacts, sending them a cassette of our music (even though they knew who we were), "waiting for the call," and then getting placed low on the bill and making squat for playing.

DAMON ROMERO: Booking agents for venues, especially in Seattle, they just wanted four bands who all sounded the same to play a Wednesday night, while in Olympia and [in] the earlier punk-rock scene even in Seattle, there was more variety. That was what I liked when I first started going, was you'd go, see four bands, all completely different. I think that the music industry in Seattle quickly jumped on the bandwagon and every bar wanted to be "that club" that had the grunge bands.

While trying to break into Seattle, Olympia became Nirvana's home by virtue of Cobain's presence and the warm acceptance the band received there.

GILLY ANN HANNER, Sister Skelter/Calamity Jane: I first saw Nirvana when they played my house for my birthday party. [*Author's note:*

I'm still in awe of this.] The guy I was dating at the time was playing bass in Sister Skelter, Chris Quinn; he knew Kurt. I decided that I wanted to play for my twenty-first birthday, that we should play at my house and he said he knew this guy and his band—that they were really great. So we decided to go find them, drove around town over to his apartment. Chris went in and asked, "Hey, want to play a party?" They said, "Sure, we'll play." That's it. I worked at the library at the school where they had a Media Department, and you could use the media equipment for school-related projects, so I checked out a PA, microphone, speakers, and everything—we got that from school, brought it home, set that up, and then played the show. My house was completely destroyed in the morning—my front window was broken out by someone slam-dancing and falling through it—it was great! I thought these guys were real rock 'n' roll—a real band. My band opened up, Kurt sang a song with us . . . my boyfriend told Kurt, "Hey, we're going to play 'Greatest Gift,' want to sing with us?" He said, "Yeah, totally, I'll sing that with you!" So we did that song and he sang with the other two singers in Sister Skelter.

The power of love clearly played a big role in Olympia's musical matchups.

PAUL KIMBALL: I was seeing a girl . . . and she was playing with Gilly in a group called Sister Skelter . . . I sang "Drunk in My Past" that night with her band, which was really fun. Pretty sure that's how Lansdat Blister wound up playing that one. When Nirvana was playing that night, the room was so packed I took one look in and walked right back out to the yard.

ALEX KOSTELNIK: Everyone in Oly knew who they were and respected them. I was upstairs throwing hastily made Molotov cocktails at a car on cement blocks down below . . . I heard this throbbing, thundering sound coming from downstairs and was compelled to run down and see. The long-greasy-haired blond guy who looked like a roadie for the band—turned out he sang! He played guitar! I was immediately attracted to Krist—he was tall like me and had a beautiful scrolled black bass. He played it so low his wrists looked like they were going to fold in half. Bob Whittaker, later to manage Mudhoney, fell through the living-room window. So many people were in the kitchen jumping up and down that they snapped the water pipe running in the floor below them. Bob came the next morning on his bike and responsibly fixed the window.

Beyond the happy revels, Nirvana's niche in Olympia was very clear; there was a vacancy at one end of the sound spectrum.

SCOTT HARBINE, Beezus and Ramona: The Olympia scene was pretty mellow. Nirvana was definitely the heaviest band on the bill. One of the bands before Nirvana was playing sort of a hippie jam rock and Hendrix covers. Nirvana was a definite surprise to what I was expecting . . . I remember telling Cobain that they reminded me of a punk AC/DC. He told me that my band reminded him of Echo and the Bunnymen which at the time felt like a compliment. We had a good conversation about bands like Green River and the U-Men, but my AC/DC comparison seemed to bum him out.

ALEX KOSTELNIK: They were the undisputed heavyweight kings. There is a *sound* in every region/town—there's a little microclimate where everyone is huffing each other's pheromones. Nirvana sounded like we all wanted to sound, like we were all trying to sound. But they did it like it was effortless (later I learned it was just the opposite) like a 747 doing a ballerina dance just for the hell of it because they could . . .

GILLY ANN HANNER: They all looked like dudes, basically—they didn't look like an Olympia band at all, which was great! There was K Records, Calvin, playing that stripped-down poppy do-it-yourself vibe, the childlike quality to the scene and to the music. Then these guys—they were rock 'n' roll; heavy, loud, and good. They were really rocking.

PAUL KIMBALL: The first clear memory I have of them was at that show in the field outside of K dorm. They were definitely "rockers": leather jackets, long hair, that kind of thing. But other than Dave sporting a redneck-style mustache, they didn't stand out as hicks . . . They were cool: I remember them being very sloppy and sounding like crap, but that pretty much described all of us . . .

For all the talk of Nirvana's pop side, they were rock first, and in 1988 Washington, good pop kids played Olympia, but super-bad rock 'n' rollers hit Seattle. Similarly, for all the positives of Olympia or Tacoma, if a band wanted some degree of commercial success, Seattle was where it was at.

BRUCE PURKEY: All the big touring acts still went through Seattle. All the money and studios were in Seattle. Pretty much, if you wanted to make it, you were eventually going to Seattle.

JUSTIN TROSPER, Unwound/Giant Henry: Olympia has a long history of weird sociopolitical dynamics . . . this weird antisuccess mentality. If you take notice, most of the people that came out of Olympia succeeded after they left . . . It's this place where people develop and test ideas like a lab. Honestly, there's only so far you can take it there, and I recommend going somewhere else to be successful. People here don't necessarily support artists that want to expand their horizons outside of a small, like-minded culture. In a way, it is really conservative and closed-minded, even though it is a really welcoming place for people who may not fit into mainstream society. There is so much collective community-oriented social behavior that it can become stifling to be an individual that deviates from that collective . . . It is this place that attracts outsiders, like the Island of Misfit Toys. It is the outsider town to Seattle.

5.0

Sub Pop and *Bleach*
June 1988 to January 1989

Nirvana's support in Olympia meant top billing at house parties, but their focus on Seattle meant trying to stir interest in a new and far more competitive stomping ground. Their first Seattle show was to half a dozen people; the band canceled a show in May when no one showed up; a July show drew only twelve spectators. Nirvana was a bunch of out-of-towners with zero pull.

CHRIS QUINN: I can understand though they got a lukewarm reception in Seattle early on. Melvins did the same thing, making the transition to bars. They played the Vogue—that's the only time they were lackluster; it wasn't their environment, they weren't used to it. For Nirvana, it meant transitioning from the kind of excitement of playing at parties to a more snobby Seattle thing where they were out of their element at first. I can tell you that Nirvana, from my perspective, compared to the other bands in Seattle, were an underdog for a while—and with everything moving so fast, even if it was just six months, it felt like a while.

KEVIN WHITWORTH, Love Battery: Nirvana were from out of town, so they obviously weren't part of the scene. There really wasn't a "scene"—there were forty or so people who traded members of bands on a monthly basis. It was like musical chairs for a while, until it stopped . . . There was exactly one crowd, and they (we) went to all the shows. We all knew each other, slept on each other's couches, borrowed equipment, and traded band members.

GEOFF ROBINSON, Blood Circus: Many did not take them seriously. We (my band-mates and I) all knew just based on their songs that they were a force to be watched . . . They were confident and polished, but their equipment and possibly their drummer, held them back—in my opinion.

SCOTT VANDERPOOL: I do vaguely remember Jon [Poneman] and Bruce [Pavitt] sitting at the edge of the stage on opposite sides like bookends, Bruce rocking back and forth autistically while this rather average but noisy bunch of hair farmers played.

JOSH HAYDEN, Treacherous Jaywalkers: I'm not even sure it was Nirvana that opened for us . . . When we got to the club, we were told that the singer of Nirvana was sick and that Nirvana canceled. I was told the name of a different band that was opening . . . I've read online that Nirvana did indeed play the show. Kurt alluded to this gig in some early Nirvana promo material . . . I vaguely remember watching some of the band that did open the set. I think they were loud. I don't think I stayed for the whole set. I don't think many people were in the audience, I'd say maybe ten people . . . I never met the opening band, but we did kind of acknowledge each other from across the room. I remember they seemed kind of nerdy and shy, or maybe that's because I was nerdy and shy.

Money was crucial throughout this period and Nirvana's sound would suffer because of the compromises made due to simple poverty.

JACK ENDINO: There was a terrible-sounding guitar amp that Kurt brought to the studio . . .

GEOFF ROBINSON: They were from a Podunk logging town and their equipment was more cheeseball than ours—which we felt was next to impossible . . . I just remember our first gig with them and Kurt playing through a Silvertone [Sears Roebuck] amp. I remember thinking, I thought *I* had it bad.

CHRIS QUINN: I was at a party at this little house called the Caddyshack . . . The whole house was the size of an apartment—it was this shacky thing. That's the first time I saw Nirvana play and I was blown away . . . They seemed very driven and they had their own PA. They had seemingly ramshackle equipment, but they were really good! I'd seen a lot of music by then, a lot of good bands, a lot of bad bands—they were *good*.

TOM DARK, Knife Dance: You did not have the same technology/exposure thirty years ago, you had to really go out and do it yourself. Back then it was about playing out, fliers, word of mouth, fanzines, college radio, and putting out your own record. With each new band, you get to know more people of all aspects of the scene; that helped out [in] going, putting on shows, what clubs to play, information on where to record, press your records, what zines to send to in order to get your product reviewed . . . the whole networking thing. It was such a big mystery yet exciting . . . Audiences were great back then, always up for something live. The media picked up on things from time to time, but nothing huge. That's why people did zines instead, as we did not count on bigger press to get the word out.

Having a demo tape was the first step for most bands, but Nirvana had neither the budget to pay for pressings nor the inclination to make and sell records themselves.

GEORGE SMITH: There were a lot of cassettes getting passed around—that's what bands could afford to do, so getting a cassette release was no big deal. That didn't feel the same; you could just do it in your house. Vinyl, though—that took real support.

RONNA MYLES-ERA: Olympia was a safe place to be a band, because you could just release your own stuff. You didn't need someone else to release it. We tried to get on K, but Calvin would say to me over and over, "Why don't you just release your own stuff?" We did have some cassettes that we would sell at shows and also give away.

If inclined, and with a little more in the way of resources, Nirvana could have followed the DIY route; the underground was full of penniless labels started by musicians.

ED FARNSWORTH, Napalm Sunday: We started our own label because we had to. We didn't fit with any of the existing hardcore labels . . . Shark Sandwich wasn't much of a label; we released two singles on it, both our own. In those ancient times before the Internet and digital recording programs, you needed to record and release something physically tangible to be legitimate, and singles were the most affordable way to do that. And let's face it, they're also pretty cool, particularly for guys like us who had grown up buying singles. We didn't have the money to record an album's worth of material . . . So we saved our gig money to pay for recording and pressing the forty-five.

RONNA MYLES-ERA: We had some good reviews and did some touring. This sparked interest from Lee Joseph, who ran Hell Yeah Records . . . We thought they were this big L.A. label . . . but it was just one guy who ran the label out of his small house . . . The record kept being delayed until finally Damon [Romero] and I decided to fly to L.A. for ourselves . . . It was eye-opening. Lee was great but just didn't have the time or the money to push the release. We ended up working at Epitaph stuffing Bad Religion records . . . It did eventually come out, though, and we managed to go to Disneyland!

PETER IRVINE, Cordelia's Dad: You are not alone in never having heard of Okra, and that illustrates our problem—it was a very cool label, but was basically just one very nice, dedicated guy [Dan Dow] working out of a record store in Ohio. There was no staff. The first time I met Dan, I proposed doing a video—it's a miracle he didn't tell me to fuck off right then . . .

TOM DARK: Amphetamine Reptile from Minneapolis wanted to do a seven-inch, and a Cleveland label, St. Valentine, inquired about doing a twelve-inch EP . . . And nothing happened with either. In the end I took four of the songs, formed Hit & Run Records, and released an EP, then later ended up releasing the *Wolf Hour* album on Hit & Run with a license deal with Double A Records in Europe too.

MARK ROBINSON, Unrest: My friends and I started TeenBeat when we were in high school. I had always been interested in music and fascinated with records. The main reason that we started the label was just to have people hear our music, since we had no clue as to how one would go about performing an actual concert. Having someone else release our record seemed like an unattainable fantasy at the time so we just had fun and did it ourselves. The original releases were just a lending library. Only one copy existed of each release and we lent them to our friends for a few days so they could give a listen.

RICK RIZZO, Eleventh Dream Day: Amoeba was a one-man [Keith Holland] label—basically my college friend who had money because he had a good job in engineering. Our first two records cost almost nothing to make. There was no support beyond the production costs. We did all of our own press, set up our own shows, printed our own shirts . . . I worked at a record distributor at the time, in the shipping department with Dan Koretzky, founder of Drag City . . .

JED BREWER, Thornucopia: Lather Records was started by my friend Mike and I . . . It was just a way to release my own stuff and my friends' stuff. I never paid for my friends' bands' releases. It was just a way to have it under one label to hopefully give a little more profile to the releases instead of everyone doing separate self-releases . . .

Beyond the egregiously famous Sub Pop and K Records, the Northwest was not devoid of other labels.

PAUL KIMBALL: Dana [Rich] from Bluebird Records out in Enumclaw, he had a label called Horton/Reflex, and was basically the insane patron saint of underground music on the outskirts of the Seattle area. He seemed completely unfazed by the low chance of financial return on his projects, or maybe he just knew something no one else did, but he put out great stuff in cool packages that nobody was really clamoring for. I always admired the hell out of him, and wished he'd catch a break somehow.

GEORGE SMITH: He owned a record store where you could get real music, one of those little beacons.

LISA SMITH, Dickless: Up Records was started by our dear friend Chris Takino [RIP], who was a true music fan and probably didn't make what he deserved in his short life for all the hard work . . .

CONRAD UNO, PopLlama: Tom Dyer from Green Monkey Records, he recorded in a closet essentially, and had a great fun little record label like I did . . . if you were a band with a product (or a circle of friends with bands with product), you made up a label name and stuck it on there for fun, same as now; that's essentially why PopLlama started. The great thing about starting a record label is that as soon as you have a name and a tiny bit of success, people out in the music world assume a certain level of functionality. We were barely functional ever. I really loved recording the music I liked, and making some records, but the rest of it was not really up my alley. Promotion and bookkeeping are really no fun. My studio (and everyone else's for that matter) was busy, busy, busy. Everyone wanted to record . . . It all worked fine for the little performance that was PopLlama and Egg Studios.

LARRY SCHEMEL: eMpTy was a local label that put out our records . . . They were an independent record label in the truest sense of the word; we would go over to Blake [Wright]'s apartment to hand-stuff singles . . .

STEVE MORIARTY, The Gits: Daniel House was fired from Sub Pop . . . he was doing distribution, so he focused on C/Z, which was "the other label" in Seattle. There were a few other small ones, but he seemed to have the resources of Sub Pop at his disposal because he'd taken them with him—distribution especially . . . They would make posters for us, that was about it—and they had a publicist.

MARK PICKEREL, Screaming Trees: Velvetone was really just born out of the studio that recorded our first few releases [Albright Productions]. The staff was made up of Sam Albright, who owned the studio; Steve Fisk, who was house producer; and myself for a little while. I did tape duplication and mailings; I even got high school credit for my job there. We also did tape duplication for K Records . . . can you imagine? I actually got school credits for listening to hours of Shonen Knife, Girl Trouble, and Beat Happening while getting paid minimum wage!

SLIM MOON: Kurt's ambition was to get a record label to put out a Nirvana album. He talked about it a lot. So did Krist.

Luckily for Nirvana, Sub Pop took an interest first. But to be fair, Sub Pop was barely one step up the ladder, at least initially. Bruce Pavitt's brand had started as a radio show, then a fanzine, then a tag for cassette compilations, then a newspaper column.

BRUCE PAVITT: The audience was small. The first issue was printed in an edition of five hundred; the first cassette [SP#5] sold two thousand. Collectors shopping in indie stores and other fanzine writers were my primary audience. I did get a lot of write-ups because the information I was providing, reviews and addresses of obscure indie releases, was rare . . .

LEIGHTON BEEZER, The Thrown Ups: This was a time when future grunge alumni were more like grunge freshmen.

One exceptional strength lay in Pavitt's decade-long grounding in underground labels and media—his understanding of record collectors, scenesters, and fanzine writers. Few people had spent so long cataloguing these networks. Yet it wasn't just Nirvana that had trouble scratching together cash. Following a 5,000-edition compilation in 1986 it was a full year before another Sub Pop release could be attempted. Sub Pop was still a strictly local name well into 1988.

JOSH HADEN, Treacherous Jaywalkers: The show was booked by Global. We were just following their scheduling, I wasn't familiar with the Vogue beforehand, and I really don't have any memories of it other than it was a typical dingy little rock club that smelled like beer . . . I wasn't aware of Sub Pop or the Seattle bands . . . I knew of Soundgarden a little later when they came to L.A. to sign with SST.

What changed in 1988 was the addition of Jonathan Poneman, who provided some cash and a touch of business acumen. Poneman and Pavitt officially incorporated Sub Pop in April 1988 amid their first contact with Nirvana. Bruce Pavitt describes his proudest achievement as "letting people know that culture starts at home. You have to support local scenes and independent artists if culture is going to move forward. We helped create a model for that." This gut instinct was backed by intelligent decisions to focus on a specific identity that encompassed sound, visuals, attitude—expressed live, on vinyl, in the press; everything was advertising.

STEVE MORIARTY: They did a few things right . . . like buying a couple of vans and putting their bands on tour—the hardest thing to do in those days was to book a tour in the US. It's a huge country. Gigs don't pay; if you were lucky, someone would call ahead and send posters, but if not you'd be playing to four or five people, maybe up to forty if you were really lucky—all for fifty bucks. You spent more on gas than you made on T-shirt sales. So Sub Pop invested in a couple of vans and sent their bands on tour, which was a very smart thing. And they had a publicist who would get ahead of the shows—Nils Bernstein—who would send articles and hype the bands.

DAMON ROMERO: Chad and Kurt had met at some previous time at the Community World Theater when their bands played together but didn't really remember that. So I introduced Chad to Kurt, as I knew they were looking for a drummer—Chad was a great drummer, really wanted to play in a band, one that worked and played a lot. So I got those two talking to each other—I think it was at the Community World Theater at that March 19 gig . . . Chad and some of my friends came down to watch Lush. My girlfriend actually suggested I should introduce those two, so I did. Chad was in the band pretty quickly. He did an audition then started playing with them. I was really psyched about that—Chad's a great guy and he was good in the band.

Their early drummers—Burckhard, Foster, Crover—had been a link backward to Aberdeen; Channing was the way forward, residing on Bainbridge Island near Seattle. He was also a younger guy with a far gentler spirit. Then again, maybe the calm demeanor signaled his physical confidence, as implied by one anecdote that made me chuckle.

LEIGHTON BEEZER: No one would mess with Chad . . . Even though he was the smallest member of the band, he had been studying Tae Kwon Do for quite a while and would kick your ass if you messed with him. Tad [Doyle] found out the hard way one night, when he told Chad he could outplay him on drums. That happened one night at some party in the U-District. Tad went first, and he was excellent. He had been a drummer in H-Hour. Chad took one look at Tad, then proceeded to destroy the entire kit with his fists and feet. Tad's eyeballs opened as big as saucers—remember, he is a big dude, probably outweighing Chad by two hundred pounds—and Tad said "Fuck this shit," and left.

Just as Cobain's amplifier earned cockeyed interest, Channing's equipment would draw attention . . .

PAUL KIMBALL: Chad was definitely good, and his drums were just a total visual statement.

ABE BRENNAN: Chad used to play these black drums that flared at the bottom—can't remember the brand, but it was a distinctive look. He obviously wasn't as good a drummer as [Dave] Grohl, but he was solid . . .

SCOTT VANDERPOOL: A fiberglass-shelled make of drums with big swooping bells at the end that was about the uncoolest kit you could have back then . . . endorsed by jazz guys like Billy Cobham.

ED FARNSWORTH: The drummer was playing Staccato drums, those weird, curvy drums that the guy from Bow Wow Wow plays in the "I Want Candy" video. That was totally cool.

SHAMBIE SINGER: Their drummer was a tiny guy and his drum kit featured the most bizarre rack tom set I'd ever seen. The toms were long and curved—like an elk horn . . . Those freaky-looking drums made more of a lasting impression than anything else.

Making people look could do no harm to a band wanting to be noticed. The visual contrasts within the band were significant.

GEOFF ROBINSON: I remember having several beers at the Vogue with Krist, and saw him in DC when we toured with Les Thugs. Krist was tall like me, so we kind of hit it off, even though he was nearly ten years younger . . . I liked that their bass player was out front, in the open. I admired all the great bass players in rock and I could tell that Krist admired them too by the way he played.

ABE BRENNAN: Krist stood out—or up, I should say. He was a towering individual, and he moved well onstage, swaying, bouncing, swinging the neck of his bass around. Kurt didn't move a whole lot, but he was intense when he sang, and he played with an edge, a physicality, that appealed.

SCOTT VANDERPOOL: Chad was a drummer so he and I got along just ducky. Krist, of course, is very tall, as am I . . . But I'm only six-four and I always enjoyed having to look up at someone for a change. Local artist and guitarist Whiting Tennis is also super-tall. We were like the "I could never fit in a Ferrari" club.

It's telling that there was more note made of Novoselic than of the future iconic front man.

PETER LITWIN: Back at that time, they didn't seem to be a very exciting live band. Kurt seemed kind of shy onstage. I think Krist and Chad were a bit more animated, and Kurt wasn't . . . My stand-out memory is just what a nice bunch of guys they were . . . I remember Kurt as being a quiet, kind of shy pothead. Krist was super-cool and has always been a really friendly guy.

GEOFF ROBINSON: Kurt had a huge chip on his shoulder (I now know it was because he was picked on by jocks in Aberdeen, and three members of Blood Circus were over six foot tall—I'm six-six), so we didn't interact with him too much . . .

SLIM MOON: The main "audience interaction" . . . was just Krist being drunk and grabbing the microphone to say something weird or funny. That started early . . .

Sub Pop made use of what advantages they had to get Nirvana's name out.

SCOTT VANDERPOOL: I met Jon Poneman when I started doing radio at the University of Washington's then all-volunteer not-so-student radio station KCMU . . . Mark Arm followed me on-air Friday afternoons . . . all the future Sub Pop band members that worked with Bruce at Muzak would call in with requests . . . I ran live sound for a lot of Poneman-produced rock shows, and played briefly with him and Gary Thorstensen (later of Tad) in his band the Treeclimbers before he quit to make Sub Pop a full-time concern.

JAIME ROBERT JOHNSON, Crunchbird: The first time I heard "Paper Cuts" by Nirvana I was down at the Comet Tavern one night and they had KCMU on the overhead speakers, who were playing the song. Hearing that was a revelation to me because here was a band thinking about rock in the same way I felt I was . . .

PETER LITWIN: I was listening to a local radio show called *Audio Aces* on KCMU and heard a Nirvana song. I immediately called the DJ (who happened to be Jonathan Poneman) and asked him who it was. I loved it! I loved the heaviness of it; it reminded me of the Melvins, but with more melodic vocals. I just know I loved them at first after hearing that song on the radio. I think that same week I went and saw them play one of their first shows in Seattle at the Vogue. I was one of six people at the show. They were great.

Poneman's presence at KCMU got Nirvana on-air almost immediately while Bruce Pavitt's work at the Rocket meant by the time of an April 24 show, the fliers and listings already showed "Sub Pop w/Nirvana."

Of Nirvana's eleven Seattle shows in 1988, three were branded Sub Pop Sunday. Instead of trying to promote individual bands, Sub Pop used the prestige they'd earned from existing successes and sold that connection to audiences; buying a Sub Pop release always meant buying not just the band but the label, too.

SHAMBIE SINGER: At times on that tour we were booked to play with other bands either from Seattle, or with a Sub Pop release. Usually both. In some cases it was clear Sub Pop had booked us with other bands on the label in order to promote the label itself. I recall, for example, being one of the bands on the bill for "Sub Pop Night" in Houston, Texas. I felt like putting together Sub Pop bills was part of the whole Bruce and Jonathan Motown hit factory aspiration.

The label also used their many friends to get Nirvana out there.

SCOTT VANDERPOOL: I think Jon asked me if one of his bands could open a show we already had down there . . .

JOE GOLDRING, Amorphous Head: At our first show in Seattle, Jonathan Poneman happened to be there. He liked a couple of songs and paid for us to go into the studio with Jack Endino to record a seven-inch for C/Z . . . One of these tracks ended up on the *Teriyaki Asthma* compilation (also with Nirvana). So when Nirvana were heading down to San Francisco for the first time, Poneman asked us to put together a gig at an appropriate venue . . . so we booked it at the only place we could; the Country & Western saloon. We also gave them a place to crash at George [Miller—Amorphous Head guitarist]'s house—George suspected they were some kind of weirdo Christians . . . I have no idea where this came from.

SHAMBIE SINGER: They'd put out the single "Big Cheese"/"Love Buzz." Loved it. Especially their version of "Love Buzz." Think a chick named Shannon who was a DJ at WOZQ [Smith College] played it for me one afternoon when I was hanging around the station.

Sub Pop made the call that Nirvana's cover of Shocking Blue's song "Love Buzz" should be the A-side for the single. The decision made perfect sense; it was the most pop-oriented song Nirvana possessed, and the provenance of the song was a talking point for musos.

GEORGE SMITH: At that show I remember them playing "Love Buzz" and being very taken by that song, a little piece of the crowd thinking, Hey, these guys are pretty good . . .

LINDSEY THRASHER, Vomit Launch: I really liked them because they covered "Love Buzz" and I'm a Shocking Blue fan and had never heard anyone cover that song . . . I remember telling Kurt how much I loved "Love Buzz" . . . They played with Tad in Chico once and I asked him to please play "Love Buzz," which they were going to do anyway.

The single wasn't just Nirvana's first release. More important to Sub Pop, it was the inauguration of the Sub Pop Singles Club, a series aimed at collectors that quickly needed to secure an audience so the label could gather sorely needed member fees—which is why Sub Pop was so particular about the release, insisting on a particular song and sending Cobain back to the studio to rerecord vocals.

SCOTT VANDERPOOL: I do remember thinking it somewhat brilliant they'd covered that obscure Shocking Blue song . . . Managed to hang on to a test pressing of "Love Buzz" that Jon gave me to play at KCMU . . . sold it on eBay about ten years ago during some financially tough times . . . got quite a lot for it, which sort of made up for Sub Pop never paying me my sales commission.

It was a first vindication of Nirvana's efforts, too—something they marked with a pointed joke.

RYAN AIGNER: You've seen the "Love Buzz"/"Big Cheese" single? Have you noticed the inscription on the vinyl? Around the label it says "Why don't you trade those guitars for shovels?" That quote happened during a rehearsal with Robert Novoselic, myself, and a friend called Brett Walker. We were at Krist's house; we'd gotten together after school . . . trying to rehearse and learn some cover songs. Krist came home, came upstairs, listened to what we doing, and gave us his opinion about what was going on, helped us out—showed us some guitar leads he knew—then Krist and Robert's father came home. He was a construction worker and he wasn't happy about this noise, so he came upstairs to the boys' bedroom, forced the door open. He was yelling. Krist was yelling back, "Aw, leave them alone! They're just kids, you know!" Finally they let him in. We didn't know him well; we introduced ourselves and let him know who we were. And he says with a frown on his face, "You kids, why don't you kids go sell those goddamn guitars and buy something useful like shovels or something?" That's where the quote came from—many years later, the story had a mythological life-span and kept coming up. They found it pretty funny so they had it engraved.

The front cover of the single was a statement of intent foregrounding only two textual elements; the band's name and Sub Pop's—all Sub Pop releases enforced this equal billing. The style was so identifiable that Steel Pole Bath Tub and Melvins would eventually put out a parody.

MIKE MORASKY: The idea to parody the Mudhoney/Sonic Youth split seven-inch was the Melvins'. I think they originally wanted to do it as a split with Nirvana, who I think were uncomfortable with the idea. We were big Sonic Youth fans, so we immediately volunteered. The Sub Pop explosion was just getting rolling and people were taking Sub Pop so seriously that the Melvins, us, and Tom [Flynn] at Boner Records found it funny to take the piss out of them a bit.

Sub Pop latched onto the old Detroit Motown wisdom of making a label synonymous with a location—ergo Soundgarden's "Sub Pop Rock City" song. They created a situation where it was hard to mention music from the state of Washington without the label's name appearing.

PETER LITWIN: On our show posters we started seeing "Seattle" and "Sub Pop" before our name. We did do one seven-inch record on Sub Pop, so that might be why concert promoters thought they could benefit from associating us with Sub Pop.

PETER IRVINE: One thing we saw was that at some of our gigs in Europe, the promoters would toss around the "Seattle" adjective in the marketing either as a bold misdirection, or else a geographic misunderstanding.

SHAMBIE SINGER: They were explicit about trying to marshal a particular sound they could market. I think at one point maybe Danny Bland—a Sub Pop PR guy and member of the band Cat Butt—likened the Sub Pop approach to Motown. He felt like Bruce and Jonathan were pretty proud of that strategy . . . Jonathan, who I knew the best of the two of them, was very candid about cultivating a certain sound and image for his label as a primary means toward financial success.

KURT DANIELSON, Tad: Sub Pop was an unbelievably supportive, visionary, fertile, and energetic label, one with a genius for innovative promotion . . . In a way, they were extensions of the band itself in terms of creative input when it came to things like ideas for album titles, contributing creatively to ideas about promotion and image . . . We always knew that both Bruce and Jon believed in the band, and this gave us a great sense of self-confidence. This was one of the greatest things about Sub Pop: how supportive they always were, even during the toughest and most tense times. We always felt as if whatever we accomplished ourselves musically, it was for our benefit as well as for theirs. It was a family atmosphere, and there was a sense of family pride, a feeling that whatever we did, we were doing it for the good not only of our own band but also for the other bands as well as the label itself and beyond that for Seattle and its music community.

Sub Pop's focus on regional identity wasn't particularly unique; the label was reproducing a common underground trend of the period.

TOM DARK: By 1983, cities and record labels everywhere started to put out lots of compilation albums, putting their scenes and bands on the map. For some reason, northeast Ohio didn't have one, so I decided to put one out myself. While helping out bands, putting on shows and benefits, I raised enough money to put out the *New Hope* compilation album on my own New Hope Records.

DAVID YAMMER, Bayou Pigs: Houston was good because of its size and its geographical location. We were sort of a halfway point between Austin and New Orleans for touring bands . . . Anomie Records was run by Scott Ayers [and Bliss Blood] of the Pain Teens. We recorded a song at Scott's studio for the *Houston Loud* compilation that was released in 1988. Actually it was Bliss and Scott who suggested that we change our name to the Bayou Pigs from the Bay of Pigs (it seems that there was a band who already had that name), and it made sense since Houston is known as the Bayou City . . . Anomie Records and Scott Ayers were a driving force in the Houston scene—he's hardworking and bright if not outright brilliant!

C/Z Records had planted the Northwest seed in early 1986 with the *Deep Six* compilation. In 1988, the new label caught up with a compilation that would feature only the second Nirvana original to see release, "Spank Thru," on *Sub Pop 200*.

JAMES BURDYSHAW: *Sub Pop 200* was Bruce Pavitt's next compilation release after his US compilation *Sub Pop 100* from 1986. *100* was from a bunch of indie-punk bands across the US . . . For *200*, Bruce wanted to showcase all the Northwest bands he loved . . . He really dug Cat Butt from day one and wanted to have us on his Northwest compilation. There was nothing formal about handing over the song;

it was simply to have Jack Endino mix it and give it to Bruce to include on the record. No money was exchanged or contracts signed. Bruce was running the label out of his apartment at the time . . . It's still a compilation, which never sells as well as a full-length release by one single group, but I made more money off that one song than anything I've ever put out. The first check was a $450 payout from Sub Pop about seven years after the record was released. Then there was a residual trickle for the next couple years.

SCOTT VANDERPOOL: We got a song on *Sub Pop 200*, but Jon said at the time "I'm not putting you out; you're a twee jangle-pop band." But then they put out the Walkabouts, so go figure. I made fun of that, even though I'd known Chris Eckman since junior high school PE. "They're sensitive hippies with big amplifiers!" . . . Bruce loved that and used it in their promo shit . . . In any case, they liked us just enough to put one song on a compilation that I think over the years made each of us about $800 total . . .

Nirvana probably made not a penny off this release for many years to come. But given the label's relaxed attitude toward it, the band must not have had huge expectations.

LEIGHTON BEEZER: I ran into Bruce at the beach and sat down next to him. I said that I heard Sub Pop was putting out a compilation album, and he said yes, and I said he should put the Thrown Ups on it and he said sure. It was a simpler time.

TERRY LEE HALE: Grant Eckman, drummer for the Walkabouts . . . told me that one of the bands that was supposed to be included on the *Sub Pop 200* album had missed their deadline for submissions and that if I had a song ready and could get it to them immediately I might have a chance to be included. I just happened to have two recently recorded songs ready to go . . . I put them on a cassette tape and got it to Jon/Bruce right away. The rest is history. I don't remember even having a conversation with them.

While awaiting *Sub Pop 200*'s release, Nirvana continued at a leisurely pace—three shows a month at most, all usually bottom of the bill.

ABE BRENNAN: We opened the show, Nirvana played second, Swallow played third, and then Soundgarden finished things off . . . Nirvana—we were into them by then . . . The thing that stood out for me was the songs—they rocked, but there was a pop sensibility to many of them; and underneath it all lingered a sense of emotional raggedness and desperation. Or maybe that's hindsight . . . "Floyd the Barber" is the first song I remember hearing on the demo tape that [John] Purkey had—that was my favorite song then, super heavy and syncopated—so my strongest memory is them playing that song and me hurting my neck via ridiculous head banging. Soundgarden made a mistake in the first song, quite a jarring gaffe, actually very noticeable, and they all looked at each other and laughed. Then they proceeded to destroy. It was nice, though, seeing a band that good make a mistake.

KEVIN WHITWORTH: We'd just finished recording our first half dozen songs at Reciprocal with Jack Endino, and he called to say that he had this band in the studio, and that we should go and see them while they were playing in town. So we all went down to Squid Row, which was just a couple of blocks away anyway. The crowd at the small tavern was thin. I am sorry to say I was not particularly impressed, other than observing how tall the bass player was, compared to the singer.

His impression was not much changed a few weeks later.

KEVIN WHITWORTH: The Annex Theatre on Fourth Avenue downtown. "Love Buzz" had been all over KCMU by this time, and it was great—but it was a cover, so it was hard to get a handle on their music . . . they just stood around and swayed in prime shoegazer fashion as they played the first time I saw them, and they were much the same at the Annex. It's been said that opening for Mudhoney and Tad opened their eyes, and I believe that's true. Mark and Tad had always been crazy onstage after Tad came out from behind the drums, and before long Kurt was jumping around too.

October 30, 1988, saw a piece of Nirvana's future mythology falling into place.

JASON MORALES: All the dorms were lettered A through whatever, and it just so happened that K Dorm was the last in a line, so that's where they'd put the people who were inclined to party and get crazy. It's where I saw Nirvana for the first time: the legendary party that shook the floor so hard it caused structural damage? That party. Just one of those early keg parties where there were so many people stuffed into the second floor jumping up and down that it damaged the floor of the dorm.

SLIM MOON: Kurt always had a theatrical flair, it's just that the way that flair got expressed changed appropriately when the venues got bigger and the audiences got bigger . . . opening for Nirvana at K dorm, I got mad at Ian [McKinnon] and kicked over his drum set, so he punched me in the face. That was the first night I ever saw Nirvana smash their instruments, and I've always suspected that it was partially motivated by Kurt being unwilling to be upstaged by the violent drama of our set just before theirs. We broke up live on the radio a couple weeks after that.

PAUL KIMBALL: When Kurt smashed his guitar at the K Dorm Halloween party I was in the hall with no visibility to the band. But I remember people howling, just going ape shit, and then seeing someone charging out the front door with the neck of a guitar raised above their heads.

A lightbulb went off when faced with that reaction; gear smashing rocked. Just as Jimi Hendrix's guitar burning was provoked by his competitiveness with Pete Townshend, Nirvana knew live performance was a friendly contest. This wasn't the last time those they played with suspected one-upmanship, but what the hey, everyone was doing it.

ROBIN PERINGER, Heavy into Jeff: I did almost burn down a Seattle club after lighting my guitar on fire. I had done this a couple of times, but on this occasion, Michael [Anderson] stepped on the bottle of lighter fluid, spreading it all around the stage. We did finish the song, though.

A final key aspect of the Sub Pop aesthetic was the sense of humor; as far back as 1986 *Sub Pop 100* carried the message "The new thing, the big thing, the God thing: a mighty multinational entertainment conglomerate based in the Pacific North West." The label even released the ironically titled *Fuck Me, I'm Rich* compilation, paraphrasing a line from Mudhoney, when the money certainly wasn't rolling in. The label was constantly self-referential—everything was intended to reinforce Sub Pop's budding mythos. Jokes were simply the default communication. Consider the following gorgeous whimsy regarding the *Sub Pop 200* party, Nirvana's last show of 1988 . . .

LEIGHTON BEEZER: I was invited to play by default, I guess, since it was a record-release party and all the bands were on the bill. But from here on out it's hard for me to give an accurate answer, since I got very seriously drunk that night and my memory is a little fuzzy . . . They were really just another band among equals at the time . . . But here's what I do remember. Kurt and I used to occasionally have a beer together before he played. He used to stink for some reason . . . like, really bad BO. And so, one night, as a joke, I brought along a roll of my girlfriend's deodorant and gave it to Kurt before he took the stage that night. He laughed, and then quickly disappeared. The next thing I knew, I saw Kurt onstage with Nirvana, rolling some of this stuff on, like, in the middle of a song . . . I can't remember which one. He then picked it up and showed it to the crowd. The band stopped playing, looking kind of bewildered. Kurt held up the deodorant, Teen Spirit, and said something like, "Leighton Beezer said I stink and gave me this. Now I smell like Teen Spirit." . . . A couple of weeks before the *Sub 200* show, Kurt stopped by my house on the Hill, just to shoot the shit. He picked up my guitar, a Squire Jagmaster, as I recall, and played these four chords for me. He said he'd been listening a lot to the first Boston album and wanted to use those chords in a new song he'd been working on. I said, "But you're ripping off 'More Than a Feeling,' dude." He smiled and said nothing.

Returning (alas) to consensual reality after Leighton's teasing, of note is how casual the release party was and how little Nirvana mattered.

GEOFF ROBINSON: I admit I still have this awful mental image of a cocktail bar with canapés when I know that's utterly false . . . It was just another gig for us. The big draw was that we would be able to play with our friend Jesse Bernstein. I am still kicking myself for not getting to know him better, and mostly for not patronizing his material and other venue appearances more. He was truly a genius, and to this day I rank him up there with Burroughs and Ginsberg. Once Blood Circus got to know Jesse, our output appeared to me to be more amateurish than I had ever imagined. He was a master, and I miss him. He would probably call me an emotionally indulgent jellyfish for saying so, but there it is.

MARIA MABRA, Hell Smells: Jesse . . . He was hard to get to know, we were kicking it with him . . . I was in the trailer where he died, where he killed himself, just days before he did it—that was a shock, we were all like . . . It just came out of the blue. "Did you hear what Jesse did?"/"What?!" It felt crazy. I see people now with his T-shirts and I always say, "Hey, that's a Jesse T-shirt!" and they say, "Yeah, he's cool."

JAMES BURDYSHAW: I kept hearing things about Nirvana but didn't see them live until summer of 1988. They played with Monica [Nelson]'s band in Seattle at a new club called Squid Row. I didn't really think much of them that night. They were super-loud and sloppy. They fell on the stage and screamed a lot. Kurt seemed very drunk and Monica told me she thought they sucked. I could hear the Melvins influence, for sure, but thought Buzz [Osborne] did it much better. I was thinking, What was all the buzz about these guys? I saw them at the Vogue in late August and liked them a little bit this time. They were tighter and started playing heavy riff songs instead of just screaming, but it wasn't until I saw them open the first night of the *Sub Pop 200* record-release party at the Underground that I really had a change of opinion. They played first of five bands that night—before the Thrown Ups, even. The place wasn't even half full and I stood with Rob Roth [of Truly] and both of us were dumbfounded. I remember him saying, "Damn, these guys suddenly got really good!" I can distinctly see Kurt and Krist playing with confidence and going into the songs seamlessly. Then I heard Kurt sing these melodies I'd never seen him do before.

Although Nirvana ended 1988 still just a footnote alongside greater legends, they could still feel genuine hope for the year to come. Their music was getting released: They'd recorded an album initially entitled *Too Many Humans* but soon to become known as *Bleach*. They were now an established presence in three regional music hubs and could enjoy the holiday season with friends in Seattle, Olympia, and Tacoma.

6.0

First Tour, First Lessons
February to July 1989

Two years' work amounted to only thirty shows for maybe a few hundred Washington natives, plus two original songs out. But January saw completion of Nirvana's first album, and some songs were already impressing their fellow musicians. Unfortunately, it'd still be months until *Bleach* would see release, and Nirvana was still just a local name.

NATHAN HILL: King Krab were playing at a club called the Vogue and they were in town recording *Bleach*. They came down to the show and played us the rough mixes out in our van. It blew us away. At that time Matt Varnum was the only one in the band who was old enough to drink in a bar, so we drank in the van. It was a good time.

STEVE TURNER, Mudhoney: Well, the first time I saw them, at the Vogue, I thought they were OK, a bit too much of a Melvins influence maybe. Then they quickly came into their own, more confidence, more hooks. By the time we played with them in California . . . they blew me away. So much energy! And Kurt rolled around on the ground at one point and somehow managed to balance on his head while still playing guitar . . .

The question remained whether Nirvana would make it past local buzz, whether they would make the first cut and then succumb before leaving a lasting scar.

Nirvana's first step outside of Washington was a logical one: Portland.

BEN MUNAT, Grind: As far as how connected Portland and Seattle are . . . there have always been Seattle bands coming down here to play and Portland bands going up there. A band could actually easily do Vancouver BC, Bellingham, Seattle, Olympia, Portland, and Eugene as a little mini-tour, with no more than a couple hours' drive between each . . . there has always been a rich local scene in Portland.

For a band that had started while one member lived in Tacoma, another in Olympia, and their drummers in Aberdeen, the distance was no big deal.

JAIME ROBERT JOHNSON: What made Seattle special to me was the fact in the space of one week, I could see Black Flag, Paisley Sin; head down to Portland and catch the Obituaries and Napalm Beach; head home the next night and catch a set by the angular artiness of bands like Infamous Menagerie doing a show with Lethal Gospel, or go see Skin Yard; then on the weekend catch Malfunkshun playing in a shoe store, go down to the Vogue to catch the Mentors, and for my Sunday hangover go hang at the Comet, where the bartenders had extremely good taste in music.

DANIEL RIDDLE: Portland was much like Seattle in that it had many talented players and groups but its lack of a so-called music industry allowed for greater musical community, as where Seattle had a music scene. The difference being one of cooperation versus competition.

SETH PERRY, Oily Bloodmen: As I see it, Portlanders [on the whole] have always had a slight inferiority complex when it comes to Seattle, even though they like to see themselves as equals, if not superior.

JOE KEITHLEY: It's got a really active punk scene—one reason a lot of people moved from California, as they couldn't stand it or couldn't afford it so they would end up in the Northwest. Portland currently has a better music scene than Seattle because you can live there cheaper than you can in Seattle, and if you want to go play in Seattle or Vancouver or down to California it's just a few hours' drive so it's pretty centrally located and you pay half the rent.

Portland became another staple of Nirvana's gig diet; Seattle and Olympia are the only places they ever played more.

RENÉE DENENFELD, Caustic Soda: It was an amazing, lively, outrageously active, and usually friendly music scene. In the beginning out of punk houses—there were famous punk houses, like Ether 13 in Eugene or Dirge in Portland—the clubs came and added more impetus. But being the rainy Northwest, the music was always largely born and created in basements . . . largely created by outsiders; street kids and rejects and poor kids and dropouts. It was not a college scene at all. It was very warm and welcoming to an incredibly diverse array of people . . .

GILLY ANN HANNER: Portland was like the Wipers, Poison Idea, the Accused . . . More punky, but punky in a way that people knew how to play their instruments—I'm not saying that no one in Olympia knew how to play their instruments but . . . you didn't *have* to play your instrument; it was almost like reverse-snobbery in a way, it was kinda weird . . . Tam was teaching herself to play drums: "I can't chew gum and play the drums at the same time! I'll mess up!" Heather, she could sort of sing . . . They were the cool people in the band. I was not cool, because I could play guitar and I didn't have crazy hair . . .

The hub for music in Portland was the Satyricon, and Sub Pop had made sure local tastemakers couldn't fail to miss what they were building.

GEOFF ROBINSON: "Touch Me I'm Sick" was on the legendary juke-box at Portland's Satyricon. Eight months prior, "Six Foot Under" launched a newly coined "grunge" sound on the same jukebox.

ERIC MOORE, Rawhead Rex: For all of us in the Northwest it was ground zero for punk rock and all kinds of cool music. Check these bands out if you want the *real* story about who influenced Kurt: the Rats, Dead Moon, the Wipers, Poison Idea, Sado Nation . . . playing on the same stage with those guys or even drinking beer with them was, like, "The Big Time."

BEN MUNAT: [It was] entirely black inside. It had some art on the walls, but it never really changed . . . it always had that black, DIY aesthetic . . . there were definitely stretches where it was pretty much the only punk/indie-rock game in town . . . Even if I didn't go to a show at Satyricon on a Friday or Saturday, I would usually wind up there around closing to find out where the after-hours party was.

SETH PERRY: That was our home. We were usually there at least five nights a week, just hanging out and drinking beer. George, the owner, or whoever was booking would just offer us shows, although I'm sure Rich or Dale were probably in their ear a fair amount . . . There were drug dealers all over the Satyricon . . . At one point George installed a system that constantly rained water down from above to try and keep the dealers from hanging out against the front of the club. For the more hardcore bands more often than not IV heroin and co-caine use was just part of being hardcore. The culture of the Satyri-con was so open and nonjudgmental (and nihilistic) that hard drug use was not considered uncool or undesirable.

Nirvana was hooked up with Mudhoney for a Sub Pop bill there, then with local favorites the Dharma Bums.

DAMON ROMERO: There was a little bit of showmanship. I rode down to Portland with Nirvana in their van and I remember the show at the Satyricon, Kurt smashed a guitar at the end of that show. It was one he'd bought at a pawn shop super cheap, spray-painted, then brought out for the very last song then smashed it—it wasn't an impromptu spur of the moment thing. Maybe the first time, out of frustration—people loved it. Kurt was really good at giving people what they wanted—he believed in it. I remember speaking to Chad, out on their US tour everyone in the band was getting sick of playing "Love Buzz" but Kurt said "Look, that's what everyone knows us for, we've got to deliver." He wanted to give people a good show.

A return to the Evergreen State College in February brought echoes of the past; Dave Foster was now playing with Helltrout, and Psychlodds was led by Ryan Aigner, another Aberdeen friend and Nirvana's semi-manager in the early days.

PAUL KIMBALL: That whole set of dorms [of which K Dorm was one] were brand-new in the fall of '87. The thing was that they had decent-sized living rooms [and two two-bed bedrooms], so if you moved the furniture out you could put a band in there as well as thirty, fifty people. The K unit just happened to wind up with some serious partiers living there, both upstairs and down, so when they threw a kegger over there it would take over the entire building . . . Helltrout all took mushrooms that night before we went on, just to see how long we could keep it together. As it turned out, the answer was "not very long." I left before Nirvana even went on that night, but don't ask me where I went! I have no idea . . .

There was perhaps some lingering (non-chemically induced) discomfort between the bands but this was a tight-knit scene and any awkwardness soon passed. Kimball's previous band, Lansdat Blister, had played with Nirvana more than any other local act and he was a resident of the Alamo band house, so it was unavoidable that their paths crossed.

PAUL KIMBALL: My connection to them was really through Dave Foster being in our band, and because they'd kicked Dave out of their band I felt vaguely patronized by Krist the first couple times I met him. But he warmed up, as did Kurt . . . We were having a party at the Alamo, and at one point I walked into the kitchen to find Krist Novoselic and Dylan Carlson standing at our kitchen counter in front of a huge pile of pot. It was a bunch of shake, not buds or anything, but these guys had a two-man assembly line going and were rolling joint after joint and handing them to anyone who walked by. Needless to say they gathered quite a crowd, and before you knew it pretty much everyone in the house was walking around with their very own joint hanging off their lips.

The presence of Psychlodds was a display of Nirvana's determination to support their friends and fellow musicians; something they would carry throughout the life of the band.

RYAN AIGNER: So one day we're sitting around talking about my guitar and that I wished I was better and how I admired what [Kurt] was doing and how he'd written a large catalog of originals and trying to understand how he did that. He said, "Get your guitar out, plug in—show me these riffs." So I showed a few little things I'd done and he looked at me and said "Ryan, those are songs." I said, "They're just riffs, I don't know how to arrange them, they're not enough . . ." He said, "No, they're enough. More than enough. That's a full song actually. This is where you need to start—this is adequate." . . . He said to me, "You just need to start a band." I said, "Well, we don't have any songs." He replied, "No, you don't understand. You just get a drummer, get a bass player, find a room and set up regular rehearsal, once or twice a week, you'll go in there, you'll play these little things you have over and over, and two things will happen. One; song form will come, and two; you'll mechanically practice your craft and get better and better each time you rehearse. The function of forming a group of people who have the same goal—it'll do the work for you. You don't get it all arranged then start the band—start a band and the songs will come." . . . Shortly after, this was end of '87, early part of '88 I actually started the band . . . and it was Nirvana who said "We will do these shows with you." Two of the three shows the Psychlodds did—we only did three concerts ever—two of them were with Nirvana. The reason was that it was Kurt's dedication to his previous statement. He felt he should also support us by telling us that if we wanted to play a show then they would play it with us . . . that's what I gave to them, too—I gave them encouragement and this positivity and that's all they wanted from anybody. When the Psychlodds went out and played, Krist and Kurt wouldn't come up and say "You were really awful, you really sucked" though we kind of did—they would say "You guys did all right, it sounded pretty good, keep up the good work." We tried to support each other and we tried to be positive.

DAMON ROMERO: [Kurt] cared about people, he cared about other musicians. I don't think he really liked Treehouse's music, but he was always supportive of us—he'd say "Great job on the single! I like what you did with the drums!" He'd always find something constructive to say. Always nice about it. I think he liked Lush a lot—it was more crazy, more up his alley. We played a show that Kurt and his friends came to and he started rolling on the floor and doing a worm dance to our music—that was cool.

Nirvana had meanwhile acquired a second guitarist, Jason Everman, a friend with sufficient admiration for them that he invested his own savings to cover the recording costs of *Bleach*.

PAUL KIMBALL: I know that they had buzz around them that I felt was largely undeserved. To my ears they didn't deserve that buzz till

Jason Everman joined . . . it wasn't till the show Helltrout played with them at Reko/Muse . . . that I found that I finally genuinely liked them, that was a great show, and with Jason on guitar the whole thing really gelled.

Cobain was still learning onstage, and as a trio the burden was on him to carry a substantial portion of the band's presence while juggling guitar and vocals. Everman's purpose was to take pressure off by duplicating the guitar work—a tricky position given that success meant the absence of error rather than any dramatic addition.

RONNA MYLES-ERA: I remember thinking that maybe it would free up Kurt to make more mistakes, but I don't recall thinking that [Jason] added too much to the sound. It's always a little strange when you see a band for a while and then they add someone . . . He was also another "quiet" and shy guy, it seemed, so I didn't even really talk to him much. He seemed nice enough though, and he was a really talented guitar player.

The band made a quick hop to California to play a February 10 show supporting the Melvins.

JOE GOLDRING: We had seen Mudhoney and a few other Seattle classic-rock-sounding bands when we had been up there, so we sort of suspected these guys would be the same type of thing . . . they were pretty quiet, just some small talk, I suspected a bit of a drug vibe with Cobain, or he might have just been a shy dirtbag. Novoselic was the most friendly—seemed like a very nice chap. The drummer had a crazy-looking '70s drum kit—red flag there . . . But when they got going we became engaged—they were nothing like the Sabbath rehash that we had witnessed up north! I think they had another guitar player; honestly I can't say a thing about him . . . The drummer was a bit of a throwback . . . Bass was interesting but it was definitely Cobain who drew you in; his singing and guitar sound owed more to Public Image than Led Zeppelin . . . There was an energy in the room emanating from this grubby little bloke—we all felt that. They obviously needed to work out the kinks . . . they were not the band they were about to become; the clues were in Cobain's trip—there was something deeper going on within him.

They then joined Mudhoney on Saturday.

LINDSEY THRASHER: We were playing with Mudhoney, who I only knew a little bit about but I had heard they were great. They were immediately super-funny and easy to be around. They asked if their friends Nirvana could open the show [for free] since they were on tour and didn't have a show that night . . . I talked to Krist a lot that night. He was super-nice and gave me his number to call next time we were in Seattle (or wherever he lived).

But that's where the roaming sputtered out. The band played only one show before April 1, after which, again, a splurge of four shows gave way to a month off.

During what shows they did play, however, there had been a sea change; they'd become a name everyone remembered once witnessed.

RONNA MYLES-ERA: When they played around town, they weren't that good, I mean, they would mess up a lot and Kurt was off-key . . . their songs were strong enough to "carry" them even if they were totally destroying their own song. It was painful for me to watch them sometimes for this very reason! They were entertaining and things would always get smashed. In fact, when they would show up at a party, they were a lot of fun, but it seemed like Krist would always break something. I remember thinking that I wouldn't ever invite him to my house!

DAMON ROMERO: Krist would often get out of control at a party—at a Christmas party once, everyone dressed up and, being civilized, he came in and destroyed the place—did a flying dive onto the hors d'oeuvre table, got kicked out. Another party, more of a rockers' party for New Year's Eve—he let off the fire extinguisher and sprayed a bunch of people with that horrible dry dusty material—he got away with it.

MIKE MORASKY: I'd met them briefly at a show with the Melvins in San Francisco but just as a visiting member of the audience. When they rolled up to the Vogue in Seattle, there was something kind of young and goofy about them, like they'd just barely managed to actually make it there. Since we'd already been on a couple of tours, they were also the "new guys," and being from an even smaller town than us . . . they just seemed like nice guys struggling to get out on tour and not being particularly organized about it.

GLEN LOGAN: The draw for that show had much more to do with Nirvana and Skin Yard. I hope and think we helped the bill, but we were not the big draw at this show . . . Nirvana were one hundred percent in the moment. There was no pretense; what you saw is what they were. There was a vital recklessness in what they did, and I mean that in the most positive sense. We . . . leaned to more of the rock side of this sort of music and may have paired better with a band like Alice in Chains.

Preparation for *Bleach* lingered; photography wasn't finalized until after an April gig in Olympia, which continued to demonstrate Nirvana's reliance on nontraditional venues.

RONNA MYLES-ERA: Reko/Muse was a space that was created to be an art space and a music space. It was also a collective. I don't recall knowing what exactly the name meant. It was basically just a big echoing room, but it sounded great when it was full of people. The things I remember most about the show . . . was Krist throwing my old bass in the air and just barely catching it each time. (I had recently sold my bass to Slim Moon and he had loaned it to Krist.) I kept freaking out that he was going to smash it . . . The other thing was that I brought my own PA for the show and it ended up on the cover of *Bleach* . . . Usually local bands didn't get paid. The money would go first to the venue to cover costs and most of what was left would go to the touring band if there was one. I'm sure we had enough to buy beer, though; it was a pretty packed night.

BEN MUNAT: Blue Gallery was an actual art gallery. It was in a typical store space in northwest Portland. So, not a very big venue. Maybe a couple hundred people if you packed it out. The walls were completely white and had art on them, which changed each month. I can't remember if they took the art down for shows . . . We had actually set up the show to have Cat Butt headline. But a few days before the show, the bass player for Cat Butt cut his hand opening a wine bottle (he was a waiter) and could not play. They referred us to "this cool band from Olympia; you'll like them." I further recall that it seemed like the only people left at the show by the time Nirvana went on were the opening bands and our girlfriends . . . They blew us away. I remember thinking, These guys are gonna be big. Of course, at that point "big" meant they could headline a larger hall.

DAVID TRIEBWASSER, Grind: Nirvana tore it up, and during their last song Kurt started rolling around the cement floor while playing guitar. I remember him bumping up to each of the eight or so audience members like a playful pup, soloing the whole time, mopping up spilled beer, discarded cigarettes, and shards of glass with his frayed flannel shirt.

JAMES BURDYSHAW: It was cheap and easy to put shows on at art galleries or warehouses, as opposed to doing them in a nightclub . . . the Center on Contemporary Art was, and I believe still is, a collective in Seattle to promote and exhibit contemporary art of all types. When Larry Reid became the executive director of the group, he started bringing in punk bands to put on showcases locally. The space where the CoCA event was held with Nirvana was actually a group of empty buildings that used to be porn shops on First Avenue. Larry got funding to lease the space and converted it into a two-room gallery with a large floor space for people. It was way too small for the Sub Pop show, but he did it anyway . . . I'm sure you read about the washtub backstage that had been full of Schmidt or Black Label beer? I stayed back there after about half of Mudhoney's set and drank a bunch of beer. It was super fucking hot in there, no A/C, and it was a massive sauna of sweat and sticky bodies. My friend Luke was given bags of sugar to sprinkle on the crowd and he threw mass quantities of it at the people, so the floor looked like it was coated with maple syrup—one of Larry's ingenious ideas, I believe. The show was booked as "Sugar Sweet Sub Pop" . . . I dipped my hand into what was now cold-ass ice water in the washtub. When anybody walked through the door, I'd flick water at them. Matt Lukin [Mudhoney] got super annoyed by this and squawked at me. Then Kurt comes in and looks happy I sprayed him. He asks me to dunk his entire head in the tub, so I do it. I started getting nervous when it seemed like a minute went by and he was still submerged in the ice water. Then he springs up and joyfully exclaims a big "AAHH!" and thanks me. During their set the sound was so muddy and the air felt like hot molasses soup with all the sugar in the air. I don't recall a single song they played. Just a huge swell of people gyrating back and forth while Erik [Peterson]'s older brother Ed lay prostrate on the stage under Kurt's legs. Later that night, I was stuck outside on First Avenue with my L5 combo and Strat. David [Emmanuel Duet] wouldn't take me back to where the gear was because he had too many hipsters and girls in his minivan. I was pretty pissed off at that point. I looked down the street and saw Kurt and Krist walking and got their attention, waving them to come back. They turned around and headed toward me looking like Mutt and Jeff from the old comic strip, heads bopping a little and big smiles on their faces. I asked if they were going south and could drop me off in west Seattle. Kurt looked confused and said he was sorry they couldn't, but he didn't want to leave me there either. He said something like "Oh man, I'm so sorry, we aren't going that way." Luckily for me, these uber-cute young girls offered to get me home, but first I had to go with them to this party. Everything worked out for me.

Sub Pop's strategy was working—each new band was seen in the light of past Sub Pop successes, making fans more likely to take a shot on something they hadn't heard. This benefited *Bleach* upon its release in June.

ROBIN PERINGER: I was a fan of Green River, who played my hometown when I was in high school. Friends told me that this new band, Mudhoney, had formed out of Green River and were playing L.A. while I was living there. I went and saw them at Club Lingerie, opening for Sonic Youth . . . I was hooked. I started buying whatever Sub Pop put out, which is how I bought *Bleach* and I loved it.

LORI JOSEPH, Bhang Revival: An old boyfriend in God's Acre who worked in a record store turned me on to *Sub Pop 200*. I loved it and then followed all the bands on that label after that release. It made a *huge* impression on me. I went out and bought a wah-wah pedal! I was like, Holy shit this music is soooooo freaking awesome. I followed Nirvana and saw them every time they were in town. I think in 1989 at Club Dreamerz and then we followed them to Milwaukee. There were ten to fifteen people at this show. I remember they were hanging out in front of the venue. I told them if they put us on the guest list I would give them the door cover directly just to make sure they got some money.

CRISPIN WOOD, The Bags: I hadn't heard *Bleach*, but I knew about it. There was a bit of hype around Nirvana at the time because they were on Sub Pop. I remember hearing that they recorded *Bleach* for $600. We took pride in the fact that, the year prior, we recorded an album (*Swamp Oaf*) in less than twenty-four hours and paid only $800. So we were kind of like, "What?! $600? How did they do that?!"

Bleach was released after Nirvana was on the road, so most audiences had no chance to pick up a copy. Even bands they'd be accompanying during the tour were unaware of them.

ALAN BISHOP: June of 1989 in Tempe Arizona. We pulled up to the Sun Club to unload through the back door and do a sound check. There was another van parked there with three younger guys milling around it. I approached them and they introduced themselves and asked if we were Sun City Girls. They said they were very happy to play with us, that they listened to our music, whatever, was a bit awkward as those moments tend to be and I was doubting that another band was on the bill that night—it was only supposed to be two bands, us and Crash Worship from California. Then I'm like, whatever, they're here and must have been added, and asked what the name of their band was and Kurt said "Nirvana." Of course I started fucking with them and said, "Oh, so we're gonna reach Nirvana tonight are we?" Don't remember anything else about them until they started playing. What I remember most about the set was Krist being so tall on that stage with a low ceiling, and his head kept banging the ceiling during the set and it was quite amusing. Their sound, to me, was very similar to many bands that were coming through town at the time, nothing really set them apart for me.

CHRIS DESJARDINS, Stone by Stone: I have no recollection of Nirvana opening . . . I frequently would not get to the club until right before the set, so I probably just missed them. It was a turbulent time in my life and shortly after that I renamed the band the Flesh Eaters, which had always been the main group name I'd used off and on since 1977.

DAVID VON OHLERKING: The Axiom was fantastic. My band played there every Wednesday for a long time . . . It was nasty and dirty and there was a couch that was infested with crab lice. If you were an ass-hole they would make you sit on it while you waited to get paid . . . My punk-ass rhythm section opted out long before the show, but oddly showed up . . . the Nirvana show had thirty people max, probably twenty with sixteen people paying, then the guests and friends . . . They were awesome, loved them. My rhythm section didn't get it . . . the small crowd were fairly static and undemonstrative—it can't have been much encouragement for them but they rocked it . . . I liked the rhythm guitar player a lot. Awkward and charming dude.

Like in their early Seattle days, Nirvana had to prove themselves afresh. They would earn a few converts both through performance and general likeability.

TIM KERR: I already knew some of the songs and thought they were a good band but it wasn't like "Oh my Gawd!" It was just good. It was not a big club, I remember that. We were sharing the backstage area . . . One newspaper chick [*Public News*] announced that they would change the world but not everyone believed her.

DOUG GILLARD, Death of Samantha: Nirvana's set starts and we had no idea Kurt broke his guitar. I could have lent him mine if we'd known, but he chose to just not play. He had a black dress on . . . They were hungry and this was their Boston show, y' know? . . . My memory of that show was being at our van in the parking lot with Dave Swanson getting dressed, changing clothes, and Krist Novoselic saunters over from their beat-up white van, a fifth of Myers's Rum in his hand, big white T-shirt, and very happy, saying, "Hey, are you guys from Death of Samantha? I'm in Nirvana." He couldn't have been nicer or warmer . . . already really sloshed and slurry when he came up to us, but he was sweet as can be.

ED FARNSWORTH: A Sunday night. By that point, Dobbs was starting to get some of the shows the Khyber would have otherwise had (and probably would have done better with, although they weren't open on Sundays at the time). As I recall there was barely anyone at the show. I wanted to see Nirvana because some of my friends whose taste I respected were fans. I remember dismissively thinking as they played, They sound like a crappy hardcore band . . . Everyone was pretty nice, although I also remember everyone looked very tired—I imagine they had played either NYC or DC the night before and goodness knows how long they had been out on the road.

TOM TRUSNOVIC, Monkeyshines: One of them—Krist or Chad, I'm certain—thanked me for covering "Stiff Little Fingers" in Monkeyshines's set. I thought that was a nice gesture, more friendly than would seem customary . . . That Elvis/Alice Cooper backdrop did not bode well . . . They had *stacks*, I mean, heavy-metal *STACKS* of amps, and were unwilling to turn down even when the maxed-out PA was insufficient for vocals and the volume began to thin out the crowd, who headed outside to drink in the parking lot . . . "Dive" and "About a Girl" aside, it was assertively audience unfriendly sludge-grunge . . . at some point someone in front straight-up requests "something fast," and they respond with one of *Bleach*'s slower numbers. Not in a mean-spirited way, just "Hey, this is what we are doing."

DAVID YAMMER: My main memory is standing out front by the door leaning against a wall, looking at a van parked across the street parallel to the club on McKinney. It seems that the members (or at least some of them) were sleeping in the van. It had been dark for a little bit—sound check was over—and we would be opening the doors soon. It was a slow night . . . Anyway, I was leaning against the wall and this hippie/Goth/punk chick who had lived on the West Coast for a while came up to me and started raving to me about Nirvana—I had never heard of them before—saying that she couldn't believe that more people weren't there yet. She went over and woke them up and started talking to them. They looked like normal, scruffy rock 'n' roll musicians . . . The Axiom was the kind of place we would go to hang out even if no one was playing. The owner, J. R. Delgado, would let us in to shoot pool or whatever, so even on a night when there was a relatively unknown band playing there would be people there to hang out—the whole thing was low-key and despite my vagueness I do remember it as being somewhat intimate and, of course, *loud*! . . . Most performing musicians—on that street level—drop the stage persona when not up on the boards, and are almost unassuming in nature and not too demanding of a club's staff. In fact, one may not even realize that they are the band until they get onstage.

JON WAHL, Claw Hammer: I remember when Kurt first entered Al's Bar before sound check. He was a grouch and wouldn't talk. Novoselic apologized on Kurt's behalf, claiming the traffic into L.A. was brutal. Probably very true . . . This Nirvana gig was up there in the gnarly gig realm. I wouldn't consider them as inexperienced, not at all. They had their shit together. It was an amazing show. Sweaty, heavy-handed rock 'n' roll done by junkie Seattleites. I was a fan going in there and a fan walking out. I remember the stage collapsing in chaos in the last chord of the last tune as Kurt lunged himself into the drum set to end the whole thing. Walking out of Al's, the ears rang and the beer buzzed. What else can you ask for? And then a handful of fans buying the not-officially-available, hot-off-the-press *Bleach* from Kurt and company from the back of their van.

Nirvana left odd impressions wherever they went.

DANA HATCH, Cheater Slicks: Broke-ass twentysomething punkers . . . We were standing in the parking lot smoking pot when Nirvana arrived. A couple of them joined the circle and one had some hash in a pouch around his neck. We thought from that, their name, and their VW van they were hippies . . . Kurt seemed really pissy but maybe just wasn't feeling well.

DAVID VON OHLERKING: They were a weird mixture of hippie and punk, like Hüsker Dü—not nervous; happy dorks . . . Didn't know who they were at all . . . They looked broke like us.

TOM TRUSNOVIC: They seemed a smidge ragged-looking, but not punk ragged, you know? Like Midwest flannel pothead outcast ragged. Ha! They were hiding out in the van most of the night, it seemed.

LLOYD WALSH, Swaziland White Band: Originally the gig we were offered was for a birthday party . . . we were her favorite band at the time, along with the Happy Dogs, so that was how the gig was created. When we showed up to play, Alfred, the owner, came up to me and said, "Sorry, guys, there was a fuck-up, this other band is touring from Seattle, do you mind if they play?" Not that he was really giving us a choice, I mean who's going to say no? Anyway, Nirvana sheepishly approached us to discuss the order of bands and we offered to open for them . . . they played second and the Happy Dogs ended the night. After the gig they crashed at one of the Happy Dogs' places.

JOHN FARRELL, Swaziland White Band: Our fangirl was Wendy . . . I remember sensing that Nirvana was a bit aloof at our humble gig and did not want to unpack a whole lot. When they came out of their van with hand-wrench outlines spray-painted over their curtains thereon, they looked like smallish hippie types just out of the spin cycle. I do remember they eventually got out some Marshall amps and began to rock the house down. I was impressed.

DENNIS FALLON, Swaziland White Band: I remember laughing at the big rock-star style hair flippin'/headbanger moves—too funny!

JOSE SORIA, Happy Dogs: We had a person who worked with the Sub Pop label, so everyone on Sub Pop would come through the Happy Dogs—we already knew, had their albums, were set up . . . They stayed at our house a whole day before they played and we partied the whole damn night. Krist was real friendly, knew a little about everything . . . Kurt Cobain was a little relaxed and didn't open up to you—I didn't get to talk to him for two or three hours after they got there. We had our own conversation. A little more not wanting to talk to everybody . . .

Cobain slept in the van, the rest slept on the floor . . . River Road, everybody knew our house! It was a place to go. *Elvis-Cooper*— Kurt made it, he had the Elvis thing but he painted Alice Cooper parts on it. My girlfriend had covered herself in it while she was sleeping so in the morning when the band were leaving Kurt looked at her and said, "Hey, you're cold, you can keep it." They were exactly like us—in terms of wanting to play, wanting to party, they were just really cool and like "Let's do it, let's do it man." That night it was one of my friends' birthday parties and they were coming through town and weren't even going to play in San Antonio but we said, "You wanna play? You wanna play at Alfred's?" And we did it—a really great thing. Kurt Cobain came back with the other guitarist, bought a couple of guitars here in San Antonio, I kept in touch with Krist Novoselic.

Nirvana would later recall it as a fairly rough tour. Even playing alongside one of the underground's cult acts barely netted them a profit.

ALAN BISHOP: After the show, the club manager handed me $225 to distribute between the bands ($5 cover, fifty-five people paid—add fifteen, twenty guests and it's seventy plus at the show). I called a guy from Crash Worship over and found Kurt, split the $225 three ways into $75 each and handed both their shares. The Crash Worship guy started complaining and saying that Nirvana was not even supposed to be on the bill and that they didn't deserve a third of the take, that Sun City Girls drew most of the crowd . . . so I handed him our share of $75 and said something like "Take this—you're on the road too." He grimaced, knowing there was really nothing he could say, refused the extra cash, and left.

Nirvana rolled into New York so out of enthusiasm they'd already canceled the tour's final eleven days and seven shows. Their relationship with guitarist Jason Everman had broken down.

TOM TRUSNOVIC: On second guitar, I don't wanna be unreasonable, but I love the Damned, right? That guy looked and sounded pretty fucking far from the Damned. Ha! He seemed to ooze the sort of repellent, dunderheaded machismo that I thought metal represented. Didn't he end up playing in Soundgarden, then joining the Army? Big surprise.

They didn't skip this show, however, because it wasn't just another gig. This was the New Music Seminar, a promotional event giving Nirvana their first contact with the wider music business.

SHAMBIE SINGER: [It was] essentially a meet-and-greet for up-and-coming bands, record labels, the PR community, and college-radio folks. A chance to assemble everyone in one spot and let the matchmaking happen. I think the official line was a bit less crass . . . But at heart and in practice, that year at least, it seemed mostly about getting alternative bands hooked up with independent and mainstream labels and PR groups. I think a lot of bands without record contracts came to the NMS specifically to try to find a deal. And for bands on independent labels it was a chance to showcase for the majors.

MIKE HARD, God Bullies: This was a *College Music Journal* [CMJ] showcase . . . Being a showcase pretty much means all the bands get paid the same stipend, like a hundred and fifty bucks, and sets are kept short.

It wasn't necessarily a huge event; each band had fairly casual reasons for being there.

SHAMBIE SINGER: Mike's grandmother was out of town and we were able to stay for free at her place. And generally it seemed like the trip'd be relatively easy, and the gig fun, and a good chance to see a chick I was sort of dating who lived in NYC.

MIKE HARD: I think you guys want to make it more than what it was. Like there was some kind of magic there. This was a CMJ show. A joint Sub Pop/Amrep venture, and it was work to us. We knew everyone was there to see Nirvana, so we just wanted to get out of their way, play a good set, make our statement (whether the audience wanted to hear it or not), and then go hang out with our friends. We weren't real bitch magnets or even "cool." God Bullies was kind of a therapy session for the members involved. We were selfish in that respect. We needed to do this or we would be the ones you would read about in the paper the next day, you know? So and so committed this crime because of their repressive childhood? We were acting out. I do not know what motivated bands like Nirvana. We were trying to save souls and were on a path of enlightenment.

JOHN LEAMY, Surgery: For us it was just another hometown gig.

For Nirvana it could still have been a chance for industry exposure. Instead, by the second song, a drunk clambered onstage to shout, "Fucking shit!"

MIKE HARD: They were off doing interviews all day or something. Rolled in after sound check like rock stars . . . It was because they were lazy and already thought they had a certain privilege. This is another big bullshit story; they were so poor? Any working band at this time wasn't getting paid shit. Our equipment was like gold. If Nirvana fucked it up or broke it, it would be us the next night who'd be fucked. We'd seen how hard they were on their equipment, we were not about to let them fuck up our shit . . . There may have been some confusion with all the bands and Nirvana: if we were all going to set up our own backlines or just use one band's. Maybe Nirvana hung around the venue, but it seems they just showed up, wondered if they had to unload or if we were sharing backlines, and then took off until they had to go on.

JOHN LEAMY: I stood outside smoking cigarettes during their set . . . Didn't meet them. I was tired though.

KEVIN RUTMANIS, Cows: I didn't watch the band at all that night . . . I walked up, was surprised to see how many people were there, and left. I never cared much for Nirvana—not at all at that point, in fact. I'm sure our booker arranged the show.

SHAMBIE SINGER: I talked to Kurt briefly in the dressing room . . . you had to climb down a steep ladder to get there. I recall talking to him about how dangerous it felt to climb up and down that ladder. And I told him a story about another night we'd played . . . When a huge—like six-foot-seven—dude climbed down the ladder while I was there and transformed himself over the course of about forty-five minutes into a spitting image of Marie Antoinette. Alternative-music night at the Pyramid was always Tuesdays. But on the weekends the club hosted transvestite cabaret acts. And a lot of the regular performers had lockers filled with their stage outfits in the club dressing room . . . Nirvana didn't seem qualitatively any different from any of the other "Seattle" bands then. And quantitatively I understood they were maybe on the second tier of things.

And with this last whimper, Nirvana's first tour was over.

7.0

Still Broke: Second Tour
September to October 1989

Like most bands, Nirvana was naïve regarding the realities of indie-label life and the mechanics of getting a record to market. They had poured their all into the *Bleach* sessions only to wait another half year for it to actually emerge; they endured the discomfort of their first tour while feeling almost no one could find their album; they had music on the market but no royalties in their pockets.

COLIN BURNS, Slaughter Shack: It was easy to feel very Rodney Dangerfield-ish about things. There wasn't "alternative rock" yet. The local press and college radio seemed enamored of college rock. Men with cargo shorts and jangly guitars were critics' darlings. And for a while the hardcore audience didn't know how to react either.

SLIM MOON: The process of putting out "Love Buzz" and trying to get Sub Pop to put out an album was very frustrating for them, and they talked a lot about feeling that Sub Pop thought they were hicks from the sticks and didn't really believe in them.

CHRIS QUINN: Jonathan Poneman even said at one point, "We like them as people so we signed them, we thought it'd be cool," but it felt like Sub Pop was banking more on Mudhoney and Tad and some other stuff. That isn't to say they weren't behind Nirvana, but from my level of enthusiasm it seemed like everything was "less."

Although there was undoubtedly a kernel of truth in certain gripes, there was never anything bad enough to justify Cobain's claims that the band was treated like a bunch of rednecks, or neglected, or underpromoted.

SCOTT VANDERPOOL: I could see where Kurt and Krist may have felt that way early on . . . it was sort of cliquish . . . but I always moved pretty freely among different groups, kind of like when I was in high school and had plenty of stoner, jock, and nerd friends.

JAIME ROBERT JOHNSON: I'm not gonna smack-talk Sub Pop, because they did some great things . . . I always had the idea that Bruce and Jon chose a particular group of artists to focus on and worked their way outward from that core group of artists . . . Sub Pop seemed to me always to be controlled by a really small group of people who were intent upon keeping it that way regardless of what they were doing.

STEVE MORIARTY: I didn't always like grunge. Mudhoney, they could play pretty well, the guy could scream pretty good, but they still had that element of rock stars and Sub Pop was about making them into rock stars in order to make money. And that was true with Soundgarden, true with Alice in Chains, true with Nirvana. It was about the mystique of the rock star—the antithesis of punk. So when we were there in 1989 we were thinking, We don't care about all this publicity, and how good these bands are and how long their hair is and all this stuff. We were there to communicate the fact that we're all the same and we're going to play on the floor instead of the stage and so we brought a different ethos and we had a female singer, which was also not done.

While prone to excessive honesty regarding his darkest thoughts and suspicions, it's unlikely that Cobain, in his more considered moments, didn't recognize how lucky Nirvana had been to have the support of Sub Pop.

JOHN PURKEY: Kurt just wanted to be part of Sub Pop; he really wanted to be part of Sub Pop and really liked the scene around Sub Pop at the time.

A typical contradiction: he wanted to be in the club as long as he could complain about it.

Sub Pop was supporting Nirvana as best they could.

SHAMBIE SINGER: I recall being in Seattle in May 1989, and riding with Jonathan Poneman out to a guitar store he wanted to show us . . . We were talking about Mudhoney. I was telling them how much I liked their stuff and how psyched I was that they were doing well, in terms of selling records, getting decent shows and lots of college radio airplay. And Jonathan said, "Oh, you think Mudhoney's doing well, we've got another band that's gonna be even bigger." And I asked who and he said, "Nirvana." And my disbelieving response was, "Even bigger than Mudhoney?" Which seemed impossible in May of 1989. But Jonathan was sure of it. I asked him why he thought so and he said because of Kurt's voice.

In fact, Nirvana's status as the first band with a formal Sub Pop contract, getting the first release on the Singles Club and the chance to release an album made Nirvana look a touch pampered compared to the way other bands on Sub Pop were scraping by.

GEOFF ROBINSON: I felt bands were out there to be beaten. It was raw competition. We felt we were the heaviest and could be the fastest, or the slowest. Whatever the case, loud was the prime directive.

We certainly did not live out of other bands' pockets. For the most part, with a few exceptions, we felt that they secretly hated us because we were "from the wrong side of the tracks." Many of the other bands' members' parents had money, so these guys got up there with some pretty nice equipment . . . We were working stiffs. I was working for Boeing at the time. T-man [Tracy Simmons] was a fiberglass boat builder and Doug [Day] was a landscaper. Michael [Anderson] was a chef . . . we were pretty self-absorbed with our own material and that Nirvana seemed to be the darling child of Sub Pop. That gets back to the competitive thing.

JAMES BURDYSHAW: I didn't make a living off my music then and have never been able to do that. I worked in a deli in 1988 making $4.25 an hour for thirty hours a week. I moved back in with my mother to save money so I could go on tour. In between tours in 1989, I worked temporary labor jobs, including at a fish-packing plant for $5 an hour. It was not easy. It wasn't until the final Cat Butt tour that Danny gave us a per diem of $5 a day. I always took savings with me.

CHRIS PUGH: When we were on Sub Pop, they were just barely squeaking by, not making a lot of money. When we first started they were well regarded and had some success but didn't have any money though their bands were doing well—especially in the UK. Swallow was never one of Sub Pop's favorite bands—not critically acclaimed or crowd favorites. So we did receive some support—they helped us with touring a bit—but we weren't on top of their list of bands they were interested in spending money on . . . If you're in a band where you're creating a buzz, then it's self-perpetuating and it'll start taking on a life of its own, but that was never happening for us . . . The thing about us and Sub Pop was that we were given plenty of opportunity but we weren't able to capitalize on it—if we'd delivered a record like *Bleach* then that would have been great, but we weren't able to do that.

Also, Nirvana never had to endure the grind of booking their own tours; their good fortune in finding Sub Pop set them a couple rungs up the ladder.

LISA KOENIG: We got pretty well known as the three-piece all-girl band in the area. Then we recorded an album in Seattle and set out on a US tour that I pretty much booked myself. Now, remember, we had no cell phones back then, so we would have to physically use our index fingers to dial a number. And no . . . I'm not talking about a push-button number, I'm talking about a *rotary-dial number.* Just thinking about that makes me realize how much work went into everything back then . . . These were times where we had to send out tapes or singles to the clubs through the US mail and hope they actually made the effort to (1) open it, and (2) listen to it. Then you'd have to call back and basically beg them for a show for, if you're lucky, gas money and free beer. So, you've got to have appreciation for the good ol' days. It took work.

Cobain wondered once more about a second guitarist—Ben Shepherd of Soundgarden and J Mascis of Dinosaur Jr. were considered—but it was still a trio that set out for their second tour. At least there'd been time for the album to spread.

BILLY ALLETZHAUSER, Grinch: I remember borrowing *Bleach* and having a mix tape that had the first single. We all loved it. I wore out *Bleach* and was happy to be asked to open for them.

BRUCE PURKEY: Even after *Bleach,* it seemed that they might be a moderately big indie band. Still, that wasn't saying much. Other bands like Hüsker Dü had received a bit of major-label push and still were barely known by the average person.

Nirvana was also developing sufficient chops such that the band could impress in scenes less open to punk-derived music.

JAIME ROBERT JOHNSON: In Ann Arbor because of the Stooges/ MC5 thing it was much harder to put a punk show together because so many of the people at the top of the musical food chain had already been rock stars and pretty much acted like royalty—except it was in that pathetic tiny small-town way—and honestly did not seem to give a fuck about what the punk, alternative, or hardcore punk kids wanted or needed for a long time. You had to be in with them to even get near a club gig of any kind, which for a seventeen- to eighteen-year-old homeless punk skater kid was impossible.

MIKE HARD: Ann Arbor at the time was a Republican's wet dream, despite being known as the hippie-dippy mecca of the Midwest, but at one time Ann Arbor really did rock . . . The Blind Pig is one of those legendary two-hundred-seat showcases to see a band at. In Ann Arbor, Nirvana was all the buzz. This West Coast new sound. Tad had already been through. I think Mudhoney, too. So the crowd was well prepared for the next new thing from Sub Pop. But I guess Nirvana was not prepared for the home of the Stooges and may have decided to take the night off in this sleepy little college town . . . Their set started off kind of laid back and the crowd resented it, like a lot of Detroit-area rock fans are known to do . . . the audience started trying to encourage them to rock that great Seattle sound everyone was talking about. My friend said he started throwing plastic beer cups at them, then people were flicking cigarettes at them and yelling "You suck!" as well as some other traditional rock phrases of encouragement. A few songs into the set Nirvana finally realized this audience wasn't a bunch of Republican rich kids living in the dorms, or some leftover hippies from the hash bash. Nirvana was playing in the living room of the family who gave birth to punk rock . . . When Nirvana realized they were in for a fight, they fought back, watched and waited, grabbed each other's backs and proceeded to kick some punk-rock ass. They left their bodies and equipment onstage, wrecked.

Sub Pop's efforts had spread a sometimes-lurid portrait of the band; Nirvana said later it was exaggerated, but hearing that the wild men had come to town can't have hurt attendances.

TOM DARK: I was told if they had a good show, they all threw their instruments in the air and trashed the stage, much like the Who. We did it, but not every time, it's just how we felt at the end of the show . . . When Nirvana went on, my mouth dropped. The sound/songs were so mind blowing. This was the first time ever seeing them play live, we knew there was something special about them. Krist had this painting of Elvis Presley with Alice Cooper makeup under his eyes right in front of his amp. I thought that was so cool!

BILLY ALLETZHAUSER: They roared through the set the best they could. There was good energy. I remember Kurt having trouble with a pedal or something and was a bit frustrated. There was blood all over his guitar from his hands bleeding . . . Nothing was smashed except maybe that pedal that was crapping out. I remember Kurt not wanting to do an encore because of the gear and the other guys talking him into it.

FORREST, 24-7 Spyz: I remember somebody from Nirvana's crew fighting with our guitar tech, Warren Tremeni, over stage space. We were in the back during their sound check and *boom*! The fight started! I never heard of them before that night so I didn't know their songs or set list but some of the kids did. I just remember the rawness and power of them and they were loud as hell . . . Spyz approached a live performance with great vigor! It was very active, innovative, energetic, and wild; we also are very good musicians and everyone knew that . . . Nirvana was the same with their raw approach and honesty [but] they had no *performance*. It was like four dudes pouring out their souls but it was dense and hard as hell. We were a very playful bunch; they seemed more laid back and local . . . The Outhouse in Lawrence,

Kansas, was in the middle of a cornfield and it seemed like you couldn't see a house in miles [but] they had a *huge* college fan base there. That place was like drugs, drugs, drugs, with no police presence. It was *really* sex, drugs, and rock 'n' roll. Hell *yeah*, that's *all* everybody was doing at the Outhouse. We were in the middle of *nowhere*! Now, me, I never took drugs in my life, but Nirvana was fucked *up*! It seemed like those students had every drug on and off the market. But not too much weed; it was, like, the hard stuff—heavy shit. College students back then were very brave. The music scene overall was heavy into drugs like they say [sex, drugs, and rock 'n' roll] is true, man . . . !

Wild men, perhaps. Bedraggled ones? For sure.

MIKE MORASKY: A couple of them had come down with something, maybe bronchitis? They all seemed tired and getting a small audience excited on an off night is tough even under the best of circumstances.

MIKE HARD: Nirvana were very tired. They had to have been. Everyone in a band traveling across the US knows this. Sleeping on other people's floors or [at] a very occasional hotel. No one made money. We all played for free beer and some gas money . . . On the road, money is a huge distraction. If you made money, you did not have to live on free beer, table scraps, and handouts. Money was evil: you could buy friends who had drugs and other cheap distractions from the band and the road. When you got money, you start meeting boys and girls who are hungry and you become their meal ticket. Without money, you can drink all the free beer in the world and you're just going to puke up the free pizza or pass out. This was the Nirvana I first met. Playing shows for free beer and food. If you got a free place to stay after the show, it was considered a good gig.

CRAIG CRAWFORD: Frankly, they seemed exhausted. They had been playing nonstop every night, touring in a little van with all their gear. West of the Mississippi River, travel times between cities are enormous, so getting from one gig to another can take a lot out of you. I remember them being friendly and pretty nice guys. They were frustrated by the turnout, but they played well and solidly. That being said, I don't think they were overjoyed about playing a biker bar in a rundown city in Nebraska . . . Back then you played for a percentage of the door receipts and you were lucky if you got even that. They were tired, broke and traveling in a van that probably needed much maintenance. It was really hard touring back then and it showed on them. Most bars didn't want bands like them. They wanted a band that played hit songs and looked good, which is why most bands on their initial tours played crap venues. The Lifticket was definitely not crap; it was a great dive bar who hosted tons of great bands over the years. It was always one of Henry Rollins's favorite stops when he went through town. That being said, it was also famous for large bikers refusing to pay cover charge because there was free pool inside.

BILLY ALLETZHAUSER: I admired his [Kurt's] denim blazer that had a patch of the Thing on the back that said "It's Clobberin' Time," and I refused to believe you could find something that cool in a thrift store.

It certainly wasn't as rough as the previous tour; there was more room in the van, more cash with one member gone, and more shows with relatively established bands.

MIKE MORASKY: The Flaming Lips had already been touring for years and had a relatively large college following, so the shows with them were generally well attended. On the off nights, when it was just Nirvana and Steel Pole, the crowds were pretty small . . . this was, however, pretty typical for bands like ours visiting small towns for the first time.

Pavitt and Poneman's shrewd common sense was also on display. For a Denver show, Sub Pop's Denver band the Fluid were the headliners, giving Nirvana a good crowd.

MATT BISCHOFF, The Fluid: We had an excellent fan base in Denver and Nirvana was really coming on. Denver folks always dug the Seattle bands when they came through. I remember Kurt's distortion pedal was not working correctly at sound check; don't remember why, though. He came up with something by showtime, however, and they killed it.

MIKE MORASKY: All three bands were represented by the same booking agency . . . Bulging Eye started picking up Sub Pop bands, including Nirvana, which is how they ended up joining us on that tour for some of those dates . . . After one of the shows we were staying at the promoter's apartment together and we were totally broke, as was often the case, but the Nirvana guys had a little bit of money (maybe a small "per diem" from Sub Pop?) and bought us a frozen pizza. Man, that was one great pizza!

Both the band's good vibes and Cobain's occasional moods were on display.

TOM DARK: Krist and Chad talked to us a lot through the whole evening. Kurt was very shy and quiet; he hung out with our guitarist, who was my brother [Scott F. Eakin, RIP], who was very much like him. They both took off and hung out in our van, talking and playing guitar. Before we went on, Nirvana went out to do a radio interview and came back just in time as we hit the stage. They ran up to the front, raising their fists, screaming our band name, really giving us support, along with Peter Davis from *Your Flesh* magazine/Creature Booking.

BILLY ALLETZHAUSER: While they were all nice, amiable guys, Kurt seemed further away somehow. It's almost like, when I picture talking with the other guys I can imagine their faces with a vivid crispness or clarity, where Kurt's seems more obscured in my memory. I just couldn't focus on him in the same way; he seemed kind of hidden. Maybe it was all the hair in his face, but I don't think so. He just didn't seem to be occupying the same space as the rest of us somehow, and I don't think that's me glorifying the memory.

RICK RIZZO: They didn't seem inexperienced—they were definitely pretty sloppy . . . I remember being impressed by their energy and noticed that the crowd was definitely into them . . . They smashed stuff up pretty good at the end of their set. I had a tendency in those days to wreck things up and knock things down a bit. When we took the stage I remember the first thing I said was, "I guess we won't be smashing things up tonight—Nirvana already did a pretty good job of that." It was a tough act to follow—I mean, how do you go on after that? They had blown the roof off. We did play a fun and energetic set, but damn . . . A couple weeks later, I noticed that I had the wrong notebook at home—I used to write in a spiral notebook— song lyrics, set lists, and such, and had it with me at shows. Instead, I had a similar notebook that wasn't mine. I always assumed it belonged to Kurt, but I have no proof. It's not like it said "property of . . ." on the inside flap. The only thing that I remember about it was that it had lyrics and drawings—one called "Fish Eye Man" sticks in my memory. Since it was a few weeks past the show, and the fact that the band wasn't the band of lore they are now, I stuck it with other stuff in the basement. Not long after that a flood wiped out all of my memorabilia and posters that I had saved—pages with bleeding ink and disintegrating paper.

Nirvana would later criticize the relatively one-dimensional sound of *Bleach*. They were increasingly proud to acknowledge the diversity of their tastes, even if it didn't necessarily show when live.

DOUG GILLARD: I said, "Oh yeah, cool. You guys are from Seattle and Sub Pop, right?" Krist: "Yeah, but we're not like those other bands. We're more like the Beatles. Into more melodic stuff." I said, "Wow, that's great actually" or something like that . . . it was pretty trashy, but exciting and full of energy. I didn't hear the Beatles that much in their sound that night, but their records all reflect that though.

LINDSEY THRASHER: Whenever I'd hear "About a Girl," I'd have to ask who it was. I never remembered. I think that was the only song that stood out from *Bleach* for me back then.

CRISPIN WOOD: Bearing in mind that I wasn't familiar with any of their material at the time, I do remember thinking, This sounds kind of Beatle-y, about one song during their set . . .

For all the stop-start motion, this was Nirvana's busiest year so far. Cobain, never a prolific songwriter in the first place, was now facing a new challenge: how to keep writing while on the road.

TRACY MARANDER: I know that he did quite a bit of writing while I was at work, and painted/drew quite a bit as well. He would also sit and watch TV and play his guitar, coming up with riffs or tunes (he did this a lot). Sometimes he wrote lyrics then too. Usually mumbled words until he found ones that fit, I guess. He had a lot of notebooks with lyrics or potential lyrics in them.

The relative absence of writing in 1989 is one reason why the tour had limited influence on Cobain's lyrics. The only visible mention consisted of a single, ultimately deleted, chorus refrain, "Pay to Play," the original title of *Nevermind* song "Stay Away." The referenced practice involved bars selling a batch of tickets to a band to let them on a bill, leaving the band to sell the tickets themselves to make any money. It's unclear how often Nirvana experienced this; still, it's the only tour memory that made a sufficient enough impression to be temporarily immortalized.

TOM DARK: The only time I had to do that was with my current band, Dead Federation, at a place here in Cleveland . . .

COLE PETERSON/RICH CREDO, S.G.M.: Never happened in Seattle. That's an L.A. thing. A royal pain in the ass or a very rare thing indeed?

DAVID VON OHLERKING: Fitzgerald's did something like that . . . I'm completely ignorant about how widespread it was and what it entailed for musicians. It was everywhere, especially Hollywood.

On January 6, Nirvana had never left Washington State. By October 13, they'd hit eighteen states and played more shows than in 1987 and 1988 combined. It may have been the same ol' van carrying them across the country, but it was a changed bunch of guys riding it home.

8.0

Young Band in New Land: Europe
October to December 1989

Just as Cobain's writing tailed off after *Bleach*, Sub Pop's prolific ending to 1988 resulted in a lull of releases in early 1989; the label was nearly bust. Then they took a long shot by flying out a UK journalist.

BLAG DAHLIA: Sub Pop deserves a lot of credit for hyping the UK rock mags on a largely nonexistent "Seattle Sound" while selling very few records. In the same time frame, punk bands and labels who didn't believe in paying publicists and manufacturing hype, labels like Epitaph, Victory, and Fat, quietly sold triple the product with a fraction of the media attention. Their turn would come with the ascendancy of Green Day a few years later.

Unlike the United States, where the market is split among numerous local media broadcasters, with few people reading a national newspaper and only a limited number of relatively conservative national music magazines, London exerts a massive degree of control over the British music scene. Hitting the UK made sense.

HENRY SZANKIEWICZ, Medelicious: The UK was definitely looking for something new and found it in the Seattle scene. I'm not sure if they even sold flannel in England back then.

BEAU FREDERICKS: When Mudhoney and Tad started getting big press in the UK, that was when we knew something was brewing. Seattle was getting more press in the US, but not more so than the other big US cities. The UK hype machine really sped things up and made us realize that our scene might be special.

JON GINOLI, Pansy Division: I was convinced that Sub Pop was built on the kind of hype that the British specialize in—they overrate something new into the best thing ever, and six to nine months later they're old news and supplanted by something else.

Sub Pop exploited the UK media's tendency to speak to itself, then believe that the volume of its talking heads indicated significance.

COLIN BURNS: It's hard to remember the exact source of my irritation with Sub Pop and Seattle at the time. Their ubiquity in the press. Probably a sense that we (our band and our friends' bands) were being overlooked in Boston. So, jealousy maybe. I wasn't a huge "regional pride" guy . . . But I was a firm believer in paying dues . . . The consistency of photography and design made it seem at once unified, but also suspect. Too slick, maybe . . .

All Sub Pop had to do was get bands over there to unleash the pent-up curiosity. Ambitiously, Nirvana's *Blew* EP on Tupelo plus Tad and Mudhoney releases on Germany's Glitterhouse were all to hit in October, coinciding with the tour. Unfortunately for Nirvana, their release was cut back to UK-only, then delayed. This emphasized that Nirvana was still the junior band on this Sub Pop tour.

MIKE HARD: Tad, Melvins, and Mudhoney seemed to be actually more popular with the press at this time.

CRAIG CRAWFORD: Nirvana wasn't the largest of the Seattle acts. The biggest draws in Omaha would have been bands like Soundgarden, Mudhoney, or Tad.

MURDO MacLEOD, The Cateran: Tad were the best band on the tour. They were consistently brilliant, Nirvana less so . . . Tad were the band that everyone thought might get to be really successful—I'm to this day baffled about why they didn't . . . Russell Warby was managing the Cateran, and we sent him a copy of "Love Buzz." He loved it and organized the tour, with our then-agent, Paul Bolton.

CAM FRASER, The Cateran: We'd just recently signed to booking agent Russell Warby . . . I'd sent him an early copy of "Love Buzz" and suggested they'd be a cool band for us to tour with. He agreed, contacted Sub Pop, and got things going . . . I can't remember when I got the first copy [of the "Love Buzz" single] through from Calvin at K Records, but I think I ordered twenty-five copies. I recall I sent quite a few of them out as promo copies . . . we felt we were playing in a vacuum here. Especially up in Scotland, where twee garage was the most popular, with bands like the Pastels and the Shop Assistants dominating. That said, there was an underground Oi/anarcho punk thing going on in Scotland, but we were too melodic and not angry enough to be part of that, either . . . There was a bit of a grouping around bands like the Mega City Four and the Senseless Things, but before Nirvana broke there was really very little interest in what we were playing . . . it was going so much better for us in Europe that it always felt a bit depressing to be doing the notorious "toilet tour" of the UK.

It says a lot that Sub Pop ensured two releases in Germany to one in the UK; understandable, given UK magazines were in thrall to the Happy Mondays, the Wonder Stuff—even the Rolling Stones' *Steel Wheels* was in *NME*'s top fifty albums.

JOHN KASTNER, The Doughboys: We had the same booking agency in Europe; we were all booked by Paperclip, so everyone knew each other a little bit. We would see them on tour in Europe . . . Paperclip really brought that entire generation of music to Europe, where we all had to dig down, and we came back to the Americas a better band. They were one of the most influential things that happened to the entire Seattle scene—bands that had a small thing going on around here, one hundred to one hundred and fifty people, then in Europe built this thing and it crossed the pond again. The club scene in Europe wasn't so saturated—there was one good American or Canadian band a month, so people would come see us . . . Anyone from 1988 to 1992 was part of the Paperclip scene.

With seven shows in eight days in the UK, the Nirvana/Tad tour set quite a pace.

MURDO MacLEOD: They were very tired from touring. People rarely consider the work ethic of those bands. They worked hard. Tad and Nirvana traveled in one van, us in another, but we'd spend time traveling with each other to get away from 24/7 close proximity to our band mates, which can get really tiresome on tour no matter how much you love one another . . . We had maybe three people between the three bands acting as roadies/drivers. We all humped gear, we all helped each other, and then we hung out a bit. There was no star-tripping, no egos—other than what you might expect from guys in rock 'n' roll bands—no fighting, no bitching, no bullshit . . . We hung out at the venues and hardly saw daylight, so not much sightseeing . . . They were excited in a low-key way. There wasn't much money around. Yes, we had riders—not extravagant, but enough for a dozen garrulous stoners who liked to get a bit drunk and talk shit to one another and boast to each other and show off and joke the way young men do . . . There was pot around, and maybe a little speed, but it was all reasonably low-key . . . The crowds were US hardcore punk fans, rockers, stoners, longhair misfits, *Bucketful of Brains* readers, nerdy obsessives, and a few on-message trendies.

CAM FRASER: Pay was shit. And it usually meant eating crap food and sleeping on floors. I remember that Kurt seemed pretty quiet most of the time, while Krist was much more sociable . . . Kurt seemed to spend most of the time sleeping—I just assumed he was stoned. I don't know if that was right, but it seemed fair enough given the circumstances. While touring most of us wished we were stoned . . . Krist seemed to be loving it, and I think he hung out with us quite a bit, just being funny and engaging. Kurt was already surrounded by various people and, as I said earlier, was a bit more distant at that time . . . he still had that cool, enigmatic thing going.

KURT DANIELSON: We alternated as headliners: one night Nirvana would headline, the next Tad would. A democratic spirit of cooperative equality informed that tour, and no egos interfered with a shared sense of brotherhood, which made it a very cool time for both bands. At the end of that first European tour, both Tad and Nirvana played Lamefest UK with Mudhoney at the London Astoria, and it was at that gig that we used a coin toss to determine who would play first and who second (at that time, Mudhoney was by far the most popular of the three bands in England, or anywhere else for that matter); Nirvana lost the coin toss, making it so that Tad played second. And even though Tad won fair and square, there seemed to be an aura of resentment about it afterward, though words were never spoken openly about it between the bands . . . there were no hard feelings between the bands. But the Lamefest UK was the highest-profile gig of the tour, and when Nirvana lost that fateful coin toss, it was as if Kurt and Krist subsequently decided to put an end to any ambivalence or ambiguity about who should headline in the future thereafter. The issue didn't come up until after we had returned to the States . . .

MURDO MacLEOD: My favorite memory is of the morning after the Leeds gig. We all shared this scuzzy little flat above the venue. I shared a mattress on the floor with Kurt. I still tell people I've slept with Kurt Cobain. Anyway, my memory is of being shaken awake by Tad at about eight a.m., holding a Coke-tin hash pipe to my face and saying, "Wake 'n' bake, boy. Wake 'n' bake." I also remember a lot of stoned giggling when Kai [Davidson] and I were sitting in Nirvana and Tad's van with Krist, drinking red wine and already shitfaced, just before Tad were to come on. Krist was being funny about the fact that his mum didn't approve of their T-shirts . . . They were all good people—polite, caring, open-minded, clever, funny, hardworking, honest, and deeply committed to what they were doing . . . Tad and band were supersociable. Tad Doyle is one of the finest human beings I have ever met, and he and they were excellent drinking company . . . Chad talked a great deal; Krist was funny and interesting, and Kurt was quiet and interesting. One thing I didn't mention, which maybe I should, is that on that tour Kurt's "stomach pains/cramps" thing was in evidence. Living in Edinburgh in the '80s, where heroin was rife, the first thing we all thought about a guy with that kind of complaint—rather harshly—was "junkie." No one spoke about it, except Chad, who I think was very worried about him, and I have no idea whether he actually was using heroin then. Anyhoo, maybe best not to dwell . . . I may also have not said that we had a very good time.

KURT DANIELSON: Kurt and I would sometimes share hotel rooms; and when we did, we'd often talk long into the night, sharing stories about the strange characters we'd both known while growing up in our respective small towns. During the long days of sitting in our cramped touring van, bored out of our minds, we used to break the monotony by joking around quite a bit, both of us having a black or irreverent sense of humor. One thing we used to make fun of quite often was junkies, which was quite ironic when you consider what would subsequently happen to both of us. At the time, we were desperate to laugh at anything, and the fact that we were laughing at junkies seemed anything but darkly or reflexively prophetic. On one occasion, Kurt talked about how he planned to wear bandages on his arms onstage and decorate himself with plenty of vampire blood in order to make himself look not only like a junkie but a sloppy, fucked-up one. On another occasion, we'd been talking about Charles Manson and Nazis—this wasn't unusual; we often talked about taboo historical figures and subjects for their shock value as well as because we both felt they were fascinating subjects in their own right—and Kurt asked me if I had a knife or some other sharp instrument so that I could carve a swastika into his forehead, which was something Charles Manson had done. We were touring through Bavaria at the time, and it seemed like a hilarious idea to walk around some German village while Kurt had a swastika carved into his forehead. Again, we were so bored we were desperate for any kind of distraction, and it seemed like a funny idea. Unfortunately, I didn't have a knife; but we did find a paper clip, which we unbent; and I had a lighter, which we used to heat the tip of the unbent paper clip, using it to carve a shallow swastika into Kurt's forehead. It wasn't very distinct, but Kurt was nevertheless delighted with it, and when our tour manager stopped in the next town so we could get something to eat, we took a walk through an outdoor mall or plaza lined with shops and where many people were crowded around. I recall how disappointed Kurt was when no one seemed to notice the swastika . . . certainly no one complained about it. It was a disappointment for Kurt; but it survives in my memory as an example of his sense of humor while also serving as an instance of his innate need to shock people.

Bored, engaging in jet-black humor just to stay occupied, uncomfortable, fed up . . . Cobain brought the tour to a dramatic head by breaking down in Italy threatening suicide, ranting that he thought the audience was a bunch of idiots. While Cobain can no longer recount his own feelings, one musician described the influence of his own band's 1989 tour, giving a sense of the endurance test and reality check early touring provided to young musicians.

SHAMBIE SINGER: The beginning of the end was that last big tour—seven or eight weeks, starting in the Northeast and moving counterclockwise around the entire country . . . I recall the entire time thinking it was a really tough way to earn a living even if we'd been making more money than the $5-a-day each person got from the tour fund. For me many things made it a tough situation, including the physical discomfort of being on the road—long, tired drives, smoky clubs, typically an uncomfortable sleeping arrangement . . . The boredom of sitting around every night for five or six hours between sound check and the show. Additionally, I didn't really relate well to many folks I was meeting in the clubs where we played. Everyone generally seemed nice enough. But I didn't feel like I had much in common with anyone. I was struck most by this issue in terms of our audience. Routinely at shows people would ask us to sign the Am Rep single . . . and so I had an opportunity to speak a bit to our "fans." And at the end of the day the disconnect between who I felt I was while I was pouring my heart and mind and soul into the music, and the people to whom it seemed to speak the most, struck me as odd. And maybe even a bit disconcerting. I was never able to understand why I didn't feel more kinship with the very people who liked our music the best. And soon started thinking maybe I should put my professional efforts into something different. I realize most of those "fans" were probably not even into us in particular but had more generally embraced the scene we were part of. In either case, though, I felt like I should be doing something that would allow me to have more of a connection to the other people who were part of whatever I would be doing. So after two months of being tired, physically uncomfortable, worn down, generally demoralized by the lack of connection with the people I was meeting, I figured I probably needed to do something else. It was a tough decision for me. Because I loved, and love, music. Maybe more than anything else. But as in many other realms, I've since learned, there can be a huge difference between loving something and doing it professionally . . . But I was very conflicted. I loved being in a band that had had the opportunities we'd already had. And I generally loved being in a band with Mike and Sam. They're both excellent musicians. And also had become very good friends. But when I looked down the road—even in a best-case scenario involving enough money and hotels—I couldn't really imagine trying to balance a productive career as a musician with a healthy, happy home/family life. I wasn't willing to play music at all costs. That last tour was the experience that helped me understand that.

For all the talk of Cobain's fragility since his demise, he (and, indeed, the entire underground) endured a lifestyle that involved lengthy periods cut off from any kind of stable home life. Choosing to be a musician meant accepting it might always be a life of few comforts, no health insurance, and no regular pay in return for the chance to be heard.

9.0

Home Soil
January to February 1990

Nirvana returned to Reciprocal Recording for their customary New Year recording session, devoting two days to "Sappy," one of only two songs they recorded in studio more than twice. The time expenditure showed how far they'd come; not rich, but able to indulge some musical perfectionism while jostling for third place on Sub Pop's roster.

VADIM RUBIN, Haywire: It's funny, though, that when we played with Nirvana and Tad, it wasn't clear that Nirvana was *the* band. In fact, Tad was the headliner!

JED BREWER: When I found out that we were opening the Nirvana/Tad show, I was actually a little more excited about Tad at the time.

Nirvana's arrival was perfectly timed at the crest of a wave. Over a decade of DIY efforts had created an infrastructure that provided all the elements of production, broadcast, and promotion that Nirvana needed. Even in the absence of mainstream awareness, word spread about the band, and other underground stars, via a number of means.

MATT HUNTER, New Radiant Storm King: College radio, fanzines, and word of mouth, mostly. *Spin* magazine, *NME*, and *Melody Maker* were sometimes useful, and once in a blue moon so was MTV. You'd be surprised how extensive informal networks were in the era just prior to the Internet.

GEORGE SMITH: It wasn't terribly difficult to set up a tour; there was a really good underground network of all the clubs, and generally there were a few houses where there might be house parties—little beacons around the country where it was all about the music. And our house in Olympia, the Alamo, was one of those.

TIM KERR: There was no radio or mainstream magazines for this music, so the only way you were going to find out about this was word of mouth and maybe, just maybe, you could start up a community and connect with other communities . . . By the mid-'80s things were beginning to change all over the US for this music. The scene was still small in the big picture and the mainstream for the most part was not interested, but there were more kids finding out about this "other choice" . . . There were more places to play now and shows became shows instead of crazy happenings. A grassroots network was going on so that bands could tour and college radio begin to play more of this music. Grassroots magazines writing about these scenes were becoming more abundant too.

COLIN BURNS: I feel like it was the clubs where connections were made. In those days, at least half the audience was people from other bands. It felt like a very supportive scene . . . We won the WBCN Rock 'n' Roll Rumble in 1990, which was an annual battle of the bands hosted by a Boston radio station. Maybe twenty-five bands over five nights, a winner each night, to five semifinalists, down to two finalists . . . Iggy Pop was the host. And he was my hero. And used Dana [Ong]'s amp when he played between the bands. And got my blood on his face when he picked up the bloody mike. A stage diver kicked my arm during our final song, the mike broke my nose, blood everywhere, very dramatic—but the Rumble was said to be cursed; something dramatic always happened to the winner, which was most likely breaking up.

ABE BRENNAN: Independent record stores were a good source of information . . . but many of the bands we got into we stumbled on through their touring and us playing shows with them and touring to their towns.

GLEN LOGAN, Bible Stud: There seemed to be so many local record stores owned and staffed by people who were fans of music. To many of these record-store people it was more than just a job or just a business. These people did a lot to support the local scene by stocking many of the local releases.

DUANE LANCE BODENHEIMER: Russ and Janet owned Fallout Records for a long time, couple, very nice people—my friend Tim Hayes worked there as well. It was a skate shop, comic shop, music shop . . . I always felt at home with them, very welcoming. A small close-knit group of people who loved music and thrived on it.

VADIM RUBIN: I grew up in Long Beach . . . In that area it was centered around Zed Records, an alternative and import record store that was full of great vinyl . . . This is where you found out about shows, what bands were coming to town . . . Another central point locally was Fender's, a show venue. Goldenvoice put on many of the big punk shows, and the guy running it was very close with the Zed Records guys. So I remember going to Zed's and finding out that we got a spot at a good Fender's gig for the first time.

Print media had been a link in the underground chain since the start—Sub Pop itself having been an example, given it began as a fanzine publication.

GLEN LOGAN: It seemed like more folks were writing their own music. There were also fanzines like *Backlash*, *City Heat*, and music-oriented papers like *The Rocket*. There were record stores by the score.

There were legit music venues as well as lofts, basements, and empty warehouse-type places where folks would put on shows. The *Rocket* magazine covered the scene, and for many of us it became the go-to source for info on all things local music well before the proliferation of the Internet. This probably focused the information on the local/ regional scene in a way that would not be possible in today's world. I think it made a large regional scene seem smaller, maybe a bit more intimate.

JAIME ROBERT JOHNSON: We had the *Rocket*, which was an amazing, maddening, annoying, and indispensable part of what was going on. We had peers, dedicated to building a rock 'n' roll community and playing shows together and having a great time; we had some good people who were willing to take chances.

TY WILLMAN: *Backlash* and the *Rocket*—if you were in a band, this is before Internet, that was your Internet. You would sit and look for your name, and if you were in there then you'd succeeded . . . It was pretty easy to get mentioned—I was on the cover once, but that only came when the *Green Apple Quick Step* record was out and was somewhat successful. But if you were in a band and you played, then you could get into those publications somewhere.

In 1990, *Rolling Stone* was still featuring Paul McCartney as their crucial February cover star, but it didn't matter that the mainstream music media was still fixated on bygone eras and sacred cows. Many key underground publications now had circulations in the thousands—crucially, all to people active within the community.

LORI JOSEPH: Going out and meeting the bands you liked, asking them if they needed a place to stay, and getting to know the local promoters were how we got our shows. *Flipside* was probably hands-down the best magazine that gave us the most attention back in the day. *Maximum Rocknroll*, *Flipside*, and *Alternative Press* were the only ones I read. In Chicago, WNUR was the biggest college radio station that we did interviews on and promoted all the local shows. I kept up with music by reading *Flipside* and *Alternative Press* as well as going to local indie record stores to see what was new.

VADIM RUBIN: The influential L.A. punk "fanzine" called *Flipside* . . . A really important venue that emerged there was Gilman, connected to the people that ran the even bigger punk fanzine *Maximum Rocknroll*.

JOHN MYERS: *Maximum Rocknroll* magazine was a great network. People wanted to share gigs and swap gigs. They would invite you to their town in exchange for you inviting them to your town. There was a certain camaraderie although sometimes there was abuse, too. But generally DIY people were pretty cool and helpful. There wasn't much money, though. And that was the hardship at that time. As a musician you had to have a day job and then get time off to do your shows.

The Beatles' success in the United States had occurred in part as young music fans began listening to FM radio. By the late '80s, a similar—though less dramatic—shift was occurring as stations, particularly college radio, found their niche playing what mainstream radio wouldn't.

GLEN LOGAN: There were local/regional radio stations like KAOS, KCMU, and KJET that played more than the standard AOR radio format stuff. TV shows like *Rev* featured much about the local music scene. Musically there was diversity and a degree of acceptance of that diversity that led to more of a vast number of shades of musical styles versus a few hard and fast colors or categories. The scene especially, on the west side, was incredibly vibrant.

JAIME ROBERT JOHNSON: We had a radio station that was doing the same—KCMU, now KEXP, which still to this day does totally amazing radio.

SCOTT VANDERPOOL: I made enough of a stink at KCMU that they hired me at one of the big commercial rock stations, KXRX, just before all this Seattle shit took off. I was somewhat instrumental in getting Soundgarden, Nirvana, the Melvins, Green River, Mudhoney, Love Battery, the Posies, and others on the air and *more* importantly getting '80s hairspray butt-rock *off* the air—a personal goal . . . I remember interviewing Bob Mould from Hüsker Dü and Sugar on my Sunday-night "new music show," and he observed that all the American rock stations he went to were staffed by his fans, frustrated they had to play fucking "Stairway to Heaven" every day and shit like Bon Jovi, while the people at "alternative" stations were frustrated that they had to play him instead of the Depeche Mode and Alanis Morissette they really liked.

Just as KAOS and KCMU had given Nirvana early coverage, this same benefit was extended to a whole swath of bands—an entire scene was rising.

GLEN LOGAN: There was a rise in college radio everywhere at the time and it did seem to be friendly to this genre of music (or, more accurately, these multiple types of music). The folks going to these schools were in large part the demographic that "got it" . . . That seemed to make shows at colleges more viable, especially where the college radio station was co-located with the college putting on the show.

MARC BARTHOLOMEW, Vegas Voodoo: Once we started getting airplay from the San Jose State University College radio station (KSJS) and our first studio demo cassette tape sold all ten copies at the indie record store, I really felt like we "arrived."

Just as a lot of the Sub Pop crew worked at KCMU, or Calvin Johnson presented on KAOS, a lot of musicians were directly involved in choosing the music that would go out on air.

LINDSEY THRASHER: We lived in Chico, a fairly small college town in Northern California. Trish, Larry, and I worked at the college radio station and loved music, but weren't good musicians; that didn't stop us.

BILLY ALLETZHAUSER: You wouldn't guess but Cincinnati had a great scene. I was a bit young to enjoy its heyday, but a joint called the Jockey Club had almost every major name in punk go through . . . We had a local punk radio show called *The Search & Destroy Show* that was the gel for everyone.

JED BREWER: We had one of the best college radio stations in the country, KDVS . . . What gave KDVS its great national reputation is that it was/is one of the few stations left that was completely free-format, meaning DJs could play whatever they wanted as long as it was something that wasn't being played on commercial radio. Most college stations give DJs parameters that tend to steer DJs to only playing the biggest names in independent music. I DJed at KDVS in Davis, California, during the Thornucopia years. I truly consider it the best part of my education . . . KDVS was an early champion of Sub Pop, and we helped put on shows for Mudhoney, the Fluid, et cetera. We played the shit out of those first Nirvana and Tad albums.

RICK RIZZO: WNUR (Northwestern University) was an incredibly helpful station; WXRT was a unique (to most of the rest of America) commercial station that played us early on. We got a big push from *Bucketful of Brains* in England, *Howl* in Germany, *Boston Rocker*, Byron Coley at *Spin* and *Forced Exposure*, and independent weeklies like the *Chicago Reader*. The major newspaper, *Chicago Tribune*, had a writer Greg Kot who championed our kind of music from the start.

A fresh generation had built an entirely new infrastructure required to get their sound out.

Amid this building excitement, Nirvana's life continued to be a series of opening and closing doors. On January 20, they gave their last performance in Tacoma.

JOHN PURKEY: I talked to Krist one day about maybe doing a Nirvana show and having Machine open at Legends . . . the Melvins were coming up on tour, I knew that—so I thought why not get a show together: Melvins, Machine, Nirvana, and we'll open. So I had to go through the woman who was managing Legends—I worked everything out and she took over the show. So she hired this security that were all high school kids, but they'd try to throw anybody out for doing anything, the smallest thing: somebody tried to jump off stage, they'd all come after him and try to throw him out. Matt Lukin was there, and he was really good friends with Kurt and Krist. Well, he puked backstage and the security found out and were trying to throw him out. Mayhem! That's what started it all, they were trying to kick out Matt Lukin and Matt's like, "No, I'm not going!" He even gets up on the mike and says what's happening and finally they end up letting him stay.

It was a less-than-charming location, an indication of the flea-pit circuit on which the rock underground was built. Rooms up in the roof of the venue harbored an assortment of insalubrious characters.

JOHN PURKEY: The Crips and Bloods—gangs here—they actually used to stay in here because we'd go up over the roof and there's a way to get over. You end up on the balcony area above the stage . . . there'd be all this abandoned building with mattresses everywhere and bums, or gangsters, living up there. We'd creep across, go down the balcony, and sneak into shows . . .

From playing a former porn theater in 1988 to a hangout for local gangs in January 1990, Tacoma's local color was undimmed. Likewise, having played eighty-two shows in 1989, Nirvana's live virginity was long gone. Their antics, since the first shattered guitar, had become wilder.

STEVE MORIARTY: Jonathan Poneman saw us play then apparently developed a crush on Mia [Zapata] and asked us to play with Nirvana at the HUB [Husky Union Building] Ballroom . . . It was our second show in town—we thought we had it made. But Mia didn't want to go out with Jonathan, she wouldn't tolerate him—so we fell off the radar all of a sudden. We were no longer in the Singles Club. These were regular people; the owners of Sub Pop were as notorious as people in the bands . . . It's gone down in history that the University of Washington banned Nirvana for life from playing there. I'm sure that they didn't care—they didn't play there again. It was probably two thousand people, the biggest show they'd played at the time—the kids went wild. When we played they went ape shit! We had to tell the bouncers to move the monitors and not beat people up, because they weren't used to this, they weren't ready for it. It was so oversold that somebody pulled the fire alarm so that people would leave. Then they sold more tickets and let more people in. That was just where they blew up right there—we knew they were packing hundred-seat places but . . . It was January, it was a university, people were back to school after holidays. We hung out in the dressing room, drank tequila, and they methodically destroyed the dressing room by smashing the chairs, and Krist was chasing Kurt around with the big cooler of ice they'd brought out for the beers. It was funny. They were just causing trouble, having fun, being rock stars—why not? We were in a classroom, basically, so it was like "school's out for summer": Alice Cooper! So they destroyed it— threw ice and beer all over the place and got banned. They were just out to tear it up. That was the biggest fun they'd ever had in their life . . . Onstage they were just really at the height of their game—they had the enthusiasm, lack of jadedness, lack of ego.

KAPTAIN "SCOTT GEAR" SKILLIT WEASEL, Crunchbird: The violence had been picking up with roving skinhead gangs. So the day of the show, and I arrive to learn our drummer had been savagely beaten the night before and was in the hospital . . . So now I am loading my shit in, there is one green room all four bands used. Now, understand, I am a rather large fellow: six-two, one hundred and ninety pounds. Kurt is this tiny, shy mammal. When I stepped into the hall from the loading dock he was on his way out, all greasy and pimpled in a blue flannel shirt—he looked scared shitless by my sudden appearance, this giant in combat boots (and a blue flannel I wore in as well) stomping down toward him holding the fifteen-inch speaker. I had to stop and turn my back to the wall, but he actually ducked under me . . . it was like when a cat scampers under your foot. We get the gear onto the stage and we needed to do sound check *right now*! We have no drummer! So in steps this very pixielike wonder named Chad Channing who whoops out our sound check and tells us he will fill if Sean doesn't make it. Now, see, right here I'm like, "Fucking cool!" But it also felt like I was dissing our drummer due to his situation. I relax, but Crunchy [Jaime Robert Johnson] seemed a bit stressed. I went to the green room and I met Mr. Novoselic—we were the same size! He was amazed to not have the biggest feet in the room. He truly seemed sincere . . . Finally, in walks Sean, head all wired together, can't talk, just totally punked the hospital to do this show—*nothing* was gonna stop this man. When we were to go on I was amazed to see that vast hall brimming wall to wall; this was going to be epic! I overheard comments from the other bands about how punk that was; tells a doctor to *back off!* gets out of hospital, and comes to pound the shit out of those skins.

SETH PERRY: Dale and I took a seat at the end of the bar by the front door of the club and spent all of the Melvins' and Nirvana's sets sitting there drinking beer. At one point we had an inkling to try to go watch Nirvana but decided not to, as the club was too packed, so we decided on the safety of our seats with quick access to the exit. It was quite claustrophobic in there and I remember being amazed at how many people were stuffed in.

The night before the Legends show, Nirvana was showing the Dionysian spirit of rock 'n' roll in other ways.

GEORGE SMITH: At the Steamboat Island show, there was a buzz that Kurt was on heroin . . . At that show people were talking about track marks—he had faked them up on his arms to skewer or maybe propagate the rumor . . . People were talking "Kurt has track marks," but he had drawn them, overdone. I didn't think about it too much at the time—Ian McKinnon, a popular punk-rock guy in town, had died from an overdose . . . I didn't know if it was true about Kurt and if he was just having a goof at people or if there was something to that.

JUSTIN TROSPER: Sub Pop bands were very "rock" compared to the Olympia thing, and Nirvana straddled that line . . . Kurt came out onstage looking all fucked up with what appeared to be track marks. He was pretending to be a junkie, or he was one, but in any case we all thought that was really stupid even though, and especially because, we were big fans. The Seattle bands pretended to be rock stars until they actually became them!

VADIM RUBIN: The rap on those guys back then was that they were pretty into drugs. So to me he seemed like he was a bit of a stoner.

STEVE MORIARTY: Part of the scene with the Sub Pop bands revolved around heroin—we were anti-heroin, anti-drugs, it was our common sense we thought; we drank a lot but we weren't doing drugs—not smack, anyway.

CHRIS QUINN: I remember Kurt having a lot of stomach problems back at the time I knew him—he had something going on. He had the stomach thing, and when I knew him he had no reason to make it up—for a long time I thought he didn't drink or do drugs, I thought he was straightedge . . . I never saw him do anything in that whole period—but I'm only one person. For the amount I drank at the time, the amount of people I knew drinking at parties—it was college—Kurt never seemed like he was into that; it wasn't his thing.

Rumors...

Cobain was certainly open to experimentation, at least of the musical kind. During this spell in Olympia he worked with a Calvin Johnson/Tobi Vail outfit, the Go Team; sang for his friend Dylan Carlson's band Earth; and collaborated with members of Screaming Trees on a project known as the Jury.

MARK PICKEREL: I loved the collaboration and would have loved for it to turn in to something prolific and consistent, but both bands just became overwhelmed with their own workloads and responsibilities as well as devotion to their own writing. I also have to wonder if it was a little uncomfortable for [Mark] Lanegan and Cobain to figure out how to divide up the workload—they were both such strong singers, but Lanegan didn't play an instrument at the time, so it didn't leave him much to do on songs that Cobain sang. I will say, though, that I thought it was a really magical meeting of musical minds, and if we'd had just a little more time to develop it, we could have made an amazing album!

Becoming a top draw at the "in" label meant Nirvana could live reasonably on just a few local shows, as they proved in 1990 by playing only once a month for March, September, November, and December, while not at all in June and July.

JOHN PURKEY: There was around $7,000 made. She [the promoter] paid out $500 each to Nirvana and the Melvins. Machine made $150, though we were guaranteed $500 if there were five hundred people at the show. The show turned out to be over capacity. Something like eight hundred people.

CRISPIN WOOD: We were paid $500 that night. I assume Nirvana was paid the same, possibly more since they went on last. Not crazy-great money, but not bad, either. I also know that Cobain was not impressed by the sound man that came with the rented PA. After hearing us do our check, Cobain offered our sound man $100 to mix their set. Our sound man—Carl Plaster, engineer/producer on most of our recordings—turned Cobain down. Nirvana couldn't have been hurting too badly for money if Cobain was able to offer $100 for sound.

MARC BARTHOLOMEW: The Nirvana show at the Cactus Club was our first legit paid gig. The band got $50 cash and every member got a free drink ticket. I'm sure the few friends of ours who showed up covered that $50 with their ticket price at the door. The only other benefit was the sound guy was usually cool and would record your set from the mixing board onto a cassette tape . . . After our set we hung out with the other bands, I got my free drink ticket, and felt like a big shot being nineteen years old, drinking a draft Budweiser in a big red plastic cup walking around a club. It was basically "Here's your drink tickets, get your shit off the stage."

Nirvana had ambition as well as label obligations, so they found themselves supporting Tad on a tour haring down the West Coast to Tijuana, Mexico.

ERIC MOORE: Pine Street holds maybe . . . 1,100 people? It was oversold, I'm sure, with more people than that. The idea that a large number of people would come see bands like Tad and Nirvana was sort of new at the time . . . There was a lot of talk about the lineup and who would headline. Tad was considered a bigger act in some ways, but they were all headliners . . . I think we got tacked onto the bill because one of our band members was sleeping with someone who worked for Monqui (the production company) at the time . . . Tad walked up to me (he was friendly sometimes!) and complimented me on our set. Stoked! And then . . . someone from, I'm guessing Nirvana's crew, stole my leather jacket from behind my amp onstage.

KURT DANIELSON: We met with Nirvana to discuss the upcoming West Coast tour on the day of the HUB Ballroom show . . . an atmosphere of brotherhood infused the venue. It was an exciting time, a triumphant homecoming gig after a triumphant European tour with our brothers . . . while we casually joked with Kurt and Krist about the tour in Europe and about the upcoming tour, they told Tad and me that they had decided that they should headline that night at the HUB Ballroom, as well as on the West Coast tour. Tad and I were a little surprised—not so much that they should headline but that they should tell us they were going to, and yet they told us in a kind of subtle, friendly way, and there was no mention of a coin toss—because there was an unaccustomed tension in the air . . . It seemed that Kurt had decided that he wasn't going to be put in a position in which he was going to lose any more coin tosses, especially not in America, where it seemed it was important to him to define his band as a headliner once and for all.

The "underground" tag concealed a melting pot with far more unusual sounds than the relatively conventional approach Seattle was becoming famed for. That rock edge made the Sub Pop bands unique while dividing them from many of those they played alongside.

MARC BARTHOLOMEW: I always looked at grunge as "slower punk, where you could understand the words." We were never a grunge or punk band. I think we were confused by all of our individual influences and while we wanted to be "harder," we always came out as more "poppy." I was shocked when the Cactus Club manager lined us up with Tad and Nirvana.

JED BREWER: The booking guys asked me, as a KDVS person, if they should add a local band, since it was a weeknight. I actually recommended that they just keep it two bands so it wouldn't go too late on a weeknight . . . A week later I was walking to class at UC Davis and I saw our name on the flier for the show! I guess they had decided to add us but forgot to tell us. Obviously, we forgave them for the communication breakdown. So the moral of the story is, if you want to play on a legendary bill, just say you don't want to! I think we were on the bill because we were "college radio"–sounding, but we were not as heavy and loud as them. We saved our only heavy song for the end to try and segue and/or keep up with the Joneses.

TED CARROLL, Distorted Pony: People were really excited that we were playing with Tad and Nirvana, but to a large degree we were not kindred spirits. We played very different stuff, but we were an "alternative" band and so were they and so it was kinda "stick them on the bill." . . . It just seemed like more rock 'n' roll to me. Not that that is bad—[it] just was not that exciting to me. We were more in touch with the K Records bands than anything else.

VADIM RUBIN: Both of our bands were going in different directions, theirs [Nirvana's] was a post-punk/hardcore sound. Not mainstream or anything, but different. Other bands at that time were products of the "punk scene" but were going beyond it, like Fugazi. Our band was more influenced by metal-type stuff, in particular, especially Black Sabbath.

Nirvana had now played over one hundred shows since Chad Channing had been added to the lineup. Their experience together showed.

MARC BARTHOLOMEW: The Nirvana guys were a few years older than us. We were all around nineteen years old. I remember admiring Chad's drumming and thinking we played a little similar in style, though he was much more accomplished.

VADIM RUBIN: Nirvana was great all around that night we played with them. Their drummer was good—not as good as Dave Grohl, though. They were definitely a great live band, lots of energy and had the audience in the palm of their hand.

TED CARROLL: It was packed . . . I remember meeting Tad at sound check and I think I may have overconsumed the rest of the night . . . I sat with Krist at the bar for quite a while. He was probably amused by my inability to speak coherently. I vaguely recall telling him I was not a huge fan of Nirvana. Didn't dislike them, just didn't do a ton for me at the time. If memory serves me, he was a very fun, affable guy.

JED BREWER: It was a weeknight, and there were probably about one hundred people or less . . . KDVS was playing the shit out of the first Nirvana and Tad albums; otherwise there would've probably only been about twenty people there . . . Nirvana seemed to be authentically young and hungry and rocked out pretty hard that night . . . I did notice Kurt curled up and sleeping and/or resting on the couch in the little backstage area.

MARC BARTHOLOMEW: By the time Nirvana got onstage the place was pretty packed, as it was not a big venue at all . . . Novoselic is pointing out guys in the audience who look like Kurt, and he's saying I am one of the guys who look like him. I had shoulder-length, stringy dirty-blond hair at the time and reddish-blond growth on my face . . . I've made the joke for years that Cobain stole my hairstyle!

KEVIN FRANKE, Vegas Voodoo: It was kinda crowded. I recall there being some bad energy and I didn't stick around for Nirvana . . . Tony [Macias—bassist] had heard that Kurt Cobain was "in the van." I wanted to meet him because I thought we might be able to play together sometime. (I think people can forget that Kurt Cobain was just that guy named Kurt who played guitar and sang in a band . . .) I went outside to look for the van that night too because I didn't like the vibes inside the club. I never found or talked to him, but I really think he wanted to get away from that scene for the same reason. What I mean is, he was "almost a ghost presence."

The first tour of the New Year progressed in an easy good humor, without flake-outs.

MARC BARTHOLOMEW: Tad from Tad heckled us when we ran out of material and we asked for requests from the audience. Tad screamed

"'Freebird'!" So we played "Show Me the Way" by Peter Frampton. We knew the music but not the words, so Adam made it up on the spot. It was classic.

ALEX KOSTELNIK: Timo Ellis [Nubbin] and I were in a band called Freebird. Yep, local show joke—the top heckler line when a band would break a guitar string.

GEORGE SMITH: There were a lot of jokey arena-rock trappings people would use, like people in the crowd yelling "Freebird!" or holding up lighters—you'd have, like, twenty people in the crowd all yelling "Freebird!" and flashing their lighters. We used to like to say at shows, if we were playing in Tacoma we'd shout, "Hello, Seattle! Hi!" stuff like that. Jokey arena-rock stuff.

As late as January 1994, Cobain would take the stage at the Spokane Coliseum and shout, "Hello, Ellensburg!" Good jokes die hard.

10.0

Nobody Knows We're New Wave
March to May 1990

As a now-established band, 1990 could simply have been a spell of rising fortunes for Nirvana. Instead, they entered a spell in which missteps were as numerous as steps forward. They began comfortably enough by hopping the border in March for a performance in Vancouver.

SIOBHAN DUVALL, The Bombshells: There is no such thing as a casual stroll across the Canada/US border for any band. As musicians, crossing that border is a very complex and expensive endeavor due to both Canadian and US immigration laws, and for smaller bands often involves all types of subterfuge . . . I don't even think we were aware of the term "grunge" yet. We knew the show was a big deal, as the Town Pump [500-seater] was sold out, and the show was presented by Periscope [precursor to Universal and House of Blues] . . . The Bombshells was comprised of five blond, bright, bubbly, friendly, and outgoing twenty-one-year-olds totally excited to be playing our fourth show to a sold-out crowd. Tad and Nirvana had the big dressing room at the Town Pump, and the Bombshells had the "little" dressing room . . . Which was actually the teeny tiny photocopier room in the basement. So five happy, excited twenty-one-year-old blondes went bouncing into the big dressing room to say "Hi!" in our friendly Canadian manner and were literally *frozen* out of the room by the members of Tad, who were not happy to see us at all. So we said to ourselves Ooh, a little chilly in there, and went bouncing back to our little photocopier room. Kurt, Krist, and Chad all followed us back and spent the whole night hanging out in there with us. But Chad and Krist were very chatty and outgoing, and Kurt was really quite sweet, quiet, and shy. Kurt told me that my band was "power pop," which was the first time I had ever heard that term. At the time we just saw them as another touring band and had lots of fun, having no idea of the impact they would have.

"Power pop" was Cobain's main musical interest at that point in time, as represented by bands like the Vaselines and Shonen Knife. It was also influencing his own work with simple ditties like "Been a Son" and "Stain" emerging as a result.

LEIGHTON BEEZER: Kurt showed up at my house, early 1990, I think . . . it wasn't too long after Nirvana toured Europe with Tad. He told me he had been listening to a lot of pop stuff . . . you know, like the Vaselines, Beat Happening, even the Beatles! He put on this Monkees record, I remember. Kurt turned to me that day [and] said, and I remember this very clearly, "I want to be a big star, and I'm gonna have to write songs like the Monkees to get there. If I can kind of combine the Melvins and the Monkees, my band could be huge." He then said, with that sly smile of his on his face . . . something to the effect that he would have to pretend that he hated stardom if it in fact happened, just to maintain his punk-rock credentials.

While Leighton Beezer's remark is a joke, it does capture the other influences that were coming through at that point in time. Nirvana's April recording showed them turning away from the sound of *Bleach*, yet their formula wasn't yet in place.

Only "Lithium" had the soft-hard dynamic that would dominate *Nevermind*. Sub Pop showed their devotion by investing $3,500 for a video to "In Bloom" without realizing the relationship was ending.

KURT DANIELSON: Sub Pop bands, being generally happy to be associated with the label, did not grumble about being on Sub Pop except maybe among themselves, which is to say privately. I never heard Nirvana complain openly, that is, not until they actually had offers to sign with majors . . . The Nirvana guys always wanted the most for their band, and they always had a healthy skepticism about labels in general, questioning Sub Pop's motives from the very beginning, but that doesn't necessarily mean anything. After all, Sub Pop helped build the band, and the Nirvana guys knew that. At the same time, they were never satisfied, always looking for ways to become as big as they believed they should be. If Sub Pop couldn't keep up with Nirvana's vision, at least Sub Pop allowed that vision to evolve.

SLIM MOON: Sub Pop sold a lot of records. No other label from Seattle or the Northwest sold anything close.

This success was relative, however. No indie label was making vast money and Sub Pop was built on a crate load of IOUs; band members working in distribution would take the chance to sell their own self-issued music in lieu of actually getting paid.

SCOTT VANDERPOOL: The *What-part-of-we-have-no-money-don't-you-understand?* days . . . we would sell our own label shit to record stores right along with the Sub Pop stuff.

ROD MOODY: Sub Pop had some great people working with them, Charles Peterson, Danny Bland, Jack Endino, Lisa Orth, Rich Jensen . . . and they did the best they could even though they usually could not rely on a paycheck. Jon and Bruce had brilliant ideas but no money, which meant they had to be very creative . . . and cagey.

A lot of the bands would hang out in the Sub Pop offices, grab free records, see what the label was up to, demand money . . . Me, I stayed out of the way.

KEVIN WHITWORTH: Sub Pop was a big Ponzi scheme and everybody knew it. We were all trying to con some major label into throwing us lines before the ship went down. Some of us were lucky in that regard. If anything, it became *less* professional as time went on, with my poor girlfriend (now wife) having to go and pound on Pone-man's (as she called him) door every month to get the rent check. But we were one of the few bands on salary at the time—which was enormous to us. We were being paid to play music. We knew our rent was covered, and that was big when you're on tour. And they never bounced a check to us, which was also big, since that was their standard MO in those days.

GEOFF ROBINSON: Keep in mind that this was a small town with a small scene and definitely a small label . . . Bruce and Jonathan were very busy securing funds for, and engaging in, record production . . . To be brutally frank, I do not believe the money was so much an issue for us . . . It was the employees hired to do our advance promo packets . . . They did not even make follow-up phone calls to clubs that we were slated to play, let alone sending advance promo packets. Half the shows on our tour didn't even have posters. Booking agents told us Sub Pop was nonresponsive when it came to promo, so opening bands created posters and did our advance promo in that way.

BLAG DAHLIA: We came from the Midwest, where being in a band was about on a par with child molestation, but less respectable . . . we were on a label called Sub Pop, which was morally opposed to giving artists any money. That's why every artist left the label. But unlike all of them, we were too scary to attract any major labels, so we did a lot of starving and dope dealing and living off girlfriends.

KURT DANIELSON: Whenever you mix friendship with business, it's going to get complicated. And it was even more complicated when you consider how the dynamic that governed our interactions with them was conditioned by their personalities and how they interacted with one another, making it so that Bruce was the one we talked to about some things and Jon was the one we relied on for others.

Nirvana wondered about the indie route, but few, if any, could offer more than Sub Pop.

DOUG GILLARD: There was never enough money with Homestead, I think we all felt. But they did press and release the albums, and included us on two pretty great label compilations . . . The problem lay somewhere in Homestead's ownership and parent company, but I mean, we recorded everything on our own and on a shoestring (*with* a shoestring, it sounded like, at times). They had great A&R, thanks solely to Gerard Cosloy, who is still a tastemaker to this day. He found and signed a lot of artists that shaped what became known as indie . . . and championed some worthy established folk that no longer had a home.

JON WAHL: Everyone wanted to release a single with Sub Pop. But Sympathy for the Record Industry was quite prolific and through that, and the fact that we all lived in Long Beach, many projects happened. I used to typeset for Long Gone John and he'd pay me in a burrito and a beer. Good times . . . SFTRI gave no booking or promotional support whatsoever. That was all done by the individual bands. He'd pay you in a small percentage of pressed records, which you'd turn around and sell on tour. It worked good that way.

ANNE EICKELBERG, Thinking Fellers Union Local 282: Here's a comparison that pretty much explains what Matador was like then: Rough Trade took us out to a big Indian meal, then back to the offices to get high and listen to the Butthole Surfers' cover of "Hurdy Gurdy Man," pre-release. Matador asked us to come to their office really early in the morning and gave us a couple bagels and said they didn't have much money. So obviously we went with them.

Rough Trade went bust soon after, so the bagels were a wise choice. Then again, Sub Pop was achieving amazing amounts on a minimal budget.

ROD MOODY: I personally thought it was insane . . . an incredibly gutsy and brilliant move on the part of Sub Pop. I mean, really [*Sub Pop 200*], a fancy triple-LP boxed set from a label that was broke? But it served its purpose and showed the world what our little secret was all about. We never got much money from it, but the recognition was the benefit, even though we were quickly overshadowed by many of the other bands.

Everyone in the scene knew the guys at Sub Pop personally and had respect for them and what they were doing.

GEOFF ROBINSON: Honestly, I do not remember the Sub Pop Sunday event that much, since we were playing so frequently anyway. We were gigging at least two times a week and sometimes three or four. We did not depend on Sub Pop for money because we knew that they were footing the bill for our time at Reciprocal—so we didn't pester them about money. We knew they were broke because they told us.

DUANE LANCE BODENHEIMER: We were very fortunate to have people that supported us in the life that we were doing—like Bruce from Sub Pop, Mark from Mudhoney, club owners as well—so we were fortunate enough to play with a lot of these bands that were up-and-coming . . . Sub Pop put out stuff for us, eMpTy Records put out stuff for us and were behind us one hundred percent . . . The label was Ian Wright and Volker Stewart (in Germany it was Musical Tragedies and here it was eMpTy). Most of our stuff was engineered by Jack

Endino—super-nice guy. Really easy to work with, put up with our crap . . . I can't express how grateful I am to Bruce and Sub Pop . . .

The supportiveness of Sub Pop meant Nirvana was at least slightly more comfortable when back on the road in April.

CRISPIN WOOD: When we arrived for the six-thirty sound check, Nirvana was loading in. (They had a station wagon with U-Haul cargo trailer) . . . Just another band on the road with not much change sums it up pretty well. We'd toured the country and were well aware of what they were up against. You need enough gas to make it to the next town. It's hard to save any money, hard to do laundry, you have to think frugally about expenses. Nirvana probably woke up on somebody's floor the day after the Man Ray show and drove to another state . . . In actual fact I probably saw more of Nirvana via their sound check than their actual set, of which I saw only two or three songs. I wouldn't say they sounded tight, or necessarily well practiced, but they didn't sound bad, either. Cobain spent a portion of the sound check playing guitar on the dance floor in front of the stage, as if to better hear the PA mix. We were definitely underwhelmed by Chad's playing. What impressed more than anything else was Cobain's songwriting . . .

Nirvana was still not quite top rank, however, either in venue selection or standing.

CRISPIN WOOD: Man Ray was a dance club; rock bands almost never played there. When we heard about the show, the reaction was a bit like, "Man Ray . . . didn't Divine perform there a while back?" My recollection is that the Man Ray show was a "co-headline" gig, which probably meant both bands were paid the same. Nirvana closed the show, though.

FORREST: One of my coworkers from the stock market in New York was there; we called him Spud because of Idaho Potatoes. He was home on vacation and brought his whole family there . . . You couldn't get a bee in there; it was like they never saw an all-black band like Spyz before, and I bet because that was the first time we ever played there. Nirvana came on before us. They did extremely well, but they were very typical like any local band—nothing special about them . . . Nirvana seemed like a band traveling the road to build up a following without much support like local bands do now but, like Primus, they seemed to have had a little fan base and yes they did have a van if I can recall. I know they didn't have a bus; that's a fact—and they did set up their own gear onstage. I don't remember where they slept or ate or if they even had a hotel to go to—those were beautiful days, man, I tell ya . . . Beautiful with plain raw talent and no excuses.

DANA ONG, Slaughter Shack: MIT was an odd place for a show . . . The show took place in a low-ceilinged basement of a frat house. Nirvana was so loud, I had to listen to them from the dressing room upstairs—we all shared a dorm living room for a dressing room . . . I liked the first Nirvana album, which was the only one out then, loved Soundgarden, but I didn't jump on the grunge bandwagon . . .

COLIN BURNS: We played in a basement, in a corner, with cables marking the edge of "the stage." It was less than a mile to the Middle East in Cambridge—one of the best live venues in town—but it felt as though the people from this dorm never left campus, or even their dorm. I convinced myself they were manufacturing LSD and rarely saw outsiders. This perception was mostly due to the insane reaction we got from the crowd that night. And that I'd never seen 90 percent of the audience at other shows . . .

MATT HUNTER: Even in 1990/1991, there was already a post-punk canon that was heavily regional (Minor Threat if you were from DC; Mission of Burma if you were from Boston; Ramones/Sonic Youth if you were from NYC . . .). Nothing about Nirvana indicated that they were radically different stylistically from the rest of what was going on in the US at the time . . . You could argue that they were latecomers even in Seattle. That said, even in 1990 they were a big deal on the indie circuit, and had some measure of "star power," for lack of a better term.

Nirvana had always blurred the line between sloppiness and passionate abandon, which manifested itself on the tour.

DANA ONG: I don't think either band was very professional at the time, coming from an era of Jesus Lizard and Black Flag; being a little reckless and almost falling off the edge of the stage was common at live shows. We may have tried to play tight, I can't remember. They were probably looser, more expressively raw, because we were trying to stay true to the structure of how we practiced and recorded our songs. Their approach had more emotional urgent appeal . . . Chad wasn't as tight as Grohl, but their style was more messy at the time, so he was fitting.

TIM SOLYAN, Victim's Family: His playing was indeed sloppy, but I thought that was part of what brought the magic to it. I enjoyed watching Chad at those shows and always felt it was unique . . . I was surprised at how tall Krist was, and as soon as they started he was hopping up and down and his head was just about hitting the low basement ceiling. The stage at this club was only about six inches high, so we squeezed up nearly in front of Krist to get a better look. I was blown away to say the least! Thunderous bass and grinding poppy guitar. Kurt screaming and Chad and his sloppy chaotic thumping. It was rad to say the least! At one moment I lost sight of Kurt (who really only had the spot he was standing in for space between the drums and the crowd) and I looked down and he was on the ground on his back squirming and writhing out the guitar part for the song! At the end of the last song Kurt jumped backward into Chad's drums and sent them and him sprawling and their set was over.

MATT HUNTER: Those guys already seemed like rock stars, and were treated with no small measure of awe by the crowd. J Mascis did sound for them that night—he was already kind of a legend on the indie circuit. As a band, they sounded very much top of their game, tight and powerful, even if the result sounded kinda derivative . . .

PEYTON PINKERTON, New Radiant Storm King: Kurt was *everything* and the band seemed dwarfed by his even-then-iconic presence. Krist constantly tried to add to the energy of the stage with his lumbering antics, but he just came off like a kid who wasn't getting enough attention.

ROBERT HAMPSON, Loop: I remember Krist just loping around and sort of pogoing. Kurt was rolling around all over the place. I think he spent more time on the floor than standing up. They looked like they were all having a blast. But it's not really what I like to see on a performance level. I guess I thought it was comedic and goofy. I liked the sound, but the show more for the noise than the stagecraft.

The tour wasn't devoid of bonhomie, either, with Nirvana's usual mellow attitude meaning others readily warmed to them.

CRISPIN WOOD: We did spend a fair amount of time in the dressing room together—lots of goofy joking around. The dressing room was downstairs, below the dance floor, and fairly large. Old sofas, funky random things. The club manager brought down a case of beer. I don't remember those guys drinking much. Lots of smoking, though. We were on a first-name basis with Krist by the end of the night. We hung with him lots, and with Chad as well. We didn't hang much with Cobain, who was surrounded by fans the whole time. Probably college kids. He was ensconced on a sofa in the dressing room, conducting interviews. My recollection is that some locals did a video interview with Cobain—just Cobain, or mostly Cobain, not so much the rest of the band. So while we stood partying in the corner with Krist and Chad, Cobain sat in the (college/indie) media glare.

TIM SOLYAN: The next show was in Ann Arbor at a club called the Blind Pig . . . Being the fifth show with Tad for us we were all becoming "tour friends" and the atmosphere was fun. I met Krist at this time as well and he was equally a very nice and friendly dude and we all chitchatted about our bands and touring Europe . . . I was sitting on a small couch and Tad was sitting in a chair across from me and we were talking. Just then Kurt walks in and jumps on Tad's lap and hangs on him with his arms around Tad's neck. Tad says, "Merry Christmas, little boy! What would you like for Christmas this year?" Kurt then says, "I'm not so happy with you Santa Tad . . ." Tad: "Oh really? And why is that?" Kurt: "Because last year I asked you for a rubber fist shaped like this" [gestures with his hand in a tight fist] "but instead you gave me a rubber fist shaped like this!!" [makes a gesture with his hand with all his fingers pressed together and straight forward] We all laughed.

LORI JOSEPH: Everyone was very nice and talkative. I remember Kurt brought along his own oolong tea. Chad was super-cool and I remember being bummed when he wasn't in the band anymore. My fondest memory is the show we played together in April of 1990. We were the opening band on the bill at Chicago's Cabaret Metro. They asked when we would be on and then ran out and got some food so they could get back in time to see us play. How freaking awesome is that? They were well oiled in the sense when you go on tour and play your songs every day you get very good. Definitely still grunge but with better venues comes better sound and all things better. Playing for ten people in a shitty club with a crappy PA versus one thousand people with a great PA does a lot for any band. Always some gear smashing. I remember their trailer full of broken guitars in the back of their van . . . As far as Nirvana goes, no, I never thought of them as being mainstream or ever getting that popular. I had seen them several times with ten people in the audience.

Yet, at times on this tour, there were clearly frustrations building.

CRISPIN WOOD: Right before "About a Girl," one of the band members asked for more light "so we can see." I know the lack of light was a problem during our set. Man Ray wasn't in the habit of booking bands, so there was no house PA or lights. The club rented a PA for the show but didn't bother with lights. If I were to guess, the stage (which was a permanent fixture) was for DJs. There were probably one or two spots, no mounted rack of lights like you usually see at a rock show. It was dark onstage, and that definitely had an effect on the playing.

At the MIT dorm show Novoselic upset some of the audience by tearing one of their mascots down.

COLIN BURNS: There was a common room that was the "backstage" area. I can't remember if this was before or after our set, but definitely before Nirvana played. A friend of ours began de-tuning Krist's bass. Then proceeded to take the strings off completely. It may have started as a prank, but felt almost malicious by the end. I didn't know what was behind it. And it made me uncomfortable. And I left the room. I think if it had been anyone's gear I would have been uncomfortable.

DANA ONG: We didn't have a nice introduction. While Nirvana was onstage, a friend, who will remain anonymous, took all the strings off Krist's bass. He wasn't a fan of Nirvana, maybe he was drunk, I don't remember. But the next day I got a call from another local band manager who told me we were weren't allowed to open for Nirvana again; we were banned! That's hilarious that Krist may have defaced some part of MIT and then was upset about the string incident, if the account of his actions are true. Wouldn't that be a little rock 'n' roll hypocrisy?

VICTOR POISON-TETE: In all honesty, fanboys, I don't remember anything memorable about the ten-minute temper tantrum "FM Jesus" might have thrown on that particular night, as I secured my personal belongings, exchanged pleasantries with friends—I believe I saw Iggy Pop at the rear of the club (not an actual friend, but you will take me serious if I drop a name), and prepared to walk the four blocks from the Pyramid Club to my apartment, and prepare for work the following morning . . . in the middle of the first song Kurt started flinging instruments and kicking amps; it seems the current drummer continued to fall off beat; and Cobain, still somewhat asleep, couldn't "find a pony to ride." I believe they played maybe ten minutes, and although people where eager to hear them, the overcrowding of the club and length of time already spent standing and pushing for airspace resulted in an early night.

Things came to a head on April 27 at a Hampshire College benefit show for Amnesty International.

PEYTON PINKERTON: Novoselic had just shaved his head the night before after being heckled off the stage by David Berman, later of the Silver Jews in Hoboken! He looked like an eight-foot-tall five-year-old.

PETER IRVINE: Krist might have been on something, but to us he was friendly, chatty, and even apologetic. I recall hanging out with him outside the venue. We were next to the backstage parking area, and he came up and engaged in conversation. He told us that Nirvana had a really terrible gig the night before, underattended, and out of frustration he had shaved his head . . . Hampshire College did have a thriving music-appreciation scene. They had funding and a good group of organizers who brought in a lot of cutting-edge bands. The

Amnesty show was just another of a series of events at Hampshire that consistently brought in interesting new bands.

JIM ROY, Sweet Lickin' Honey Babes: Just Gobblehoof, Cordelia's Dad, and Nirvana were the big fish. So basically, the folks putting on the show had most of the Hampshire bands that were active on that bill. It would have been practically impossible for us not to be playing . . . I knew who Cordelia's Dad were, and liked them; I didn't know Gobblehoof and I didn't know Nirvana at all. At all! I mostly paid attention to getting set up/wound up for our set, and beer . . . there was some generalized pissing contest between Gobblehoof and Nirvana and this had escalated to the point that Cordelia's Dad got fed up and played a free acoustic set out in front of the venue.

CHARLES SHIPMAN, Three Merry Widows: We played right before Gobblehoof . . . They dithered endlessly during their sound check so that we never got to have one and had to rush up and start right away when they finally got off. Terrible breach of etiquette—we took such things very seriously in those days! And then one of their guitar players continued fiddling with his pedals even while we were trying to start, so our drummer went up and screamed in his ear, "Get the fuck off the stage!"

PETER IRVINE: Nirvana was late. There was some problem with the sound, so we kept waiting to do our sound check. At some point there was some talk of switching the sequence of bands . . . I overheard someone ask, "Who is Cordelia's Dad?" and I believe it was J Mascis who responded, disparagingly, "They're just an Amherst College band." This was annoying, as we actually had a good following in the area (above and beyond a typical "college" band), and were appropriately placed on the bill . . . What Mascis was suggesting was that we get bumped to an earlier spot so that, I think, Gobblehoof, who were friends with Nirvana, be put in a more prominent spot. After waiting around some more it became apparent that we were not going to get a sound check. I don't know if it was Nirvana's fault, or someone else, but the whole show seemed to be falling apart. We were annoyed at the petty jockeying and feeling disrespected, so we decided that instead of playing inside, we would play an acoustic set outside. When we moved outside, a lot of people followed us . . . We had no way of knowing but were told by several people that there were far more people watching our set outside than were inside watching the other bands. In some ways this night encapsulates our whole career—when faced with the threshold of popularity, we take an intimate turn, break the rules, and end up outside.

The line between mischievous and annoying depends on whether one is on the receiving end.

PEYTON PINKERTON: They got in trouble with security for stealing loaves of Wonder Bread from the commissary at Saga after the concert . . . Everett True—the Brit journalist—was traveling with them and I think they were really working the Beatles' *Hard Day's Night* shenanigans and doing stupid rock shit. Krist kept stealing the beers that were meant for all of the bands (about ten bands played in total)— taking them out to their van in his pants—making several trips. Bands would come off stage and find no beer waiting for them. The young woman sponsoring the benefit kept getting more beer for the bands— out of her own dollars—yet Krist kept taking them still. Same for cigarettes. We had someone buy us cartons of cigarettes up in Vermont, where they were much cheaper, and they brought them to us at the show. Nirvana kept bumming smokes off me so I gave them a pack. Later I caught Novoselic going through my backpack and taking several packs for himself and the band. When I went to grab my backpack he just gave me this dumb little-boy look like *What did I do?* I got a bad vibe off of him even before he started hoarding everybody's beer and smokes. He presented himself as a real dick in several regards from the moment I came in contact with him until their van drove away . . . He was so rude to the "rich college kids" who were paying to hear his band . . . I hate that cliché rock-star shit—he acted like they were sticking it to the man but ended up just fucking over some poor students (like the girl sponsoring the event) holding a benefit for a worthy cause . . . From stage he more than once yelled at kids in the back of the room (a room which was almost entirely a slam/mosh pit) to dance their "rich" asses off. The people in the back by the kitchen doors were actually work-study kids who had to work and clean up at the show to pay for school.

The tour was certainly not a high for Nirvana; they'd been booed offstage and had equipment break down, then added to the ugly vibe by taking it out on their own drummer, upsetting other musicians and generally acting sullen.

DANA ONG: I don't remember Krist being reckless or destructive, he was sitting cross-legged in the dressing room when I met him, surrounded by goggly eyed rockers . . . I remember Kurt being moody; he was kind of a black cloud when they arrived at MIT. I don't know if he even introduced himself. I'm sure if he was using at the time [he] could've been in a nasty state of withdrawals or waiting to get high . . . Having met the problems of my own addictions, I understand why he may have been less than charming that day.

TIM AARON, Gobblehoof: Cobain liked us—gave the band a hundred bucks after the show when he heard we weren't getting paid. I remember him sitting outside, side stage, on the loading dock just kind of chilling solo and he seemed like he was thinking—wanted his space.

CHARLES SHIPMAN: There was a negative vibe coming from that crowd. Hard to put a finger on, but they definitely didn't seem to be enjoying themselves.

PEYTON PINKERTON: Kurt was shy and fairly amenable to casual conversation, but he shut down after getting stoned and just kind of slumped into his chair in the band room and watched Krist and his mean-spirited behavior. We did manage to talk about Scratch Acid's first EP and how we both loved Rey Washam's drumming on that record. He also knew J Mascis was coming to the show, and you could tell he really was worked up about hanging out with someone whom I presumed to be an idol for him.

CRISPIN WOOD: As for visible signs of tension, that's so hard to say. Touring can be exhausting, tensions come and go. Cobain wasn't particularly friendly. Was he always that way? I have no idea.

ROBERT HAMPSON: I didn't really care for the Seattle scene. It was filled with too many bar bands that riffed on the sub–Black Sabbath angle or the overearnest, self-indulgent Pearl Jam types . . . They [Nirvana] definitely were a band apart from the "Seattle sound"; they had something a little extra. I guess you can count me as a fan, so I was looking forward to playing with them . . . The drummer was nowhere to be seen backstage, so I didn't meet him. Krist just seemed like a very tall and shaven-headed goof. I tried to talk to Kurt and say how much I liked his records and the show. He just literally blanked me. Didn't say a word. Looked straight through me. So, I just left him to his own thing. I walked away and just thought, Fuck him, arrogant miserable cunt!

JIM ROY: Nirvana didn't make a big impression on me at the time, But Novoselic impressed me as a figure onstage, and played well enough that I approached him after the set to congratulate him, "Great set, dude, you're a monster up there!" And he just totally shut me down, "No, I'm not," and walked away. It stung, so I was done with them and didn't give them another thought until my band had broken up and their band was all over MTV. For a long time, I disliked them out of principle.

11.0

Intermission
June to September 1990

Cobain retreated to his one-room apartment and spent much of the summer cocooned there. While Nirvana barely played as a group, this time alone would bear fruit in the form of an entire suite of new songs; Cobain's most prolific spell ever.

GEORGE SMITH: As far as Kurt the person, he was fairly reclusive—you might see him out at shows, at a party, but he definitely wasn't out a whole lot. Not terribly social. He wasn't particularly awkward; he was friendly—not just a wallflower—he just didn't seem to be someone who craved social attention. He stuck to his own circle. When I knew him he was staying in Olympia, at Tracy's house—that's where he lived and he just spent an awful lot of time there.

JOHN PURKEY: He had a lot of pictures of Jesus and crosses, a collection of them behind the couch . . . almost like a shrine but not that he's doing it religiously. Above it was one of his paintings—I remember that. Kurt and Tracy's place smelled like rabbit shit; they had birds and rabbits, sometimes there'd be a rabbit running around.

SLIM MOON: I really loved Kurt's visual art, his sculpture and painting. Also when he lived with Tracy, they had a lot of animals, rats and turtles . . . I loved his gentle nature. I loved that I introduced Kurt to the music of Lead Belly and he loved it so much.

RONNA MYLES-ERA: I wouldn't say that Kurt, Krist (I only knew him as Chris), or Chad ever really rambled around town . . . Not in the early days. I don't recall them being in bars much. They were stoner types, usually home listening to or playing music. I would see Kurt around; he lived next to Slim Moon and I would hang out at Slim's house sometimes. They weren't showy people at all . . .

Channing bowed out on May 17, 1990, having endured his comrades' increasingly aggressive antics on the last tour: glass thrown at the wall behind him as he played, his kit demolished with him beneath it, a jug full of water gooshed over him.

PEYTON PINKERTON: Chad Channing seemed like he already knew his days were numbered but was real nice and humble—at, like, five-foot-two, he and Kurt really seemed like hobbits next to Novoselic's giant frame. Chad just stayed outside the band circle and seemed like he didn't want to be involved . . .

RYAN AIGNER: Chad was the really shocking one to me, because he was pretty punk rock, alternative mentality, came from Bainbridge Island—artsy, hippie, cool—he had the background, he wouldn't be questioned as hard as Dave [Foster]. Dave they were still like, "Dave you're still wearing that redneck baseball cap, what's up with that?" Asking him, "Maybe your culture, your style, needs to be more like us . . ." Chad had that. Why and how they ever got to where they felt like he wasn't a good enough commitment I never did know.

DAMON ROMERO: I feel he got a bit of a raw deal in the end; they weren't super-professional about how they kicked him out. He put up with a lot—he toured with them all through the United States, all through Europe; he put in the work to help them achieve success.

It's hard to keep together—every band I've been in has broken up—so I have respect for people who can be mature enough to keep working together.

Just as Nirvana's last shift in drummers had coincided with their move onto Sub Pop in spring 1988, this one happened as a potential major-label move was in the cards.

Nirvana had been a relative latecomer to the Seattle scene, and then they were a latecomer to the major-label whirl surrounding the Northwest.

MATT HUNTER: Well before Nirvana became a global phenomenon . . . Seattle was already being combed over by A&R people because of Soundgarden and Mudhoney, and a bunch of other bands (as early as 1986, in fact).

SHAMBIE SINGER: By 1989, I felt very sure about the major-label future of many of the bands who'd been part of the Sub Pop scene. Or the alternative scene, as I knew it then. I don't recall the label "indie" existing until after all those "indie" bands weren't part of the underground/alternative scene anymore. It seemed like more of a marketing/cultural meme than an accurate description of what I considered to be alternative music. I remember hearing stories about all the major-label reps that were showing up at alternative music venues like the Pyramid Club in NYC to scout out bands. And stories as well about all the money being offered to bands. This was all in 1989 . . . I wouldn't characterize what was happening as a new "openness" to alternative music per se. To me it just felt like labels were following each other in a mad rush to not miss out on the opportunity to make money. And maybe not for the most rational reasons—i.e., that they could actually make money on alternative bands. The whole scene had a sorta frenzied gold-rush vibe about it. Which perhaps is a bit cynical, but, hey, as I mentioned, I was always more of an SST kinda guy.

Mother Love Bone went to Polygram subsidiary Mercury Records in 1988; 1989 saw the Posies, Soundgarden, and Alice in Chains heading to DGC Records, A&M, and Columbia Records respectively; and both Pearl Jam and Screaming Trees went to Epic Records in 1990. Nirvana was merely following the example of others.

MARK PICKEREL: It was after seeing the success of groups like REM, Sonic Youth, Hüsker Dü, and Camper Van Beethoven that got us all wondering if there was any room for a Northwest band at the top. Then after one of our own signed with A&M (Soundgarden), it was a mad dash for all of us to get to the next deal . . . We were lucky enough to share the same management as Soundgarden, Susan Silver. She could charm the skin right off a snake and that's exactly what she did for many of us—delivering us major-label contracts with her good looks, charm, and her sharp-as-a-knife smarts and know-how!

With the band almost entirely on pause, Cobain embarked on his most prolific twelve months of songwriting. Tracy Marander had ended their relationship and moved out, leaving Cobain dallying with Tobi Vail of Bikini Kill and mostly sitting at Pear Street.

DAMON ROMERO: Kurt was sort of . . . not reclusive, but he didn't go out very much—he tended to stay at home. He was a charismatic person; he had people coming to *his* house! He had a lot of social contact because people would come to him. I saw him more at his apartment than I did out on the town. I knew him well enough, I'd go there and we'd watch movies. They had tons of records and he had a lot of pets, too—aquariums, turtles, rabbits or something, a whole bunch of pets—a packed place. He was listening to all kinds of music, he had the punk-rock independent stuff but I remember going one time and he said I should hear this record and he was listening to the Knack *Get the Knack*, and I was like, "Really?!" He said, "Yeah, it's a great record." I thought commercial products like that were taboo; he thought it was great and told me I should totally listen to it. He listened to a vast spectrum of music.

JASON MORALES: I was in Music 6000 [a legendary music shop in Olympia] once . . . I was quite a shy guy. At that point Kurt Cobain was more of a mysterious dude—I didn't know him that well—but sitting in there once Kurt walked up next to me, tapped me on the shoulder, said, "Hey, you're in Helltrout, right? I really like your band." I just told him thanks . . . He was a normal dude, slightly shy, but for the most part nothing out of the ordinary. There was a certain air of stardom around him, he was on Sub Pop, *Bleach* was a great album— Sub Pop were local heroes at that point in time. He didn't act that way though, just a nice guy. Honestly, not really the kind of guy you'd see at parties—more of an introvert.

GEORGE SMITH: I remember when talking to Kurt, spending hours talking about music, that he was sort of an odd little man. Getting into his world, he was in this dark little room littered with posters and stuff. He wanted to play me a record he said was really neat, really meaningful . . . He played it and it was just some local homespun, non-label-backed recording of some really dumb rock band—butt-rock. Dumb. Really artless. I'm so unclear why he was so taken by it but he was playing it and just looking at me—he was being really reverent toward it. I can understand, I like music like that sometimes too, where it's just so earnest and bad that it's good. But being there, unsure how to respond—I couldn't tell what his angle was; did he see the quality there or was it just so bad it was good? I think it was that it was pure, no put-on, just somebody doing their best to rock with what they had. It was pure. And it was bad. He just had this dark little cave as his hangout in that house.

While he may have been quite an insular individual, Cobain was certainly a driven one. In the run-up to recording a video on March 20—with vague intentions to sell tapes on tour—Cobain put in his homework, as well as making clear what the future held.

ALEX KOSTELNIK: I knew Kurt from around town; he had an old cruiser fat-tire bike he'd ride downtown. He ate at the China Clipper a lot . . . Kurt had been spending a lot of time indoors during the day-time, at his girlfriend's town house on Pear Street. He taped literally hundreds of television advertisements and anything else gross and funny that TV had to offer. I gave him a quick tutorial on how to edit bits of video together, end-to-end. It was well understood that this was going to be simple and straightforward—play live in front of a green screen with the TV stuff playing in the background . . . By then they had done the Sub Pop thing, "Lithium" was played for the first time in a recording at this video session. I remember Kurt saying that they wanted to leave Sub-Pop because "they're sexist." Kurt said he was going to use the videos to try to get a new, different record contract . . . the Evergreen State College had a *very lenient* loan policy—students could routinely check out, for free, whole PA systems, Nagra portable recorders, Neumann mikes. Later, Mexican black-tar heroin flooded the Northwest and theft came into full swing. No more gear party for the A/V nerds . . . The film students were a small bunch of kids at the Evergreen State College and Jon Snyder called me up and asked me to run a huge heavy studio camera in the TESC student televi-sion studio. It was spring break and all the staff were gone—it was time to do whatever we wanted! I got a cement bicycle parking stand from the loading dock outside and stuffed it in Chad's kick drum because every time he hit the kick pedal the drums would inch forward on the draped green-screen fabric. I put masking tape on Krist's legs so they would show up on the chroma-key. Otherwise he was a floating, legless bassist. We did "Lithium" for a sound check because I wanted to make sure Krist's bass could be heard on a tiny television speaker.

Remember, this is 1990. Greg Babior did sound. He was in a band with Slim Moon called Witchypoo. Jon Snyder ran the control room and directed the camera motion. My other best lady friend, Maria, and my buddy Geoff ran a second camera. Geoff had to just be the muscle—the camera rigs weighed three hundred pounds . . . Krist paid me with a large pizza and $40 in $1 bills. I wasn't complaining. One of the boys came and got a copy of the tape later. They also took dubs that night . . . Kurt always had everything planned out. He looked like a homeless janitor/weasel; was quiet as hell, shy as hell, but what he did in his "spare time" was nothing short of amazing. He'd thought and rethought the plan probably ten times before coming in. Jon was a great collaborator too, I'm sure he added direction. You know how it goes: highly motivated people with a reason to hustle things . . .

Cobain's early artistic urges had emerged as all sorts of curious home experiments; one example was "Beans," which included sped-up vocals, acoustic guitar, and a helium-voiced intro skit.

RYAN AIGNER: The time I heard "Beans" for the very first time—Kurt came out to my car, I was up at Krist and Shelli's house, and we sat in the front and listened to it on the cassette tape in there and I was really confused as to what that was all about. He was pretty excited about it. It's overlooked that there was a sense of humor, there was a softer side—it wasn't one dimensional, this torrent all the time. Kurt was a charismatic guy and a funny guy and shy at the same time. I remember after the show at Squid Row, Kurt was asking all these questions, "What did the guitar sound like? How was my voice?" People can't imagine him being insecure about his voice—most people are focused on [how] he had this ferocious powerful voice . . . They can't imagine how insecure . . .

Cobain's 1990–1991 spell was far more focused on a particular type of song. A majority of the music that would emerge in the final years of his life would all be written at this time.

DANIEL RIDDLE: Krist and Kurt were roadies for their friends in a band called Earth, who opened for my band, Hitting Birth, one night. We all hung out in their Ryder rental box truck, smoking pot and talking about music. Kurt did not say much until my band mates mentioned that I had been listening to the new Pixies album nonstop, driving them all crazy. Kurt perked right up, exclaiming, "If you like the new Pixies album, you're gonna love our new record. I rip the Pixies off on every tune!" Like a lot of people in that loose musical community of the time, he was funny and knew when to reveal his feelings.

The brevity of Nirvana's career often hides lengthy losses of momentum; mid-May to late October was only a blip before the anointed ruler of the Nirvana drum stool made his grand entrance; Nirvana genuinely didn't know who would drum for them.

GEORGE SMITH: There was this weird thing where Kurt asked me to audition to play drums, but it didn't feel like an audition, it felt like "We *want* you to play drums" and we'll go up to Seattle and see how it goes. But I didn't realize he kinda handed out his business card to every drummer—I've gotten that sense since then! It ties into his response to me that he was waiting for me to call him but we'd left it that he was going to call me. He told me something like "I wanted you to love it and be so into it that you'd come back and beat my door down demanding to be in the band!" If he was flirting with a lot of musicians I can see him waiting for the one demanding to be in, the one interested enough. I was also somewhat reticent because by that point I'd heard that he was somewhat of a taskmaster . . . He had a distinct impression of what he wanted each composition to sound like and was not shy of telling each musician what they were going to play very precisely. I'd not been in a band like that—it wasn't the way I liked to do things.

JOSEPH HAYDEN, I Own the Sky: Kurt was frustrated and knew I was a pretty good drummer . . . Kurt expressed some concerns about Chad and the future of the band so I told him I was interested if a time came when, and if, they needed someone to fill that vacancy. I was given a cassette tape of some newer songs they had a demo recording of . . . I agreed to fly up to Seattle and see if things clicked . . . we ran through some tunes at their rehearsal studio. I remember we just played the songs through without Kurt singing any lyrics along. I also remember what a crappy-sounding drum kit was there and regretting not bringing at least my own snare and cymbals with me. It seemed to go pretty good and they assured me my playing was good. They were scheduled to play some shows with Dan Peters around that time up there. We talked about me moving up there.

Nirvana's musical friendships were good for throwing up candidates; the band considered J Mascis, who declined but passed the invitation to a friend.

MATT HUNTER: My good friend George Berz was asked to fill that slot on J Mascis's recommendation. He said no, obviously, largely to stay with his band Gobblehoof . . .

LISA SMITH: We ran into him somewhere then went bar hopping. There were some great dive bars there that were not overrun with hipsters at that time. We ended up at this bar that serves clear Screwdrivers . . . mostly American Indians hanging there. We all got shitty drunk and Kurt leant over and threw up in the corner then ordered another! We were cracking up. Later that night Kerry [Green] was driving and our second bass player, Jennie Trower, and Kurt were in the back making out . . . Let me clarify: that was after his long-term girlfriend but before Courtney started stalking him. We like to give Jennie shit about kissing Kurt *after* he had barfed! . . . He also looked at me and said, "Hey, we're looking for a drummer." Think he was just being nice, but on a more serious note he asked about my friend Rey Washam in Austin because he was a big fan of his. Rey was one of my biggest influences out of the drummers that are still alive.

They'd thought about another female drummer, Patty Schemel, and their old friend John Purkey auditioned with them too.

JOHN PURKEY: Kurt talked about wanting to find someone like John Bonham; it made sense. That's what he told me: "I want to find a drummer like John Bonham." He was basically turning me down nicely.

Part of the trouble was that Nirvana was centered on Cobain's vision; not just anyone could play the rhythms in his head. When asked whether he actively plotted out drum parts, Tracy Marander recalls, "I didn't see him doing it when we lived together, plus he had no drums in the house. I am sure, though, that that might be one of the reasons they went through so many drummers."

AARON BURCKHARD: "Floyd the Barber," that bit at the end where we're all playing the main riff—all of us together, then it's just the drums on their own? That was my idea . . . Drummers don't get much respect . . . Kurt would just show me what he wanted, then I could do my own thing; he didn't mind that.

RYAN AIGNER: "Mexican Seafood," "Downer," "Mr. Moustache," for example . . . I remember Kurt physically sitting at the drum kit tapping out specifically what he wanted played, where and when for each one of these songs. He was writing the other musicians' parts—but he wasn't saying they couldn't improvise. Like on "Love Buzz" when Kurt does the big blown-out feedback, phase-shifting solo, all that bass work Krist does, Kurt had nothing to do with it. That was Krist's

personal knowledge of music and theory and how that worked. Kurt
didn't have to teach these guys how to do time and tempo; they understood, they could do what was asked of them. He would simply
say, "I wrote this song, I wrote a part for the bass, for the drums, and
this is how it goes"—then they could play it. That's not easy! Kurt told
me one time, "Being in a band is not that spectacular. You can be in
a very successful band like the Beatles and it doesn't take this great
amount of mechanical ability. You can have somebody that has 80 or
90 percent creativity and 10 percent mechanical ability and you'll be
a fantastic band. Or you can take a guy that has 99 percent mechanical ability but only 1 percent creativity and he'll wither away in ob-
scurity and no one'll give a shit because he's not creating anything."
My thinking about Aaron and Krist is they came to the table with
that functionality. Aaron doesn't need to be taught how to play drums;
he knows how to play. Krist is the same way, he was capable—he's a
good guitar player even, he plays very nicely. Kurt got accomplished
musicians.

Having been offered a tour for eight shows in August, Nirvana temporarily
shelved the hunt for a new drummer and got an old friend to join them.

DAVE NAZ, Chemical People: We were big fans and they were very
cool guys. Dale Crover from the Melvins was playing drums. The promoter had booked us in San Diego several times and knew we were
big Nirvana fans and asked if we wanted to open for them. We were
part of the Cruz Records family; ALL and Big Drill Car, later Skin
Yard . . . Skin Yard were a good band with Jack Endino and Daniel
House. Daniel put out the Kiss covers album with Nirvana, ALL,
Hard-Ons, Chemical People . . . The grunge bands were always cool
to us. There were no huge egos as far as I can remember . . . Keep in
mind the capacity at the Casbah was one hundred people.

DON FLEMING, Gumball: Sonic Youth, for many years, especially then, made a point of looking for what they thought were the most fun, cool local bands wherever they were playing and asking them to be on the bill—which is drastically different from the bands who come to town and either have a band who travels with them or just takes whatever band gets put on the bill. Nirvana was one of the ones they really loved and started doing more shows with.

This was the first tour Nirvana had been offered without their own label mates. Also, Sonic Youth was at its reputational peak, so this was the greatest exposure Nirvana had yet had to show Cobain's maturing writing.

BEAU FREDERICKS: Hearing "In Bloom" for the first time at the Moore Theater show really impressed me. They were far better than Sonic Youth that night. And I love Sonic Youth.

Back in 1988, Sub Pop had made the smooth move of arranging the marriage of their "crown jewels," Mudhoney, to the underground's most respected band.

SHAMBIE SINGER: The fact that a Sub Pop band was splitting a single with Sonic Youth made Sub Pop seem like a bigger deal. Sonic Youth was one of the super "big" alternative bands at that time, as I recall, in terms of airplay, record sales, concert turnouts, buzz.

The rising label became a desirable association for ambitious bands; referring to their own single on Sub Pop, Hole's bassist Jill Emery recalls, "It was definitely something that seemed like you heard more than any other place; it almost became manufactured, like, unless you were already doing it, and from there bands flocked there just like major labels later on wanted 'their next Nirvana' . . . this is where I say that was all calculated on Courtney's part, not the music but all the business side. She would have made a great lawyer or business manager . . ."

ERIC ERLANDSON, Hole: Hole's first tour was a West Coast run in June 1990. We met Jonathan and Bruce, along with a few other Seattle scene luminaries. They saw us play, and after a bit of Courtney's snake-charming, offered us a Sub Pop single. We recorded it in L.A. with a different producer a few months later. I flew up to Seattle with the master tapes in November 1990, and mixed it with Jack Endino. It was the same night of Nirvana's infamous Off Ramp show. We worked late into the night comping Courtney's vocals and never made it to the show.

Sub Pop enjoyed the reflected glory and spewed out singles with most major names of the era. Its success rivaled that of the Dischord label, which, in the early '80s, had made itself similarly synonymous with a city (Washington, DC) and a new sound (hardcore.) Sub Pop also shared some of the same challenges.

DON FLEMING: Dischord in the early days had no interest outside of the bands that all sounded like Dischord bands, so that was fine, that was why it worked, but I think in their case they became successful as much as they did because the guys there worked so damn hard. It was a very small crew there that ran an extremely efficient label and did it very well. I think that's sometimes the difference. I don't think it's even the bands who are on it—with some labels you get one band that sells a lot of records, or gets picked up by a major and the indie makes a lot of money, and that's more the case with Sub Pop: they ended up with a few bands who sold a lot of records.

Like Dischord, the label had ridden a signature sound into the dirt, had branded itself *the* grunge label and now faced difficulties broadening appeal.

MARK DAVIES, Thinking Fellers Union Local 282: As far as Sub Pop goes, I think my attitude by then had become that Sub Pop was pretty narrowly focused on grunge, and I'm always a little disheartened when a genre starts to crystallize into a standardized sound. It seemed like that was already happening, and it made me somewhat disinterested in where it was going. But I don't know if I was being fair to them, since I wasn't tracking what they were doing very closely.

Sub Pop's bosses were barely into their thirties and unexpectedly successful.

CRISPIN WOOD: Sub Pop put Seattle on the map in a big way, and the rest of the world came to associate Seattle with grunge as a result.

DUANE LANCE BODENHEIMER: Bruce and Jonathan are highly intelligent people and have a great sense of humor—it was overwhelming for them. They were awesome, they thought they could make some money at it and joke about it at the same time—it was sarcastic. Then look what happened! . . . Bruce is a very down-to-earth guy, warm, nice human being . . . Loves music. Very supportive. We were shocked when they were like, "We want to put a record out for ya"—they did it. They helped us with a van and everything. Very grateful for that. We were all friends, so they just brought us in one day and said, "OK, record some songs with Jack, we want to put out a record." So we picked some songs, took them to 'em; they released one single then we did a double single . . . It was real casual. No expectations. When the *Wash* CD was released, someone called it "the worst Sub Pop release ever." We took that as a compliment. They also released some stuff by Poison Idea—one of my all-time favorites.

MARK ROBINSON: K [Records] was all about having fun and making your art. Sub Pop wanted to be a commercial success. For the K release, Calvin just asked us to do it. Bruce at Sub Pop, the same thing. The Sub Pop thing seemed like a bigger deal, since their single-of-the-month club was so hugely popular, but it had been a dream of mine to do something with K for years.

As well as having exhausted the hard-rock-meets-punk amalgam they'd built themselves on, an increased presence of non-Washington bands—even if they were the cream of the underground—diluted Sub Pop's brand, making it look more like just another label.

Meanwhile, Nirvana had settled the matter of their drummer, finding a friend with proven chops: Mudhoney's Dan Peters was told he was now a full member of Nirvana. His anointing took place at a now-legendary September show at the Motor Sports International Garage in gloriously irreverent company guaranteed to ratchet up the excitement.

BLAG DAHLIA: We didn't give a fuck about the Pixies or the Vaselines or David Bowie. What kind of dipshits would like that?! The Stooges, GG Allin, and Paula Abdul were our grunge-era heroes . . . Nirvana were big fans of the Dwarves' bass player, Saltpeter; they knew he could really play. They never expressed any support for the rest of us that I am aware of, but Kurt never wore women's clothes onstage or jumped into a drum kit until we had done both things numerous times in Seattle and nationwide.

DUANE LANCE BODENHEIMER: The Dwarves, they borrowed our drum kit the first time they came up—destroyed it, and we got into a huge fight then made up the next day and became best friends. I think that was a Halloween show. I was dressed up as a girl and when the Dwarves were playing I lobbed a bottle at Blag and hit him right in the forehead. He chased me around . . . A lot of people didn't like us just because we were dicks, not intentionally so but . . . when you're drinking and stuff . . . We weren't violent—it was mostly internal violence, we would fight with one another a lot. Me and Neil [Rogers] would get into it onstage—don't know what caused that, love the guy to death, best friends, always were.

Certainly Nirvana playing in dresses wasn't an uncommon move. Many minds thought alike.

DANA HATCH: There used to be a big pile of trash in the back of that club and I'd look for some kind of prop to use onstage. That night I found this old Big Ethel–type dress and put that on. Merle [Allin, bassist at the time] gave me a wig he had and his girlfriend made up my face so I played in drag. When Kurt wore a dress on *SNL* a few years later I liked to say he got it from me, but it was hardly an original idea when I did it.

The show kicked in with the Derelicts.

DUANE LANCE BODENHEIMER: I've no idea how we ended up on the bill with them—we just said, "Yeah, OK, wow . . . we're playing . . ." I had no idea how many people were going to be there—to us it was like a fucking arena . . . I remember walking out and seeing all those people, I got serious stage fright—it was awesome . . . When I came out there were a lot of rocker-type people there. I think I said some stuff like, "All right then, you long-haired hippies . . ." just talking some shit, stage banter, trying to be charming. A good show, a lot of our friends upfront yelling at us, calling us rock stars. There must have been over a thousand—to us that was . . . wow. To bands used to playing on average a hundred or less, that was scary.

Then the Dwarves kicked off.

BLAG DAHLIA: There was a charged atmosphere that night, that's for sure. We were more concerned with getting enough gas money to get home, though. We drove up from San Francisco at Sub Pop's suggestion for what turned out to be $100. None of the supposedly cool indie bands on the bill or allegedly cool Seattle promoters offered us anything else. But hey, they were the "nice" guys and we were a bunch of real "assholes" from California . . . I know that there was general fear of us because of the bloodshed at our shows, and a general fear of our onstage nudity and the female nudity on our record covers. Seattle was, and is, a very asexual place. Although, I always managed to get my dick sucked there!

DUANE LANCE BODENHEIMER: Somebody threw a whiskey bottle and hit the Dwarves' bass player in the face—he started bleeding. They had that whole violent aura about them—very confrontational.

BLAG DAHLIA: I would have loved to have seen Nirvana that night. I had enjoyed their sets several other times all over the country. Unfortunately, our bassist was struck with a bottle thrown from the audience during our set and I spent the rest of the show at the emergency room with him. Concerned promoters, our label, and fellow bands on the bill all pitched in to help though, it was really beautiful . . . *Psych!* No one from Seattle helped out or gave a shit . . . The vibe around the band [Nirvana] that night at Motor Sports was more like dumb-ass drunk ex-jocks from Aberdeen in Kmart flannel shirts. And because it was the Northwest, fat chicks.

The Melvins tore it up and finally Nirvana burned it down.

DUANE LANCE BODENHEIMER: Kurt was really passionate . . . lot of punks didn't like them, hated that "grunge" word too—I can't stand that word. But Kurt was a purist, he loved punk rock; what they did was honest rock 'n' roll. He loved all types of music—loud, dirty, real, honest lyrically. The really hardcore punk rockers weren't big fans. It was simple, raw rock 'n' roll. Krist came up to me after the show and was like, "That was a great set!" He was really nice. There's a story before that when he and I were at a show, Poison Idea was playing, a fight broke out—Krist got in a fight, I tried to step in and help and he told me, "Fuck you! Mind your own business!" so he got his ass kicked, he was hurt, and I walked up to him, "Yup . . . should have let me help ya."

It was only here, in Autumn 1990, that Nirvana finally overtook their former mentors by ceasing to compete on someone else's turf.

BEAU FREDERICKS: For me, Nirvana was a good live band then, but they could not match up to the Melvins as a heavy intense rock trio. The Melvins were consistently crushing it live, as I am sure Nirvana would agree. Nirvana came into their own when they tapped into their melodic gifts.

12.0

New Blood

October to December 1990

Unfortunately for Dan Peters, there had been a change of plan. On August 3, Cobain and Novoselic saw Dave Grohl play with Scream. Grohl was invited to audition and accordingly flew to Seattle on September 21. The next night he was in the audience and on September 25 Cobain announced on KAOS Radio that Nirvana had a new drummer. Seven weeks from first glimpse to closure. This was a band that knew to snatch at the hand of chance, and the choice met with approval among the Northwest's musical cognoscenti.

RYAN LOISELLE: [I] saw Scream and I was like, Oh my God! That drummer is incredible! That guy's crazy! And we used to hang out with Krist Novoselic when he lived in Tacoma; we'd go to his house and hang out with him and his wife before they were popular. I remember Krist coming to me super-excited, "Dude, we got a new drummer, the guy from Scream!" I didn't even know his name I was just like, *Yes!*

PAUL KIMBALL: I do remember meeting Dave Grohl the first time at a bar downtown called King Solomon's, and Kurt seemed as animated as I'd ever seen him when he introduced us. Scream had played in Olympia not too long before then, and after that show Dave was somebody a lot of people had noted for his awesomeness on drums. I'm guessing Kurt felt like he'd scored pretty big.

BEN MUNAT: I remember being somewhat incensed: How could they get rid of Chad?! Then I met Dave and found out that he was one of the nicest, coolest musicians I'd ever met. I still felt sorry for Chad, but Dave was awesome.

DUANE LANCE BODENHEIMER: Dave Grohl, never had a problem with him . . . I think he had sex with my girlfriend, but I dunno and I don't hold a grudge. I loved Scream; the guy was a great drummer.

Photogenic, personable, just twenty-one but already a powerful drummer, Grohl made a real difference to Nirvana's live persona.

SLIM MOON: I would not characterize them as "professionals" until *Nevermind* came out. They were just a good solid underground band. The main leap forward was the addition of Dave Grohl, but also Kurt's songwriting evolved, and they did become more practiced with their theatricality and consistency over time.

Though Channing had already played half of what would become Nirvana's great triumph, Grohl perhaps freed Cobain to finally embrace his pop urges wholly.

STEVE MORIARTY: Chad, quite a good drummer I thought—for what they were doing. He was really solid; that *Bleach* record was a slow dirgy psychedelic style—he was perfect. He plays a little behind the beat, while Grohl plays in the pocket but just a tad faster, just above the beat: that's what created that pop sensibility for the masses—the drums. It went from being sort of a very dark sound to having something that was driving and more Killing Joke, less Black Sabbath.

Nirvana's pressing priority was that arrangements were under way for them to tour the UK. With four weeks to get the lineup prepared they wedged in practice runs at a surf club and on friendly turf at the Evergreen State College, where Grohl's presence was immediately felt.

SLIM MOON: It was a leap forward. After their initial shows with Dale Crover as drummer, the drumming was always a disappointment in Nirvana until Dave showed up.

MARK ROBINSON: Unrest was on tour with the DUSTdevils and we were holed up in Olympia in between shows . . . Calvin Johnson's K Records is there, and it was a friendly place. We were staying at the Martin Apartment Building downtown, which was essentially a dorm for indie rockers . . . We performed in a small common living room in a dormitory complex. Just fourteen by fourteen feet. Maybe smaller . . . There was a vocal PA, and that's it. Just amps and a microphone in a very small room. No sound checks, this was a party. No stage, just play in the corner of the room . . . Dave Grohl had just recently joined Nirvana . . . He's a pro, and from what I remember, they didn't seem shaky or like they hadn't played together before. This show was the first and last time I saw Nirvana perform . . . I don't think I even watched their entire set. Only a small amount of people could fit into that room along with the band performing. Probably not more than fifteen or twenty . . . At some point during our stay there we met them at the Martin. I don't remember much about it and I don't think they said much, but I do remember Kurt Cobain had eyeliner on. At any rate, we were asked to play the show and we did. It was just a normal American college keg party. I'm pretty sure we didn't get paid, nor did we expect to, as there was no admission price.

This time in the UK, Nirvana was the undeniable star and played the UK's great cities like . . . Er . . . Norwich.

SAM MARSH, Jacob's Mouse: We very nearly didn't play it on the

night—our shit heap of a van broke down on the way and we literally
made it to the venue in time to set up and perform! Bloody typical!
However, with all the adrenaline of running late we went for it once
we got onstage and released all that pent-up energy!! Nirvana's performance that night was storming—it was a reasonably small venue
and Kurt spent half the time in the audience. No after-party stuff,
everyone did seem tired, but Nirvana were really friendly and gave
us lots of praise!

JEBB BOOTHBY, Jacob's Mouse: I remember that we almost didn't
play the gig because Hugo had an A-level re-sit the next day. Both
Hugo and I still lived with our parents and although they were mas-
sively supportive of the band and our music they had got a bit pissed
off that the band was distracting us from our studies leading to some
pretty poor exam results in the summer. In the end we played the
gig, but Hugo had to drive home early. Rock 'n' roll! Nirvana all
seemed pretty tired, as you would be after a long European tour in a
Transit van. Maybe Kurt was a little more aloof than the other guys,
but they were all really welcoming. Like all the bands we played with
at the time, you just talk about music and I guess because our van
had broken down that was a good icebreaker . . . There did seem to
be a bit of an end-of-term feel to the tour party. I think they were heading home after the Norwich gig. I got the feeling it had been a bit
chaotic. I think the tour manager had jumped ship and the booking
agent, Russell Warby (who later took us on), had taken over for the
last few dates . . . While we were playing I saw two guys sitting down
in the front of stage really getting into it, sort of head-banging and
rocking out. When we came off stage these two guys came up to us
and it was Krist and Dave from Nirvana. They were really enthusing
about the gig, which blew us away. I remember Krist wanted a record.
We had just released our first EP, *The Dot*, and had a box with us to
sell. But he explained, "Being the end of the tour, I don't have any
money!" I think I swapped one for a T-shirt. I still have the T-shirt. I

wonder if he still has the record! I remember them playing songs from *Bleach* and "Sliver" (I think they were over to belatedly promote "Sliver"). I also remember them playing a load of more melodic songs that I didn't know but more in the style of "Sliver" than *Bleach*. I guess these were the songs they were about to record for *Nevermind*.

HUGO BOOTHBY, Jacob's Mouse: Kurt came onstage afterwards when I was packing my stuff away to say hello. He shook my hand and said he enjoyed the show and that we were one of his favorite support bands from that tour. We had a viola player at the time and I can imagine that this reminded him a bit of the Raincoats. We met both Krist and Dave briefly. They were nice, down-to-earth people, and I was very excited to meet this band that already seemed very famous and exotic to me, although this was pre-*Nevermind*. A year later we joined Nirvana's booking agent and he told us that Kurt remembered the show and was glad that we were with the same booking agency as them. Some years later a friend of ours was wearing a Jacob's Mouse T-shirt in Seattle and Courtney came over to say that Kurt liked the band.

After a week on the road Nirvana couldn't even spare enough cash for a twelve-inch single. However, their increasing sway did mean they were able to request support acts.

NAOKO YAMANO, Shonen Knife: We made a contract with a management office in Tokyo in 1990. The office got an offer from Nirvana about touring with us . . . I didn't know Nirvana when we got an offer to tour with them. I saw their photo and they looked wild. I was a little scared about them, but they were real gentlemen.

TIM SOLYAN: All the shows were crammed to the rafters with people! . . . When we got to the UK, we were told by our booking agent that when we get to Leeds, we will be playing at the Leeds Polytechnic College with Nirvana . . . better off getting on the gig with

Nirvana than try to compete with it the same night. So it was arranged that our support band, Arm, would play first; L7, who were on the current tour with Nirvana, would play second; Victim's Family would fill the support slot . . . we were informed that Nirvana and L7 were not happy with the lineup arrangement . . . We arrived at the gig and loaded in and Nirvana were just finished with their sound check and Krist was still onstage and saw us and gave a big "Hello!" and talked with us and told us where he found good cheap pizza just outside the venue . . . . We set up to do sound check and I saw Kurt come toward the stage. He leaned right up against it and looked right at me with a blank expression. I said, "Hey Kurt! What up, man?!" He blankly nodded at me and turned and walked away. I figured he was upset his support band was not in the support slot. Oh well. He wasn't ever really too friendly with us, as I don't think he liked our music in the least bit.

MARCUS GRAPMAYER, Arm: We had no personal contact during the whole thing. To us they were just long-haired rock stars with no interest in their environment and the people around. Why I remember is 'cause it was the only time in my life I played on a hundred-square-meter stage with no PA, no engineer, and our showtime right at the opening of the doors.

TIM SOLYAN: I watched Nirvana's set that night, which was the first time I saw them with Dave on drums, and quite frankly I thought his perfect drumming was a bit too slick compared to Chad's fumbling coolness. I am not saying I disliked it; it just was a whole different band.

Another new factor in the band's future experience was also arising.

SLIM MOON: I saw the depression. I didn't know about the heroin use, but one time he helped me move house, and while driving across town he opened the door to his car and vomited. So now in retrospect I've always wondered if he was having withdrawals.

While being interviewed for this book, numerous individuals were open about their history with drugs. I admire those who have come through fire and can look back with honesty.

DUANE LANCE BODENHEIMER: It was kind of a secret—just between us junkies, but everybody knew. Not proud of it. No glamour. It definitely came through in my lyrics, something I wrote about openly. I was the only one in my band that did that—I want to make that clear. But we had a lot of issues. It was sort of social in the beginning but in the end I was doing it alone, definitely an isolation drug. There were all kinds of drugs around . . . I first met Kurt at the Hollywood Underground, I never really got personally involved with those guys— Kurt and I shared a lot of the same . . . er . . . y'know . . . We had the same dealers.

BLAG DAHLIA: Kurt and most of us were part of a drug subculture. If he didn't do dope before 1990, I'd be very surprised. Downers and booze are closely related to dope as well. Courtney's love of dope is well documented, and Kurt lied about that all the time . . . I know lots of folks who shot up with them. If I would have been a dope fan, I'm sure I would have shot up with them too. Believable, but unverified, reports of ODs were numerous, but again, I wasn't in the room. I did see Kurt, eyes pinned, having a siesta on the roof of the Terminal Building around 1990. Nothing conclusive there, but where there's smoke . . .

DANIEL RIDDLE: Kurt had lots of dark eyeliner on because he was a musician and didn't give a fuck what people thought! . . . But really those of us with blue eyes knew that was more about hiding your eyes with pinned-out pupils when you're doing dope.

Still, Cobain was just dabbling; he was fine and if he was in a good mood all knew about it.

North West Rock Legends, 1985: Damon Romero, Andy Miller, Ben Shepherd, John Goodmanson, and Chad Channing *(Damon Romero)*

Aaron Burckhard, Nirvana/Attica, 1988 Hoquiam *(Ryan Aigner)*

Togetherness: Kurt Cobain, Steve Sundt, Kristine Proctor, Matt Lukin, and Aaron Burckhard *(Ryan Aigner)*

Chris Quinn and Kurt Cobain, October 30, 1988. Back of photo shows Tracy's statement. *(Tracy Marander)*

Chris Quinn + Kurdt Kobain
Oct 30 1988

Ryan Aigner, Krist Novoselic, and Kurt Cobain *(Ryan Aigner)*

Jason, Krist, Kurt, and Chad at WYNU, July 18, 1989 *(Hugh Foley)*

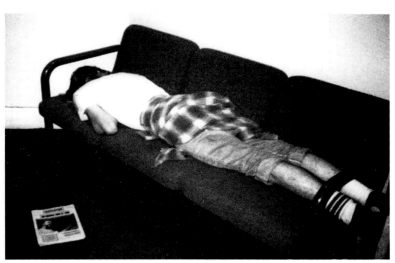

Last day, first tour: Cobain exhausted at WYNU radio, July 18, 1989
(Hugh Foley)

Kurt and Krist beneath the art of Colin Burns (Slaughter Shack), 1990
(JJ Gonson)

1992/1993 *Houdini* recording session. *From left to right:* Buzz Osbourne,
Jonathan Burnside, Lori Black, Dale Crover, and Kurt Cobain
(Jonathan Burnside)

Kurt Cobain meets
André Stella in Rio
de Janeiro, January
1993. *(André Stella)*

Clockwise from top left: Kurt at the Mia Zapata Benefit, Josh Sinder at RKCNDY, Krist at the Mia Zapata Benefit, Tad Doyle at RKCNDY, Tad at the Mia Zapata Benefit, and Dave Grohl (borrowing Josh's drums) at the Mia Zapata Benefit *(Jeri Childs)*

Kurt Cobain and Youri Lenquette, 1992 *(Youri Lenquette)*

SAM MARSH: Kurt was amazingly friendly and approachable on the night. You meet so many bands who are right prima donnas, but I always found everyone on the alternative music scene is generally friendly—all the bands were friendly that night . . . The band looked tired, as is often the way when you've been touring for ages—I wouldn't have got any impression he was a heroin user by his appearance and demeanor.

Nirvana was nearing triumph; their next show at the Off Ramp in central Seattle was a victory dance.

JOSEPH ARONSTAMN, Holy Rollers: That period of time was special because the "Seattle sound" was breaking nationwide . . . A lot was going on in Olympia, so there was a lot of crossover and intra-town support. Basically, a convergence of time, place, and great bands and other musicians (in the audience) that form the backbone of a "scene" . . . While you live it, you don't realize that you are actually part of a historic and memorable social moment that is greater than the sum of its parts and outlasts what we were all there in the first place for. For us, to play and hang with a friend [Dave] and his very cool band mates, while also knowing there would be people there. For the audience members, it was a homecoming of sorts and a chance to support the cross-pollination between DC's Dischord bands and Seattle and Olympia musicians . . . a lifetime highlight!

ROBIN PERINGER: The Off Ramp was great for a twenty-one-and-over bar, plus we could walk there from Capitol Hill . . . As far as what I think makes a top band or not, at the time, I didn't really know what that meant. I had yet to have any friends who were able to even sell out the Off Ramp. I did feel that Nirvana should be making a living off playing music as much as Jane's Addiction or Nick Cave did, but that was about as high as I could imagine any Seattle band going . . . Nirvana was an excellent band, but there were a lot of excellent bands at that time. These were guys you'd see at local shows, and it just didn't seem like future rock stars would be checking out Girl Trouble on a Tuesday night. Plus, the only bands that achieved crazy levels of fame were together for more than three years.

After months just ticking over, having a permanent drummer meant Nirvana pushed on toward the destination they had set early in the year.

PAUL THOMSON, Midway Still: I think the single "Sliver" was a game changer that hinted at the brutal pop they were capable of and was played to death everywhere in London. After that single, I think there was general excitement at what the new album would be.

The band even played a New Year show in Portland to crown 1990.

DANIEL RIDDLE: I booked the show that night. I got Krist's phone number from the booking info and when I called he had remembered hanging out with us at the Blue Gallery . . . they set up most of their own gear. They had some new gear that they were getting used to . . . They knew they had an explosive, powerful new lineup and an amazing batch of songs. The sound check brought tears to my eyes. It was so fucking powerful, filled with melody and raw emotion. They used sound check to rehearse most of the set. It very much felt like the lineup was fresh and most of the tunes had never been played live . . . After the show I paid them in cash from the door. I think I promised them 60 percent and it was a $10 cover charge. I think they made $1,800. We totally oversold the door. It was so fucking packed in there, people were leaving because after a few drinks and getting pummeled by an insanely loud PA system that I rented—most folks couldn't handle it.

RENÉE DENENFELD: Nirvana was pretty popular on the West Coast at that point. The club was packed. But they were certainly not popular to the point where anyone foresaw their future fame. They were just some nice guys in a punk band that everyone liked, just like they liked other bands. I didn't feel intimidated, because I had been around Nirvana before, working in the Blue Gallery, and they weren't any different than anyone else . . . the audience was over-the-top, like always happened on busy nights at Satyricon . . . there was no backstage to speak of, just a tiny room that stank like pee. So band members always just hung out in the bar with everyone else . . . I remember after we finished, I was soaking wet from people spraying me with beer. I climbed with a friend into the sound box above the pit. It was amazing to watch and see Nirvana in all the melee.

Still . . . while Nirvana's popularity was going from strength to strength, the atmosphere around Cobain showed his keen awareness of the darker consequences of success.

DANIEL RIDDLE: With Kurt it seemed like the right thing to do was say hello and look down. He was not very interested in engaging anyone in an up-close and personal way. His band was gaining momentum and it was understood that this brings on unwanted insincere affection. When that happens, you give those people space and let them come to you or you end up on a mental list of assholes and suckups. I had a few nice conversations with Krist and Dave that night. Kurt and I did not talk much.

Cobain later confessed, in the liner notes of a reissue of The Raincoats' first album, that in this period of triumph he was "extremely unhappy, lonely, and bored." The underground music scene was a place he finally belonged among those people who had seen poverty, who had been alone—they all found friends among the injured. Portland was sympathetic to Cobain because those who played there were much the same as him.

DANIEL RIDDLE: Most of us came from broken homes and were picked on a lot in school. Humor was a defense mechanism, and playing music was a cathartic release of pain and a way to get the approval of our peers. In all my years of playing music outside of the pop culture, I've never once met a player who had a "good" relationship with their father. Every stripper, every junkie, and every musician had that pain. Why else get up onstage and jump around like an idiot? Those cats in Nirvana where just like us. We were all kids/people who just wanted to belong to something, be good at something, have a sense of community.

RENÉE DENENFELD: I "sang" for a hardcore punk band when I was sixteen. I was fresh from living on the streets and frankly, the punk community saved me. I was crashing in a house where the Wipers were recording their last album. A hardcore punk band was practicing in the space. They asked me to front them, probably because I was sixteen and could scream really loud. That band was called Sin Hipster, and we opened for Black Flag. Henry Rollins himself told me how much I sucked . . . I hear the scene has changed a lot . . . I'm not sure how much that has to do with the music getting popular. I think a more important factor is how expensive it has become to live in this city and others. At the time of that New Year's show, you could rent a run-down house in Portland for a few hundred dollars. It was possible to live and play music while working part-time. You could be someone from a terrible background, alone and in pain, and the punk community was a place to find friends and solace. Now I am not sure how musicians afford places to practice and I've heard the whole community of punk houses has died. That, to me, is sad. I don't know where the lost kids end up anymore. Those homes were havens for many of us, places where we discovered friends and art and music, and hope.

13.0

Corporate-Rock Whores
January to July 1991

Nirvana had benefited from benefactors and mentors throughout their career—the give and take of the music community. Now it was the patronage of Sonic Youth that took them to DGC Records.

DON FLEMING: I think it was very meaningful to them to be a part of the Sonic Youth party at the time. Everyone in Sonic Youth liked them a lot . . . when they [Sonic Youth] got their Geffen deal they got a deal to bring bands in—which is usually, or almost always, a deal thrown in there to make the band being signed feel like they're the "big cheese" and they can get stuff going and have a lot of power there; many more bands than Sonic Youth get that kind of deal. But typically, what happens is the label doesn't give a fuck about the bands you bring in—they'll sign one to appease you but there's a whole game in every major label—Geffen is a good example—there's power within the label and to get any band really noticed you have to get every division behind it and there's usually few people in a label who can do that. Most A&R guys don't have enough clout within their label to get everyone—Marketing, Promotion and so on—to really come out and work the record, so typically records get a little bit of work from one or two people who really like the band and like the A&R guy, but only like 1 or 2 percent get this huge push from the label. So when Sonic Youth got Nirvana signed to Geffen, it was kinda like that.

Nirvana began to make a point of playing for causes they respected; 1991 started with a No More Wars benefit.

JELLO BIAFRA: I was pleasantly surprised when I realized a lot of the grunge-era bands who initially appeared to be a full-on revival of sex, drugs, and rock 'n' roll in the lyrics and attitude department turned out to be pretty politically active and aware . . . It seemed like Green River on down was a deliberate response against the more dogmatic areas of political hardcore—they weren't going to play that sound and those lyrical angles got tossed out the door.

PAUL KIMBALL: Evergreen was a very socially conscious environment, sometimes to a fault. But we and the other bands were really feeling it. It was an intense moment. Krist Novoselic spoke at length from the stage that night, and though I remember it being less than entirely eloquent, it was definitely right-on . . . The big difference at this one was Dave Grohl. All of a sudden what Nirvana had been trying to do finally became undeniable. The songwriting, the time on the road . . . The fact that Dave could harmonize with Kurt is something that pushed the songwriting way upfront, and his drumming—well, c'mon!

TIMO ELLIS, Nubbin: That antiwar show should have been a "peak," but I remember it as one of our worst shows ever, performance-wise— also made that much more cringe-worthy by the fact that for some unknown reason I decided to wear this ridiculous one-piece sleeveless jumper type of thing . . . a pretty emotionally charged atmosphere that night, as of course people were generally really disillusioned and pissed off about the fact that a war/invasion of Iraq was likely.

RYAN vᴏɴ BARGEN, Fitz of Depression: Krist had written something he was reading about his opposition to the US war and some idiots in the crowd kept yelling at him to "shut up and play." I have to say that that was one of the things I thought was sad about watching a cool band like Nirvana get bigger; more brain-dead assholes were going to their shows. Good for business, bad for the subculture. That was another thing about watching Nirvana shift the whole perception of rock 'n' roll up to that point: dudes can get all the tribal tattoos and piercings their parents can afford, but it will *never* make them better individuals at heart. I hope some percentage of them did "get it," wherever the wind has blown them.

For a band that would later spend the *In Utero* tour halting to shout at meatheads harassing the female audience, the shift in audience wasn't a positive.

DANIEL RIDDLE: You could see that in the self-hatred and frustration those dudes and many others expressed when their bands got "big and successful." They had guilt and felt responsible for bringing the industry vampires, the violent jocks, the rich-kid poseurs, and corporate consciousness into our sacred spaces—the clubs, the parties, the underground subculture, and even our minds. It couldn't be stopped. It was going to happen sooner or later. The beatniks, the hippies, the punks, every counterculture underground movement eventually gets infiltrated, diffused, polluted, dumbed down, then repackaged, sanitized, and sold to the masses. Most of us in the underground music community saw this happen with the "Nirvana explosion" and we felt a great deal of compassion and empathy for those guys. Be careful what you ask for, you just might get it, right?

RYAN vᴏɴ BARGEN: If some redneck idiots started shit, which they occasionally did, I really liked how there were a few who were like the protectors of the Northwest pacifist punker types . . . People don't realize how outwardly violent, ignorant, and cruel some of the bastards were around here. There was no Hot Topic to create an air of acceptance around "individuality" for the redneck, just hatred and contempt for these weirdos with Mohawks wearing surplus Army clothes.

TIM KERR: After Nirvana broke big, a lot of the people fucking with us became the '90s crowd who acted like, "Yeah bro. We are with you! We are of the same cloth!" And I am sure that bugged the hell out of Kurt.

Nirvana increasingly acted on the underground's social activism. In Cobain's journal list of his top fifty albums, of four released after 1990, three were female-fronted. The other, by the Frogs, had a gay theme. Cobain would befriend Kathleen Hanna and Kathi Wilcox of Riot Grrrl legends Bikini Kill and dated their drummer, Tobi Vail, while the band attended classes at Evergreen State College.

GILLY ANN HANNER: Evergreen—it was very level, a lot of talk about feminism, a lot of feminist courses, women-focused writing courses and so on. I met Kathleen Hanna in a couple of my classes like my Women in Poetry class. Kathi . . . she was dating my boyfriend's best friend—that's how we ended up living together and she started playing music after hanging around with us, so she took up the bass . . . They coined the Riot Grrrl thing—made the fanzine, the pictures, really good work—they put together the full concept. Tobi was a really good drummer, Kathi took to the bass real quick, Kathleen's a great singer . . . I think some of that came out of the way the classes were at Evergreen—integrating pieces together. The concept of having a fanzine, a band, a certain look . . . all of that—brilliant! I was very jealous at the time. [For us it was like] "We're just a band, we're all women but we're really rocking—but we're not Riot Grrrls."

The hardcore scene of the early '80s had become increasingly male-oriented by the middle of that decade. Even venues that are now legendary in punk-rock circles were not necessarily female-friendly, even if unintentionally so.

LISA KOENIG: Tropicana—uh . . . that was sort of out of my league. I was just a young pup and the Tropicana crowd was like "professional" punk rockers . . . It wasn't a place for a female newbie on the scene— well, not me anyway, I was too scared, ha. But there were places like Reko/Muse, the backstage of the Capital Theater, the Surf Club, Thekla, Rainy Day Records, and the Smithfield . . . These places contributed to the whole Olympia vibe in the late '80s/early '90s—a time where art, music, and coffee harmoniously collided; pretty cool and way-less intimidating than the Trop.

The punk scene wasn't a homogeneous entity, however. It had both a progressive wing and a macho side.

COLIN BURNS: At the time, the women playing heavier music confused some of the audience. For an example, we played a show in Worcester, Mass., with Boston hardcore stalwarts Slapshot and a couple of Worcester hardcore bands. It was an all-ages show, packed for the first two bands. After we started, everyone but four kids left. And then everyone returned for Slapshot. Those four kids loved the show. That show definitely felt like an extreme reaction to the women in the band.

Supported for years by strong women like Tracy Marander and having been on the receiving end of plentiful macho idiocy Nirvana's progressive instincts saw them supporting anything favoring a more equal and respected place for women. There was certainly plenty to be fought over.

SIOBHAN DUVALL: Girls who played guitar were literally laughed out of guitar shops, and the music scene, although often run by women on [the] management side, was very male-dominated and sexist bandwise . . . The Bombshells once played a benefit concert for Rape Relief, an organization to assist victims of sexual violence. We were slammed by the hipster "politically correct" college-radio press, who said it was "laughable that the sex kitty Bombshells could possibly take a stand against rape." That article was written by a woman, who seemed to subscribe to the "she was asking for it" view of sexual violence. We found that very shocking and offensive to say the least.

The surge in female participation was certainly not localized, either; wherever there was a scene, there were women rocking. Nirvana's pro-feminist approach built on their close association and regular performances with a wide range of talented women.

GILLY ANN HANNER: Right before that was "foxcore"—supposedly Lee Ranaldo of Sonic Youth coined this term because of Babes in Toyland, L7, Hole . . . Basically meaning chicks playing hardcore-y music . . . I didn't see very many females playing music at the time— there were a few. Once I started with Calamity Jane, we played with Scrawl—they were Midwest, three women, the first all-female touring band I saw, super-cool.

LORI JOSEPH: I just wanted to learn to play the guitar so I wasn't just the "girlfriend" hanging out listening to my boyfriend's band practice . . . I really became interested in the lack of female musicians. I was a huge Girls School fan and was really annoyed that most woman musicians at that time in my area were nonexistent or terrible, so I practiced my guitar solos and formed an all-girls band called Bhang Revival.

RENÉE DENENFELD: Here in Portland some of the earliest punk bands were female, like the Neoboys. I think the media "discovered" the Riot Grrrl thing, but it had been happening for a long time. Only, before that point being a punk-rock girl wasn't about trying to look conventionally sexy or even fashionable. Most didn't care about fashion at all. And if we did, it was more to mock it. If I recall right, I performed the entire New Year's show dressed in an old woman's swimsuit with lipstick smeared on my face.

Likewise, it wasn't a one-size-fits-all deal, easily packaged for stereotyping. Being a female musician didn't mean automatically falling into lockstep as a gender. To a significant extent, it was Nirvana's rise that drew further attention to female-fronted bands in the Northwest, but mostly just to the media-friendly Riot Grrrl phenomenon.

MARIA MABRA: One thing about Seattle, and everyone knows this: it had the best reputation for pumping out the best rock chicks ever. When I came here to Austin it was so disappointing that all of a sudden I was a minority—are you kidding me?! . . . Courtney Love, when she wanted to create Hole, she came up to Seattle to get people—I remember when she picked Patty [Schemel] to be her drummer . . . Olympia also produced the Riot Grrrls—the worst! Oh God, chicks all of a sudden became popular . . . The whiny ones. You don't reverse sexism to get something right—those chicks had the nerve to set up gigs where guys weren't allowed to stand in the front . . . I was like, "Excuse me? Fuck that." You do not set up reverse sexism to try and fix a problem. So the whole Riot Grrrl thing is lame to me and a lot of other chicks from Seattle, and the fact a lot of us got looped into that [sucked]. I remember being interviewed and being called a Riot Grrrl, and we protested; we will not be your Riot Grrrls, your Riot Grrrl shit stinks. The guys weren't allowed in the mosh pit, they weren't allowed to punk-rock dance, they weren't allowed to stage dive and they had to stand in the back—I remember thinking, Is this fucking Jim Crow here?

RENÉE DENENFELD: The whole media focus on the Riot Grrrl thing was more about *devaluing* women as artists and thinkers and acting as if our role in music is meant to be titillating sexually and risqué. Honestly, the media didn't care about punk-rock women until we stopped being political and started looking like porn.

LISA SMITH: When you are the novelty chick band, you don't get a sound check. If we ever did we were lucky. We were usually the opening act, so then you just push your drums to the side and get entertained the rest of the night . . . We had the correct anatomy for the Riot Grrrl crowd, but who knows if we were hated or looked at like pigs singing about living on beer and sex. Kurt thought we should do the cover "Green Eyed Lady." As far as Seattle, how much more macho could you sound with tiny Kelly Canary sounding like a drunken four-hundred-pound man . . . Or Meagan Jasper in her garbage-bag dress and dog collar? Or, better yet, Mark Arm and Duane (Derelicts) in one of our dresses and all made-up! Mark asked what he should sing about and we told him to write lyrics as if he was a girl. He wrote some hilarious shit like "Tell me you love me, or I'll scratch out both your eyes . . . Tell me you love me, between both my thighs."

Nirvana lent weight whenever asked. Cobain dueted with Courtney Love at a Rock Against Rape event. The band played Rock for Choice, contributed to the Home Alive compilation, invited female-fronted bands on tour, and on occasion would chastise male members of their own audience if they spotted them molesting girls in the crowd.

GILLY ANN HANNER: We played West Coast dates, including some in L.A. that were filmed by Lisa Rose Apramian for her rockumentary *Not Bad for a Girl*, featuring Hole, L7, Babes in Toyland, and dozens of other female musicians. The film was released in 1995, and Kurt and Courtney ended up partially funding it.

SLIM MOON: The hardcore scene in the '80s was macho and sexist. But California was the nexus for the hardcore scene on the West Coast . . . The music thing that was happening in the Northwest in the '80s was much weirder and more eclectic, and women had a bigger role . . . Rock 'n' roll is sixty years old now—that's a mighty long time. It had a macho phase, but that phase was less than twenty years out of the sixty-year history, it wasn't the default "truth" of rock . . .

Even the rest of "grunge" in the '90s, which might have been made possible by the success of Nirvana, was comparatively sexist and "rock" compared to the intentions of Kurt. Many of the successful grunge-band members had been in sexist rock bands up until the moment they jumped to grunge for careerist reasons as the new trendy sound. Some bands like Alice in Chains had actually *been* Mötley Crüe–style bands up until they decided to go grunge and change the spelling of their name. I remember how pissed Kurt and Krist were when they started dressing like Kurt and changing their sound.

STEVE MORIARTY: There was an all-girl band on Sub Pop, Dick-less, but other than that you couldn't count on one hand how many bands on Sub Pop had a female vocalist until 1995. I think part of it was what they were into, part of it was ignorance, and part of it was that they weren't easy with women—they were dudes' dudes, and they didn't have much of a sympathy for a woman's voice in a band.

Sub Pop, meanwhile, made sure to get one last nugget of reflected glory by pairing Nirvana with the Fluid for a live split-single, which ended up being the last Sub Pop release for both bands simultaneously.

MATT BISCHOFF: [It was] an attempt to capture the ferocity of the live performance rather than a "polished" studio sound. It was certainly *not* to be our last of working with Sub Pop, however. Due to inability to come to terms on contracts it, unfortunately, ended up being so . . . I don't really know why that one happened. We had played some pretty damn good shows with those guys. We all shared a common love of rowdy performances. I suppose we were going to be exposed to a wider audience, but that was all pre–"Teen Spirit."

This was the first of many Sub Pop releases that knowingly piggybacked on Nirvana's status. The *Grunge Years* compilation reissued "Dive," then *Bleach* was rereleased with the previously unreleased song "Downer" to incentivize purchase.

Nirvana would place both songs on the *Incesticide* compilation soon after, thus nullifying any benefit.

For the band, only five rapid-fire shows in March disturbed their practice and tranquility, and they remained barely more significant than any of the other punk bands with whom they shared the stage.

KEVIN ROSE, The Wongs: It had a "mini festival" vibe, and there was a buzz about Nirvana. We were friends with the Doughboys; Chi Pig knew John Kastner from Chi's touring days with SNFU. Kastner was very kind to put us up in his place in Montréal for a few days . . . We hung out with him and the fellas from Voivod, and Ivan from Men Without Hats . . . Nirvana caused a stir; everyone was impressed and energized by their set. I loved Kurt's voice; everyone was saying what a great singer he was. They were heavy and powerful. I didn't know the songs at the time . . . The Screaming Trees had their own room backstage and we hung out there. I was drinking and gorging myself on deli meat; I've tried to make better choices since.

BILL WALKER, Blank Frank and the Tattooed Gods: The same month we played with Nirvana we also opened for Social Distortion, which was a big deal at the time. The show with Nirvana was a nut house; we left after we played and didn't even get to see them. I did however see some other cool shows in that particular venue around that time, notably Voivod, Primus, and Soundgarden.

JOHN KASTNER: The first night I saw them, it was a total snowstorm and it's eight thirty and Nirvana haven't shown up yet. All of a sudden the back door opens and this bass drum is thrown in. They threw all their shit into the club. This big yellow bass drum came rolling in—they didn't have cases for any of their gear. They had one crew guy, Krist's friend, and all he did was make martinis. They rented us a free hotel room and we went and had a big party in there—that was the first time I hung out with them . . . They were excited because they'd just signed their record deal, excited because they had laid down the first demos, ready for their album—they were enjoying it. Krist and Dave definitely, fun no matter what—Kurt you never knew what the fuck was going on, he never took off his gloves, he had this dark demeanor. We were watching the Screaming Trees play and I asked him, "Who are these guys?" He said to me, "He's my favorite singer in the whole world." He was a really quiet guy. Everyone was drinking beer, he had a little micky in his pocket, whiskey or something and would just take little sips. Kurt sat at the merch desk all night because they'd bought a whole bunch of white lighters and he just sat there and wrote NIRVANA in pen on them, circling the A like the anarchy sign, and sold them for a dollar each—sold out that night, a hundred lighters or something! It was when we first really bonded with them; it was really sweaty, everyone stage-dived, crowd loving it . . . they were super-tight, Kurt was dark and mean—Krist happy jumping up and down—Dave just laying it out.

JOSH KRIZ, Anxiety Prophets: We were constantly rocking out to them, and were floored when we were approached by Allen Ireland (our band promoter/manager . . .) to ask if we would be interested in opening for Nirvana. They were cool. They introduced themselves (and even offered us beers, wow!). We chatted with them for about thirty minutes or so before our sound check, and they didn't seem elitist or cocky like some of the bands that we had opened for in the past . . . They seemed fairly down to earth, and maybe a bit subdued or tired or maybe just a bit apathetic in general. But to the young teens that were Anxiety Prophets, they were like kings among men (we looked up to them in a big way) and were so surprised when they invited us to sit at their table at the Zoo with them. Their stage presence was phenomenal. The throwing around of the heads and hair, the tossing of guitars in the air, kicking the drum set, lighting guitars on fire . . . Their feel was natural and free-flowing, do whatever the hell they wanted while onstage type of attitude, and the crowd ate it up (as did we). They blew me away . . . Seeing Nirvana live really put in perspective their ability to put on an amazing show. Of special note was the lighting on fire of guitars and the kicking and breaking of the drum set during the performance. But the songs like "Love Buzz" and others sounded just as good live as they did on the studio recording.

The first true inkling of what was to come emerged at an all-ages show at Seattle's OK Hotel in April.

TIMO ELLIS: They played "Teen Spirit" for the first time live; everyone went completely fuckin' nuts . . . and it seemed like Kurt hadn't even finished writing all the lyrics yet! I remember driving back to Olympia with friends and we were all singing the melody of the chorus and raving about how rad that song was.

RYAN von BARGEN: I noticed it profoundly when "Smells Like Teen Spirit" was played. I was standing up at the soundboard with Stuart Hallerman watching Nirvana play. They had just played "Floyd the Barber." You know how "Teen Spirit" starts, the little guitar riff, then *boom*, and then the decrescendo before the first verse. I watched how everyone was brought up, and then gently sent back down to dig this incredible new tune few, if anyone, had ever heard before. I felt how badass it was. I was happy for them that they had written such a cool and dynamic tune. It was very inspirational as a musician and artist. I didn't realize it would change rock 'n' roll and usher out all that over-produced hair-band shit that had kept its place for far too long in dominance over the radio waves. Thanks, guys!

Life changed when Nirvana entered the studio in May to begin *Nevermind*. Until that point, it's no exaggeration to say that the demise of Kurt Cobain would have passed leaving barely a vapor trail in history. By late summer, *Nevermind* would still have become a fine could-have-been cult recording. It was only with the release of the "Smells Like Teen Spirit" video that flicking the blinding spotlight off became impossible.

AL BLOCH, Wool: We had been hanging out with them quite a bit when they were recording *Nevermind* . . . We'd stop by the studio and have a listen, and Grohl would come hang out with us. Of course, he was very close to Pete and Franz Stahl. One time, Dave and Kurt stopped by the record store I worked at and picked me up and I took them to a rock club where I was on the list. It was horrible hard rock/heavy-metal crap . . . I think Grohl and I got a kick out of it, so bad it was funny, but Kurt was disgusted and asked us to drop him off so he could go to a bar.

RYAN von BARGEN: We stayed with Nirvana at the Oakwood Apartments in the Toluca Hills area while we were there. We originally had no shows in L.A. and too much time off for three dudes with no money. Those kind Nirvana fellows hooked us up with a show with a band called Urge Overkill at a venue called Club Lingerie . . . I think that was Krist's doing. I remember hanging out with him at that gig. Krist was very generous and I have always appreciated the effort he put into helping us. There was talk of trying to get a show going with Nirvana at the Jabberjaw. I recall that Nirvana agreed to do the show on Sunday and the show was set for the Jabberjaw on Wednesday . . . Kurt had a sore throat because he had just finished vocal tracks for *Nevermind*. I also recall listening to their rough mix tapes and loving the tunes they were working on. The Nirvana guys would leave us in their apartment while they would do whatever during the days we were there, so with those tapes sitting around the boom box, they had to be heard, right? I am glad I never took any of those tapes . . . We got to go to Sound City on Tuesday with Krist to get Nirvana's gear . . . I saw the gold records on the wall, the carpeted walls and all that, but I wasn't star-struck or anything and I now regret not paying closer attention. How was I to know the world of rock was about to be changed forever by the recording session that had just taken place in that building? It was just one of many studios in L.A. to me. Krist gave us a cool little tour of Sound City. We got to meet Butch Vig and his assistant. At that time they were working the tune "Something in the Way" using the antiquated music-editing software . . . I watched them using a Yamaha DX7 to play notes and compare those notes to the cello recorded on the "Something in the Way" track for the purpose of retuning the cello track by adjusting the waveform on the screen. In addition to adjusting the tuning, they took out clicks and other imperfections. I was blown away and had never seen anything like that. When we went into the studio where David's drums were, I can remember seeing a music stand standing in front of the glass to the control booth with a spiral notebook on it. While the equipment was being gathered up, I paged through the notebook and read the lyrics to "On a Plain." I thought that it was so cool to be able to read the lyrics no one had yet heard but Kurt had just finished laying down. We ended up spending about an hour there playing pinball. While doing so, we ended up meeting Mick Fleetwood and Fleetwood Mac's manager . . .

Nirvana had played California plenty of times but always on underground soil; the Sound City Studios was their first step onto the mainstream's turf, the kind of place where celebrities showed up out of the blue.

RYAN von BARGEN: The show at the Jabberjaw was packed! For a show that was agreed to just three days before it was to happen, it was amazing how many people were there. Packed, I say! . . . I had the best seat in the house. The stage at the Jabberjaw was at the rear of the building if you were standing in the street facing the venue. To enter the Jabberjaw, you had to walk down a narrow alleyway at the back of the building. The stage would then be immediately on your right as you enter the venue. There was a two-tiered stage that bands would put gear on the higher tier against the wall to the back of the room, which would then be behind the drummer. It was an amazing place to see Nirvana play; on that riser, right behind David Grohl . . .

I remember Krist saying to me after we played the show, "Hey, did you know Iggy Pop is here?" Which was an amazing illustration of how many people heard about the show so quickly, but kind of a bummer, as we had been playing the Stooges' "1969" on that tour but randomly we elected to play Kiss's "God of Thunder" instead. It was cool to briefly meet Mr. Osterberg, but oh man I wish we would have played "1969" . . . I hear Nirvana's management was a bit upset about them playing the Jabberjaw gig because they were to play a show at the Palladium not long after and "the management" was concerned that it would take away interest or draw from the Palladium show. Suits! Out of touch almost every time.

As late as August, even Hollywood shows were still pretty casual.

AL BLOCH: The gig was a showcase, so people from the label (and other biz people) could see them at a comfortable venue—so they wouldn't have to make the trek to some shitty, smelly, sweaty club! . . . It was all still pretty organic at that point. I knew Nirvana's manager, John Silva, and he was pretty cool—and other than a bunch of major-label record people at the show, and that the show was on the Sunset Strip, at the Roxy, there was nothing "business" about it. The crowd down in front were all fans, jumping and slamming away. The sound probably was better than at a punk club, but it certainly wasn't overly "professional." I was standing back at the soundboard with Craig Montgomery, their sound man. It was the end of the set and they were smashing their gear and making a huge racket. I think the crowd was just exhausted, because it was an amazing show and I watched Craig push all the faders on the soundboard all the way up, making the noise even more brutal! It was unreal. After the show, there were a couple people handing out fliers asking for extras for the video shoot the next day . . . it wasn't any big deal.

Major label or no, the gentle mingling of musical life in Olympia continued. Cobain and Grohl joined Slim Moon's Witchypoo at shows in April and June.

JUSTIN TROSPER: Those shows, which were really just house parties, were fairly informal in-the-know kind of events . . . this thing like, "Hey, the Nirvana guys are around, maybe they can do some impromptu show." At one of those parties, Krist was working or something, so Nirvana became Witchypoo and then the other party was just an actual Witchypoo show with Kurt playing guitar and Dave on drums for part of the set . . . Slim did all the vocals. Some of the songs were part of the normal Witchypoo set and then these kind of noise-rock jams. As I remember, Billy Karren from Bikini Kill and Joe Preston and folks from Bratmobile may have jumped into the mess as well. It was pretty common to have people picking up or offering their instruments at the end of the night at some of these parties. Kurt did this really Midwestern acid-damage guitar thing that you hear on some of the solos on their records.

The completion of *Nevermind* was a cause for satisfaction, but for Cobain it also marked a definite end. He had been thrown out of the Pear Street house in which the majority of what now stands as his legacy was created.

STEVE MORIARTY: Kurt, I think he was just a quiet guy . . . He was just kind of a lonely, semi–street kid who grew up in a tiny town. It's like logging trucks and the smell of low tide—a pretty depressed area. Can understand him wandering to Olympia . . . I have friends who Dumpster-dived with him for sweaters to stay warm—getting in the garbage to get stuff. It was also kinda trendy back then. The punks in London would dress in ripped-up sweaters and hand-made T-shirts, that was more his aesthetic. So going Dumpster-diving they might find a bunch of clothes, sell some to a thrift store, a secondhand store—same with books, whatever they could find to make a little money.

JAMES BURDYSHAW: Nirvana were still pretty much a struggling band until *Nevermind* was released. I talked to Krist at a Sub Pop party in 1991 and he wanted to sell me his Honda for $500 because he needed money.

RYAN LOISELLE: Kurt wasn't a close buddy, but when they start[ed] getting kind of famous, he was kind of an introvert, but at the same time as being socially not comfortable, he'd seek out John and I and be like, "Hey man . . ." There'd be hundreds of people and he'd be embarrassed they were all there to see him so he'd come talk to us kinda like quiet but crazy, super-nice—the nicest guy . . . he would always find us.

There's no sign that Cobain intended to leave Olympia; the world simply began moving too quickly for him to return.

Nirvana was now right behind the leading lights of the indie scene; chosen as touring partner in June for Dinosaur Jr., another band straddling the underground/ major divide.

NEIL FRANKLIN, Kai Kln: Kurt dazzled everyone by climbing on a tall speaker and wailing on guitar . . . They sounded huge compared to the Cattle Club gig, much tighter with Grohl on drums . . . downstairs there was just one big room. They had cold-cut platters and Becks beer and I asked Krist Novoselic if they were going to eat their food (this was during Dinosaur Jr.'s set, so the food has been sitting there awhile). He said they were vegetarians so go right ahead. I did. We had polished our beer off long ago so I helped myself to a Becks or two also. I remember Kurt sitting in a chair with a towel over his head looking kinda miserable. He did say hi when I introduced myself earlier around sound check, so I did shake his hand. This is when our manager (Marc Malakie) was grilling Novoselic about their record deal and asking advice about our dealings with majors. I also had my most memorable moment of the night (in retrospect) at this point.

I asked Novoselic what the song was that Kurt said "hello, hello, hello" in. It was one of the few in their set that I didn't recognize. He said, "It's 'Teen Spirit,'" like it was no big deal—which it wasn't at the time. Little did any of us know . . . I also talked to Grohl about his previous band, Scream, which I was a *huge* fan of, still am! He was preoccupied with some lovely lady, which I could understand.

SCOTT ANDERSON, Kai Kln: Music has to really move me to get me on the dance floor or out in the pit. Was moshing to a couple tunes having a blast, then a song ended. I suddenly was wondering why my left hand was hurting so bad: looked at it and realized my bandages had come unraveled. Music was so good that I forgot I had a third-degree burn from red-hot cooking oil and was bandaged up. Played five painful gigs in that condition, but Nirvana's music ripped my flesh open again . . . [I] was walking out, saw Kurt and said hi. He lifted his head long enough to say hi back, then his gaze went back to the floor as he kept walking. Suffering my own bipolar issues . . . I could tell this guy was deeply depressed. I played more than half of our shows in a very depressed state, which is tough to keep it together. Not talking much before or after, usually not very friendly, and pretty much kept to myself most of the time. In the brief moment I met him I could feel and see the pain in his eyes and the way he carried himself.

People had stopped talking about Nirvana in terms of heaviness and started focusing on the rock/pop side of their personality. Meanwhile, Cobain's yin-yang nature was rarely affected by what was happening around him.

The underground's friendship network was already passing the word—or, more accurately, the tape. Musicians worldwide, those in the know, had copies and were whispering how good it was long before *Nevermind*'s release.

COLIN BURNS: I wasn't much of a fan at the time. I remember checking out a little of their set . . . It wasn't until a year and change later that I spent August in a borrowed car with a cassette of *Nevermind* demos on permanent repeat that I was converted.

KEVIN ROSE: A friend gave me a copy of *Nevermind* and we fell in love with it right away; a few months later it blew up.

MICHAEL McMANUS, The Guttersnipes: A friend had given me a tape of a pre-release copy of *Nevermind* a few months earlier, and I'd been listening to it nonstop.

GERARD LOVE, Teenage Fanclub: We already had a pre-release copy of *Nevermind* and it was played on repeat in the van; we all knew it was a top-quality record.

AL BLOCH: I remember talking to John Silva and telling him how much I liked the *Nevermind* album because we had been listening to an advance cassette Grohl gave us. I thought it was going to be a big album, and he asked me if I thought it would sell two hundred thousand copies. I think I told him not to get his hopes up.

14.0

Takeoff
August to December 1991

Nirvana was on a major label but still saw themselves as part of the underground, no different from their indie-label friends. In the late summer of 1991 they had just finished work on *Nevermind*—a record they had polished for months, doing everything they could to ensure it might be a hit (at least, an underground one)—and were preparing for its release in September with various industry showcases for media and record-industry executives. Yet alongside the major-label business, they were still planning an appearance at the International Pop Underground Convention in Olympia and chipped in a three-year-old song to the accompanying compilation—it was a statement of their continued allegiances.

SLIM MOON: I called them up and they immediately contributed. It was part of a two-day whirlwind in which Calvin and I were calling a lot of bands. We put together the lineup to that album in less than forty-eight hours. Nirvana were initially scheduled to play the IPU but changed plans later to play Reading. At the time that they gave me the track, we all believed they'd be playing the fest.

"Beeswax" was the first Nirvana original since the previous September. There had been over eight silent months between the *Blew* EP and the song "Mexican Sea-food" on a C/Z compilation then for the year after that, just one single and three unremarkable cover songs; Nirvana's rep had built despite almost no new music.

Nirvana would never play Olympia again. They had to cancel their festival slot to support Sonic Youth. Having performed 160 shows since the start of 1989, the band hammered out a further 76 between August and December 1991, their heaviest spell of touring ever.

DON FLEMING: The three of them all had an intense vibe, serious. Dave, super-serious, Kurt serious in a sadder way—more of a deer-in-the-headlights look at times with Kurt. But at least at that moment they were genuinely wanting to be a great band; that's what was fun about catching them at that moment. A band enjoying playing with each other, enjoying the friendships they were making. I think it meant a lot to them to have Sonic Youth being their mentor and a champion at that time, I think it gave them a lot of confidence that wouldn't have happened as much otherwise, not getting that record deal—maybe that wasn't a good thing actually . . . Backstage we were sharing a dressing room, I remember mainly that there was one bottle of whiskey and we were fighting over it. During their set Krist had taken it out and had it onstage and one of us, maybe me, snuck behind him and got it from behind the amp, brought it back to the dressing room. I loved them, a great band—Kurt was a great songwriter; it was fun to play with them. But at the time they weren't *Nirvana* yet, they were just a cool band I was psyched to see and play with.

However, armed with their new songs Nirvana was making a genuine impact.

DON FLEMING: I do remember being on tour in Europe at that time and going to places Nirvana had played and listening to [people] talk about having seen them. And the thing that was very distinct to me at the time was that the people who were mostly raving about them were women, girls—they loved the band and that was something I didn't usually see. It was usually guys—"Hey, did you check Tad? He's so fucking amazing!" Or Dinosaur Jr. or . . . It was very unusual to me, striking, to hear women raving about the band. That was something that was different and did give them more mass appeal. Kurt was a James Dean to a lot of females—he had that dark look, songs, bad-boy-but-take-care-of-me thing. Appealing. And the crowds that I saw that were really talking about them, it was one of the things that was really apparent to me. Usually you didn't hear girls talking as much, especially with punk or grunge sort of bands, it was more a guys' game, but this opened it up and that seems key to their mainstream success.

LISA SMITH: What always stood out was *Kurt*! Krist was fun to watch because he had so much energy, but all eyes were usually on Kurt. All of us girls would joke about not ever having babies with the exception of having *his*!

JOHN LEAMY: We met some girls in Sweden who were annoyingly obsessed with *Bleach*. That was the real rumblings in the distance for me. I was trying to get laid, and these girls wouldn't stop talking about that record. So, I listened to it. Ad nauseam for a *long* weekend.

Nirvana now had a timely first taste of festival crowds—just as the fruits of their summer labors were starting to leak, they were to be seen by tens of thousands.

ERIC "DANNO" JEEVERS, Paradogs: Paradogs were one of the very few Dutch bands on the Ein Abend In Wien showcase festival, we were very much the critics' sweethearts—fair is fair, we weren't too bad, either! . . . In most of the publicity, I think Paradogs had a big color photo and Nirvana a small black-and-white one. That doesn't mean we were superstars though—hell no—but Nirvana was an up-and-coming band like many others. By the time the festival was on, there was a buzz that they were the band you should go and see, because "Teen Spirit" was getting a lot of airplay and all that. I think by then we realized they should have had the color photo!

JB MEIJERS, Charmin' Children: I clearly remembered that those were the guys from the *Bleach* album and wondered where the fourth guy was. I have never told this to anyone. I really dug that record. I was a member of the Sub Pop singles club and therefore received every single Sub Pop release . . . I thought of them as the best thing ever, but I saw Dinosaur Jr. as the band that should've knocked Michael Jackson from the throne . . . Who would have guessed . . . Nirvana? Really?

With the Rotterdam festival marking the tour's end, Nirvana celebrated by making drunken fools of themselves.

JB MEIJERS: They wrecked the backline, including my Marshall. I was not cool with that . . . We shared a dressing room—we were an obnoxious bunch but I remember them pushing that a bit further . . . There was an accordion door that split the room right in two. After someone in the Nirvana camp threw a banana to us, John, our singer, closed that door.

ERIC JEEVERS: I missed the whole equipment-smashing bit, although backstage the security's portophones were buzzing and we heard what was going on. Personally, I don't get a kick from seeing someone wrecking guitars, so I went to see some other band—and later on ran into Mr. Grohl . . . Dave tried to nick our six-packs of beer. He was dead drunk, and we told him to cut it out. Like, "If you want a beer, here, you have one, but don't take a whole six-pack OK?" Then he started making masturbation gestures with the beer, and I put a friendly arm around him [and said], "Know what, let's see if there's any cool bands to check out." He agreed, but in the corridor, he slipped over some spilled beer, thought I had pushed him or whatever, and he attacked me. It was pretty easy to dodge his blows and I didn't feel like hitting him back—I mean, he had trouble standing up as it was! So, anyway, security saw what happened [and were like] "Ah, another of those Nirvana guys . . ." and they had a little chat I think . . .

September 23, 1991—Boston. "Smells Like Teen Spirit" had been out for two weeks. But local pride had muted the release of *Nevermind;* it was just one more good album at the time.

LEX LIANOS, Cliffs of Dooneen: Boston had its own thing going on and the feeling was that Seattle was trying to take over Boston's mantle as a cool music town. Honestly, at the time I wasn't a big Nirvana fan. I liked "Smells Like Teen Spirit" a bit but didn't really get it until much later . . . The bigger deal was that the local station had chosen us to open this night that the entire industry was buzzing about. The guy that essentially discovered us and gave us a shot on the radio was Kurt St. Thomas. He was the program director of WFNX and this was their show. He was probably Nirvana's biggest supporter at the time and was among the first to play their record . . . they were fine. Nothing earth-shattering. Kind of garage-bandy. Our stage and light show was much more big-venue-oriented. Probably overshooting where we were at in our career (medium clubs), but we wanted to be playing arenas and approached it that way. They just kind of got up there and played. I got zero feeling they were the next big thing and that everyone would flip out . . . Eric Sean Murphy and I were most interested in meeting the Pumpkins. But when we introduced ourselves to Billy Corgan, who I think was chatting with their drummer Jimmy Chamberlain (who I think is incredible), they were so rude it was a bummer. We said hi, that we were playing before them and we thought their band was amazing. Billy says, "Yeah, we know" and turned his back on us. Probably one of the biggest arses I've met in the industry.

FLYNN, Cliffs of Dooneen: We were so focused on what we were doing in Boston at the time. We were very aware of Nirvana and the Seattle sound but felt we had our own "sound" brewing in our home-town . . . outside the Paradise Rock Club in Boston, sitting in the band van and one of our songs had just played on WFNX 101.7, then "Smells Like Teen Spirit" came on shortly after. I remember thinking, This will be huge . . . Cliffs were on the rise in Boston. We were so into what we were doing that we did not pay too much attention to every-thing else. At least, I didn't. We won an award that night as well, I believe . . . like a people's choice award that was presented after we played. I remember MTV interviewing us and all the bands that night. It was one fantastic night that went by way too quickly! I also remember Smashing Pumpkins on the bill and there was a great buzz about them also. I don't remember a media frenzy about Nir-vana that night . . .

The impact of MTV was immeasurable to bands at the time. Nirvana had the right video, sound, and song.

GILLY ANN HANNER: When I first heard "Teen Spirit" we were in Seattle putting together artwork for our album. We went into Kinko's to copy the artwork and lay it out—it was on the radio. Everyone thought, This is awesome, what is this? It sounded so different to how they played it live. All of a sudden all of us collectively went, "Oh my God, it's Nirvana! This is their new record? They're going to be huge!" Goosebumps, that moment when we could just tell that. From then we saw their video on MTV and it was all surreal.

LINDSEY THRASHER: One weekend we went to San Francisco to play a show and somewhere I heard "Smells Like Teen Spirit." Then on the way home, we stopped at a gas station and heard it again. It seemed like we heard it five times that day and it didn't let up . . .

ALAN BISHOP: I was at work in an office that always had MTV going on the TV with the volume turned off, and I looked up and saw this band playing. They looked familiar but I couldn't place them . . . I watched the rest of the video and when the band name and song title appeared at the bottom of the screen . . . it became crystal clear: it was those Nirvana guys . . .

JOHN PURKEY: It's when I went into the shop and I'm looking at all the magazines and they're on the cover of almost every single magazine, not just the music magazines, and I just thought: Wow . . . that's when I really knew something was happening to my friends.

DON FLEMING: The label thought it was cool, but they didn't see it coming at all. There was only one guy there who was really working it personally to really push it, which was John Rosenfelder; he was the college music rep, so he would push records to college radio . . . the rest of the label didn't even realize the record was out and were caught happily surprised when the record did break. There could have been other people pushing it, but John is the one I knew and with him it was like once things started rolling it gave him even more to work with. But he was in from the get-go, before it took off.

GLEN LOGAN: My impression of Nirvana pre-*Nevermind* was that they were a cool band among the so many other incredible and cool bands in the area. They did not, however, stick out head and shoulders above other bands in the area to me. That is not taking anything away from them; it is more a statement of how strong so many other bands were. From my perspective I think they found a bit of a new voice on *Nevermind* in a way that positively did separate them from everyone else. I know some folks who perceive *Nevermind* as a sellout. I, however, think it was the opposite and actually a braver thing to do.

RICK SIMS, The Didjits: Nirvana was just another band from Seattle until *Nevermind* in terms of popularity. I know they were well liked and drew bigger crowds than us, but they weren't massive. There were certainly other bands that were "bigger," like Fugazi, but they operated on a different plane. There was an atmosphere of promotion and commercialism that revolved around Nirvana. Fugazi had an anti-promotion vibe and more of a cultlike grassroots following . . . My personal opinion is that it wasn't how well they played live that got them so wildly popular. They exuded a cool in songwriting that hit just at the right time. Couple that with a bazillion-dollar PR budget and the bubbling up of the so-called grunge movement and they hit at just the right time.

KEVIN ROSE: There was a strong current of anticommercial "alternative" feeling at the time just before Nirvana became worldwide; college radio seemed to favor SST bands with leanings toward Jane's Addiction and reverence for the Bad Brains.

MIKE HARD: The industry did not know what to do with bands like us, and of course wanted nothing to do with some of us. Rock 'n' roll reached entropy and the music of the '80s was a backlash. And of course we had Ronald Reagan saying there is a definite need for *greed*. There was still a need from the music industry to exploit this, minus the politics, but they could not figure it out, of course. So they tried using their past formula for success on the alternative scene. Alas, a cute, young, highly photogenic, twenty-four-year-old with blond hair and blue eyes becomes a poster child for grunge. Kurt Cobain fit the "Johnny Bravo" suit . . . I am sure the industry thought Nirvana seemed very safe and exploitable at first. Unintelligible lyrics, familiar chord progressions ripped from the best classic rock tunes, blond and blue-eyed front man. No apparent political motivations. Just another recycling job for the industry.

The rest of October vanished as the band romped around the Northeast then plowed a path home, gig-by-gig, across the United States.

GARY FLOYD, Sister Double Happiness: *Nevermind* hit heavy rotation in the middle of our time with them . . . I remember their road manager telling everyone backstage one night the CD had hit one million sales that day. They seemed almost embarrassed . . . All the rest of us were so happy for them and they were low-key and, as I said, really humble-acting . . . Kurt was a super-respectful and sweet, beautiful man. Punk-rock gentle kind person. After a big show one night I was headed into their room planning to say, "Congratulations on all this . . . you deserve it, so happy for you . . ." When I walked in, he said, "Hey, good show." I said thanks. Before I could go on he said, "I'm so sick of people telling me congratulations and how they are happy for me—it's all so funny and weird that this is happening." I swallowed and said, "I bet, can I get a beer?" . . . I remember being in the middle of nowhere one night in the van—dark and nothing around—some crackling radio station was on and they had a recorded intro saying in a big rock voice *the sound of the '90s* and "Teen Spirit" came on . . . We all just looked at each other and said, "Damn!" . . . The tour had been booked before it all happened so most of the clubs were too small for what was happening! It was chaotic every night . . . It was so much fun to see and hear them just rip down the walls every time they played. You could taste the energy!

LYNN TRUELL, Sister Double Happiness: We were asked to do some West Coast shows with them . . . I heard later that Krist was a fan and got us on the bill. Krist came to our backstage in Houston and introduced himself and hung out awhile and we talked about music . . . I introduced myself to Kurt in Phoenix during sound-check time. I walked up to a table where he was standing and eating his Taco Bell meal. We shook hands and had only a few words—he was eating, after all . . . I remember listening to KUSF in San Francisco and DJ Terror Bull Ted played "Smells Like Teen Spirit" on his show and he introduced it saying something like, "Nirvana may be on a major label now"—a real catchphrase coming out at that time—"but they still got their sound and it is rad!" Something like that. The seven shows we played with them were totally insane and one couldn't help feeling that something *big* was breaking out.

ERIC MOORE: Krist and Dave were really funny, outgoing, and well . . . like most of us, drunk. Kurt was very reclusive and surrounded by a coterie of people who had dyed hair and looked smacked-out . . . We opened for them the day (I think) *Nevermind* went gold in the US. And hanging out backstage with Mudhoney, watching Nirvana at their fucking peak . . . fucking amazing. I tell people all the time. That night, Nirvana was the best rock 'n' roll band in the world. The *best* rock set (and drummer) I've ever seen to this day . . . I wasn't nervous at all, but with all of the lights and cigarette smoke I couldn't really see the crowd. Oh yeah, and I made a point of stealing beer from Nirvana's dressing room. Because no one was downstairs in the dressing rooms, they were all up top watching Nirvana!

STEVE BIRCH, Sprinkler: That night is a bit blurry for me, as I was sick as a dog, running a 101-degree temperature and sweating like a pig . . . they did seem kind of dazed by the rocket ride of adulation that was hitting them. What I remember most is standing in their dressing room right after meeting them and having their manager come in and excitedly tell them that their record had just gone gold. Kurt just looked at him and said something like, "What does that mean?" . . . When Nirvana hit the stage, there was definitely a shift in the air or something, and it got *special*. That was probably the best show I ever saw them play, and they seemed happy and on the top of their game, and while Kurt was, in hindsight, using, there were no symptoms of that in this performance.

GARY FLOYD: Dallas, we played our set—people were happy—this was one of those clubs that it should have been bigger, packed! . . . All at once the crowd noise level went up double and we tried to see what was happening. All hell broke out. Later I'm hearing about the [Hells] Angels chasing the band . . . Kurt hit a big bad bouncer with tattoos on his face in the head with his guitar—oh, well!

LYNN TRUELL: All I can truly remember is that the band had to "escape" out the side door and into a cab to flee the club.

ANNE EICKELBERG: The audience was very young and acted like they were seeing and hearing God. The kids had overrun the area from well before sound-check time. We were shocked to see big lines and masses of kids as we pulled up to the club in the late afternoon. After Nirvana's set, when people were leaving, a young man grabbed my arms and looked at me with the wild eyes of the newly converted and kept repeating, "Did you hear that? Did you hear that?" . . . I know a monitor board was smashed and there was a fight and Kurt had to be snuck out of the club after their set because people wanted to beat him up . . . Nirvana had an agent or road manager who carried a brief-case full of cash to pay for stuff they broke. But mostly I remember that we had to wait for what seemed like two hours to get paid at the end of the night because of all the drama . . . Kurt was under the pro-tection of his handlers from the label (I assumed that's who, anyway). He was never by himself, and not really with his band—he was with a guy who looked like a suit. He looked remote, unapproachable, and unhappy.

MARK DAVIES: Kurt was crowd-surfing . . . the security guy jumped in and ended up getting smashed over the head with the guitar. Chaos set in and I recall Novoselic jumping up onto a really high monitor tower and crouching there so as not to hit the ceiling. Then at some point all the band was off the side of the stage and disappeared for a while. At some point there was also a confrontation outside of the club . . . there was definitely someone bleeding from a guitar over the head, and the show was paused for many minutes. Definitely an apoc-alyptic sort of feel that night . . . Kurt did seem like a bit of a wild card, like he might unhinge at any point.

LYNN TRUELL: In Tijuana, Dave was not feeling well and wanted to nap in their van, so he asked me to do sound check for Nirvana that day. Pretty cool for me. I think we played "Love Buzz," and another one or two songs . . . One of the nuttiest things I have *ever* seen was in the Tijuana club: it was three levels, and people were jumping into the pit from the second—even third—level. It was horrible, scary, and amazing, surely people were hurt! But the energy of the band and crowd was uncontrollable.

GARY FLOYD: Mexico, that was a completely one-hundred-percent-nuts, out-of-control thing to witness—packed with kids who walked over from San Diego, drunk as hell, no real number on how many or crowd control? Lynn Perko [Truell] and I were standing behind the curtain right behind their drummer in this walkway . . . Outside were hundreds of kids beating in a huge folding door. We looked out at the crowd with tons of people jumping off the third-floor balcony and the band super-loud and right behind us, the beating on the folding metal door—We were just hugging each other and laughing. I was yelling, "We're here! We are here in this time seeing this!" It was one of the big spiritual moments in my very spiritual life!

ERIC ERLANDSON: There was this "golden calf" air about them at the time. But they seemed to be having such fun, and enjoying the attention while still trying to fuck with the system the best they could. It was also the beginning of Courtney and Kurt's relationship. So that new love, push and pull of romance, was also happening concurrently. I remember running out onstage during Nirvana's encore at the Palace show and jumping on Kurt and pulling him down. Dave and Krist both jumped on top of us and it became a sweaty dog pile. Just fun fucking around!

Given the strong bond between L7 and Nirvana, plus the latter's genuine inter-est, it made sense that they paused to be the only all-male group at a Rock for Choice Benefit on the way home.

LYNN TRUELL: It was absolutely intentional that women were repre-sented at this show. L7 had a lot to do with Rock for Choice—they were its major organizers. We all felt strongly about a woman's right to choose, at that time and now. It was pretty obvious what was being highlighted—a woman's rights to choose and to rock! And we did and still do.

JILL EMERY, Hole: Sad to say I have to even think it's an issue this far in the future, if the Republicans had their way, they would close down every clinic. It shocks me there are Republican women in office who are fine with them being involved in women's reproductive rights . . . honestly at that time it felt like a swooping-in whirlwind: all you could do is play, hold on, and watch your back . . . Kurt seemed OK but basically Courtney sprayed the scene. As the drug thing escalated no one was emotionally available. Dave and Krist were supernice dudes, I would say Krist was a sweetheart and completely down to earth; I remember Dave just enthusiastically daydreaming about his own band, guess it wasn't too much of a daydream . . . It got to the point where both bands were forced (mentally) into onstage antics, Courtney being stripperish and Nirvana feeling like they had to break their instruments, it even happened with Mazzy Star just seeing how little light they could use onstage, it just happens.

Although they played the Paramount Theater in Seattle on Thursday October 31, Nirvana were onstage in Bristol, UK, the following Monday. At least they weren't alone in feeling rushed.

PAUL THOMSON: At midday nothing was happening, I was sat at home in south London; five hours later we were sound-checking in Bristol using Nirvana's backline! I think the call came from Lawrence Bell, who said that Captain America's van had broken down and did we fancy opening for Nirvana? Duh . . . *yes!* That was it, all in the van and on the road within an hour. Played a great gig to an amazing crowd and then got to see one of our favorite bands rip the place up from the side of the stage. Result! But it was just luck that we were

Captain America's label mates that we got the call . . . by the time they were due to play here (our gig with them was the very first of the *Nevermind* tour) it was clear that this was an *extremely* popular record, but I don't think anyone thought it would be *so* massive. I remember first hearing it at our press agents' and people being genuinely blown away. The audience at the Bristol show confirmed what we thought. It was a packed and very excited crowd! There was a lot of Novoselic jumping about and Dave doing his head-down drumming. The whole thing looked and sounded great . . . I don't imagine they would think twice about what they were doing onstage, just not that kind of band. They just did what came naturally. I don't think they even smashed up their gear that night!

The UK tour, like the US shows over the previous two months, had been booked without any expectation that Nirvana was anything worth worrying about.

PAUL THOMSON: The Bierkeller wasn't particularly pleasant: in a dodgy part of town, dark, smelly, maybe five hundred capacity? But for us, that was a step up! Venues in the UK for bands like us were generally small, hot, dark, and smelly. If you got a dressing room, that was a major bonus. But it suited the music and the audiences at the time. The place was rammed full by the time we started and everyone was buzzing that they were going to see Nirvana. I think there were people all 'round the stage with little or no security. I don't know what other venues they played, but the Bierkeller was exactly that, a midlevel indie venue. In London they played Kilburn National, which was maybe one thousand people?

GORDON KEEN, Captain America: Witnessing, firsthand, venues being packed night after night, the amount of people locked out and trying desperately to get in to see Nirvana, the palpable feeling of expectation and excitement from the audience inside the venues—more so than any other gigs I'd witnessed as a musician or as a fan—all led me, and the other guys in Captain America, to realize that this was special.

ANDY BOLLEN, Captain America: They played decent-sized venues in London at the Astoria and Kilburn National, but in Edinburgh, for example, they were playing in a really small club. I also remember the Glasgow QM show; we must've sneaked in hundreds of people it was so jam-packed. One show at Nottingham Rock City there were literally people weeping in the streets outside the venue, hundreds of people who couldn't get in. You could've played two nights at venues twice the size and still not met the demand.

NAOKO YAMANO: When we toured with them in 1991, the capacities of their venues were between 1,500 to 2,500, but all shows were sold out and the audience was very enthusiastic for the band. They were just breaking. The members of Nirvana, especially Kurt, was very busy for promotion booked by record label . . . We hired a van with a Scottish band, Captain America . . . We basically toured in our own van but a few times, we had a ride in Nirvana's tour bus from hotels to venues. They were very kind to us.

DAN TREACY, Television Personalities: The gig at the Astoria was a very last-minute thing for us. We got a phone call out of the blue from Kurt's manager. Apparently Kurt had asked for us. We were supposed to be on first, but ended up going on before Nirvana. I got the impression the other support bands were a bit pissed off about that. Nirvana were lovely guys . . . They played very loud! We played quite well . . . Kurt watched us from the side of the stage. We got some of their fans on our side . . . Had a brief chat with Kurt at some point . . . I couldn't understand him very well, but it turned out we had a mutual love of the Terry Jacks's song "Seasons in the Sun" . . . Kurt asked, and I think he was testing me, what the B-side was: "Put the Bone In." We connected . . . I had no inkling at all he had issues, but Kurt in particular seemed a little uncomfortable with the sudden success.

But I couldn't say what that was down to. He was very introvert[ed], shy . . . he and the rest of the band were a little unsure but also enjoying it.

Their time on the road was starting to show, with the band beginning to tire. In one petulant moment Cobain would turn a performance of "Smells Like Teen Spirit" into sarcastic comedy when irked by the demands of a TV show's directors.

ANDY BOLLEN: The demands placed on them had increased. They were very busy doing promo work for TV, radio sessions, interviews all the time. I recall a general conversation and the band were on basic wages, on a tight budget and still hadn't received any royalties. At the time the figure may have been $250 a week, a grand a month or something. I was impressed but looking back it's not life-changing. The effect of fame at that level for Nirvana just meant more and more time on the road, more shows; they grew tired but kept the momentum going.

GORDON KEEN: It was wonderful to share the time we did with a band who were genuinely blown away by the reception they were receiving and before the media madness surrounding them got to the level it did. I remember us driving 'round and 'round outside a hotel in England in our tour van with Dave Grohl clinging onto the bonnet shouting for us to drive faster. It was hysterically funny . . . We also sat with Kurt, Krist, and Dave watching their *Top of the Pops* recording when they intentionally hammed it up. At the time that was a big thing. They were worried they had gone too far, and we were reassuring them that it was just the right thing to have done.

PAUL THOMSON: We hardly saw them, really. We had to walk through their dressing room to leave, and I remember Kurt was prostrate on a sofa like he was asleep. The others seemed happy enough. I don't think they were aware of what madness was coming, they were just playing their gigs and pleased they were busy. We went to a very crowded after-show party in London after they had played Kilburn a week or so later and Dave Grohl made a point of coming over to us to tell us he thought we'd been great in Bristol, which was nice. And Dec [Kelly] ended up going out to a club with Kurt. Kurt fell asleep with his head on Dec's shoulder . . . they seemed fairly nice, normal guys at that point. A bit sleepy, though . . .

Despite all that was going on, Cobain and Grohl still took time out to play a benefit for the children's hospital in Edinburgh despite being unwell.

ANDY BOLLEN: I did see him really ill in Edinburgh. But it was more glandular, his voice was gone, a doctor was called; we actually thought it was game over, the tour would be stopped, but he made it through.

MURDO MacLEOD: The gig that Kurt and Dave did with us was not just by chance. We had asked them to do it. I called and spoke to Kurt when they got to the UK, and asked if they'd do it, as a "secret" gig, and he agreed. We got the audience by advertising our acoustic gig "with very special guests." I think everyone knew who it was going to be, because they knew we knew them, and Kurt had mentioned us, as he liked our single, and they had played in town the night before, or were playing the next night—I can't remember which. We played to an unbelievably packed room (about two hundred in a space designed for about eighty) with no sign of Nirvana. After an hour or so, everyone started to leave, berating us for bullshitting them. We knew better. Kurt and Dave showed up when there were about thirty people left. We locked the doors, they played six songs, and then we and they and a bunch of our good friends all sat about until God knows when drinking and shooting the breeze. It was lovely. I have no idea how much we raised.

Regardless of their rocketing popularity and success, they still supported their friends. They weren't saints, let alone angels, but they brought the communal spirit of the underground to whatever strange land was opening up for them.

ANDY BOLLEN: They were warm, friendly, respectful, and generous. They let us use their gear every night. In terms of approach we were a shambles, we got drunk, had a great laugh; I think Nirvana really enjoyed our company. They gave us their rider every night. They had this punk-rock sharing thing; they didn't act like a big band. I think they sensed we were struggling. We were signing on, in vans that were breaking down, it was chaos! They wanted us to play the mainland dates in Europe with them too and were prepared to let us share their bus and gear, but we couldn't afford to do it.

Amid the chaos Cobain kept writing. The band was already practicing new material.

ANDY BOLLEN: I didn't want the others to see me doing something so uncool as writing, so the only place I could go was Nirvana's dressing room. Kurt would be either sleeping or writing, or chatted with me. I can't believe now that he was annoying me by talking to me . . . I remember over the tour sitting watching them hone "All Apologies" every night. The sound caught by their sound man, Craig Montgomery, was better than the version on *In Utero*. It sounded more dramatic and powerful, the bass more resonating like Joy Division.

15.0

Falling Apart in Asia/Pacific
January to February 1992

Nevermind **had conquered** the world in less than fifteen weeks. A media awakening to the newest "must-see" phenomenon raced to keep up and proceeded to smother Nirvana with attention while at the same time whimpering that it was impossible to see them in the United States. Geffen had decided Nirvana's touring schedule prior to their unpredicted triumph and it had made perfect sense for what had been just another mid-ranking band. Nirvana's hefty touring had saturated the home market, so until fame hit, there was nowhere in the States that Geffen needed Nirvana to go.

The answer had been to hit the overseas circuit in Europe in late 1991 and then the less-traveled markets of Asia/Pacific in the New Year.

MARK HURST, The Guttersnipes: We got the support many months in advance, before *Nevermind* came out. We all followed the Sub Pop thing closely and liked *Bleach* a lot, so we were very happy to be playing with them. Everything changed when *Nevermind* came out, obviously, but we were kept on the bill, which was nice.

SHAUN BUTCHER, Nunbait: We just were playing in lounge rooms/backyards at friends' parties. We were always practicing, writing heaps of songs, and it was a bit harder than we thought to get gigs, so we entered a couple of band competitions so we could at least play. One of the competitions had a first prize of recording a single with Waterfront Records, a well-known indie record label and shop in the city and, blow us all down, we won! We recorded a bit with them, toured interstate; there was even talk about going to America to record as the whole Sub Pop thing was happening and they pegged us in that category . . . We were lucky to get some great supports with overseas bands like Butthole Surfers, Mudhoney, [and] Fugazi through a band promoter, Steve Pav, who worked closely with Waterfront and who eventually brought Nirvana out.

RICHARD LEWIS, Tumbleweed: We knew Nirvana when they were included on the *Sub Pop 200* compilation doing "Spank Thru," then *Bleach* came out. We all had a copy of *Bleach* . . . During the Mudhoney tour we did as the Proton Energy Pills, we were sitting around the pool of the Diplomat Hotel in Melbourne with Mudhoney, just hanging out, swimming, shootin' [the] shit, and getting over the gig the night before, when Matt Lukin said, "My house mate Kurt is in a band called Nirvana, do you know them?" We said, "Yeah! We love Nirvana!" He said, "Well they want to come out here, you guys should play with them." . . . Steve Pav was our manager and he was with us at the time and the deal was pretty much struck then and there.

PETER FENTON, Crow: We were in a loose arrangement being looked after by Steve Pavlovic . . . there was this Canberra mafia thing going on in Sydney. He was booking the Landsdowne Hotel and his momentum and vision took him to Mudhoney and Fugazi, the Flying Nun bands . . . I remember having a conversation with him that he was bringing out this band from America called Nirvana. I'd heard of Nirvana down at the local record store, probably Waterfront Records, but they really were one of many at the time. Sometime after that, "Smells Like Teen Spirit" broke through. In Australia, Triple J (our national youth broadcaster) presented the tour, but behind the scenes there was a wonderful lady named Jen Brennen, who later managed Crow—she was in marketing at Triple J. I remember she had to push quite hard to get "Smells Like Teen Spirit" played on Triple J. That's why Nirvana presented her with a gold record, to say, "Without you, we wouldn't have gotten this gold record in Australia." Amazing.

Nirvana's absolute triumph had derailed the plan. Yet, so close to the unexpected explosion, the label had no idea how to react. Ultimately, the brevity of the Asia/Pacific tour meant it wasn't worth the drama of cancellation. What Geffen and the local promoters could do—and did—was shift venues to larger locations.

MICHAEL McMANUS: The Australian shows were booked prior to the release of *Nevermind*, and were in smaller venues than they could have played in. They honored the existing arrangements though, which was noble of them. We got onto the show through Steve Pav, who ran Magnet . . . We heard around the middle of '91 that he was planning to tour Nirvana, and being fans of *Bleach* put our hands up enthusiastically for the support . . . A friend who worked for the promoter said they were swamped by media enquiries.

RICHARD LEWIS: The tour was arranged before *Nevermind* came out, so it was set up much the same as the Dinosaur Jr. or Mudhoney tour that preceded it—venues that held about 2,500 . . . I think the Phoenician Club held about 2,500, same with the Palace. Thebarton held a few more, maybe 3,500; ANU around 3,500 I think?

DAMIEN BINDER, Second Child: The Logan Campbell Centre held about 2,000 people. We used to call it the Logan Concrete Centre because it sounded like shit in there—not exactly known for its warm acoustics. The Powerstation, where I believe the gig was originally to be staged, was a much better, more intimate venue . . .

The tour kept Nirvana in motion while the label awaited the return of regular business forecasting.

SHAUN BUTCHER: All the hype on Nirvana exploded when they came to tour. It all coincided with *Nevermind* going ballistic and every indie and commercial radio station in Sydney had Nirvana on high rotation. Suddenly everyone [was] walking the streets in their "grunge-wear" (flannelette checked shirts—"flannies"—ripped jeans, and sneakers). We got heaps of them at our gigs, as some classed us as grunge (I even done the uniform . . . only 'cause Sydney was always cold, sneakers were cheap, and I couldn't afford new jeans!), but we were happy to go along with it. (Got people to our gigs.)

PAUL BROCKHOFF, The Guttersnipes: A buzz is an understatement. Mass hysteria, the likes of which I don't think could be repeated . . . Mainstream Australia was smitten. It changed the landscape in many ways. Kind of like losing the roof of your house in a windstorm. All of your special things, the things that made "alternative" music . . . were all of a sudden subject to idiotic commercial radio DJs. Kind of like the Dead Kennedys agreeing to go on MTV . . .

MICHAEL McMANUS: You couldn't go into a shop or café without hearing "Smells Like Teen Spirit," at least around St. Kilda, where I lived . . . The buzz started I think in late '91, and grew rapidly. It was obvious they were going to be huge, and the media activity was intense. I don't recall anything like it before or since. Once we were announced as a support, virtually everyone I spoke to was wanting to talk about it, even people who would normally have absolutely no interest in music. It was pretty exciting and it was like the stuff we'd been doing as a very underground thing was really gaining broad acknowledgment. There was a definite feeling of zeitgeist, too; it felt like a wave that was bigger than just the music.

RICHARD LEWIS: When *Nevermind* came out, it broke the banks of the narrow stream that we were all used to swimming in. People who were not a part of the scene got into it as well—"Smells Like Teen Spirit" was huge! It was a revolution! It was such a great album, it retained all the things we loved about music and punk rock but was produced so well it was commercially viable. It felt special; Australian audiences were totally aware of Nirvana's impact.

The Asia/Pacific market was not a musical dead zone yearning for good rock bands.

RICHARD LEWIS: I know Kurt was a Cosmic Psychos fan; he was also into the Scientists and Feedtime and Lubricated Goat. The stuff that was happening in Australia in the late '80s had a big impact on a lot of the bands in Seattle; the term "grunge" was used to describe the Scientists in about '87!

Like the US punk underground, the scenes in Australia and New Zealand had benefited from being able to do their own thing without interference.

MICHAEL McMANUS: Pre-Internet, there was a large geographical isolation factor here, so only a handful of bands are known internationally. In a way that made the scene here a little self-sufficient, and full of its own quirks and deviations. Melbourne had the advantage of having really strong public radio and street press to promote the scene.

PAUL BROCKHOFF: There was literally a band on every street corner in inner Melbourne . . . Some of the pub owners got wise and settled into a particular night of the week. The Tote held the Friday-night pole position. Friday or Saturday it was the Punters Club and the Evelyn Hotel. Tuesday, Great Britain; Wednesday, the Bendigo Hotel. Melbourne's music scene was strangely divided by the river: north of the Yarra and south of the Yarra. South it was like big city, larger venues. North it was a hangover from its heritage as semi-industrial, semi-high-density living. Purely in terms of numbers of punters and dollar contribution to the economy, live music is bigger and more popular than football in Melbourne.

PETER FENTON: Sydney was more a Detroit/swampy rock sort of a place but had many elements, as there was many subcultures happening at that time in the '80s . . . Sydney was the place for everyone who had run from somewhere. For a place with such magnificent geographical power, it sure had a dark, beautiful heart!

During Nirvana's tour, corporate business as usual made its presence felt, which didn't enthuse the local bands.

MARK HURST: Just before we went on I needed a piss and went into Nirvana's band room. Got stopped by some people and they nearly didn't let me in there. One of them did a sweep of the room to make sure it was empty before they would let me in and they told me to hurry up and waited close by to escort me out again. That was all a bit ridiculous and insulting; what did they think I was going to do?

RICHARD LEWIS: We definitely felt like the crew and tour party were somehow arrogant. Before the first Palace show in Melbourne, Kurt's effects pedals went missing; they were stolen. We were accused, we were locked out of our dressing room while all of our bags and dressing room was searched by the crew, and they were dicks about it too. We thought it said more about their character than ours. We knew Nirvana had nothing to do with it, it was just a case of the role going to people's heads . . . it seemed like [Kurt] wanted to hang out, but we felt like he was in the middle of a protective circle, being dragged around and told what to do, we were sort of kept at arm's length. People were all of a sudden working with a "big band"—the biggest band in the world! And it went to their heads and people we had been working with for years and been friends with suddenly became assholes.

PAUL BROCKHOFF: I remember being told by a bouncer not to try and talk to the band, or we'd get thrown out, regardless of whether we had played or not . . . Nirvana were quarantined from the outside world . . . We were allowed to drink the water once they came on but that was all, and during the performance we weren't allowed to even look at them from our band room . . . I remember feeling a little ripped off because my chance to see a really cool band had been steamrolled by the very thing that kind of music was supposed to be anathema to.

SHAUN BUTCHER: I remember walking around backstage looking for them (after I had a bit of Dutch courage) but I stumbled in on the promoter counting money and was shooed away immediately.

An additional problem was that, for all Cobain's claims that he was merely dabbling, his heroin use had become significant, if not, at this stage, all-consuming.

YOURI LENQUETTE, *photographer:* On the Australia tour obviously I saw it. I warned him about drugs in general, this one more than any other. Having experienced it myself and having had a lot of people around me on that drug—some close friends—I could see when someone had taken it straightaway. We talked about it . . . he may have started to play with it in a dangerous manner, but it wasn't quite so critical as it became . . . In Australia, though he had already started, he wasn't that much into it.

Some had long realized there was a pharmaceutical issue, but talk of other sicknesses kept the waters muddied.

MARK HURST: [I] got the impression they were overwhelmed by the whole thing and not enjoying themselves, they seemed very tired and Cobain did not look at all well. He was very thin and pale and I remember thinking he was a sick man.

MICHAEL McMANUS: Kurt didn't look that healthy, and maybe a bit giddy on his feet. But I'd seen many musicians be a lot more messed up and pull off great shows . . . I was pretty young and naïve to that sort of thing at the time too, and probably a bit star-struck.

RICHARD LEWIS: We heard about it, we attributed his quiet distance to it. But it was not out there; it was a secret, only rumors and specu-lation. It never affected their performance, and personally we did not see any evidence.

SHAUN BUTCHER: Our drummer, who was a nurse at the time, was asked by someone if he could get anything for Kurt's "stomach prob-lems." It was well publicized in the media about Kurt's bad health in Australia and the inside information was that he was a junkie . . .

PETER FENTON: They found this "Dr. Rock"—that's how Pav de-scribed him—who helped medicate Kurt. The doctor involved is now a psychiatrist, but he prescribed this medication that totally did the trick with Kurt, and from all reports he was the best he'd been for a while—at his happiest and best.

YOURI LENQUETTE: It was true that he did get sick with stomach-aches. I remember one time in Sydney, they had played some kind of small pub—a really small place. After the show he was sitting in a corner with his various pains, I spoke to him: "Hey Kurt, what's go-ing on?" He said, "I don't feel good and the car to take me back, it isn't coming." I offered, "Look, Kurt, let's go, I'll take a taxi with you." We made it back to the hotel and suddenly he was OK.

Cobain's skewed perceptions of the world at this time, and another way he re-acted to his fame, can be seem in an innocuous remark made at one of the New Zealand shows.

JULES BARNETT, Second Child: Kurt walked out onto the stage, slung his guitar on, and said, "Hello . . . this is a song off our first al-bum, which you can buy at Really Groovy Records."

This jocular intro in New Zealand speaks volumes about the whirlwind that was compressing Cobain's existence. The young man of February 1992 was barely six months away from being so poor he lived in his car. Cobain genuinely felt no one had bought *Bleach* and that he had to tell these new crowds it existed. Onstage for the *MTV Unplugged* performance in November 1993, he still introduced "About a Girl" with "This is off our first record, most people don't own it," then continued to repeat almost these exact words throughout the 1994 European tour, even at Nirvana's last show: "This is off our first record. Our first record's called *Bleach*." Even with *Bleach* approaching platinum sales Cobain was hypersensitive to Nirvana's new audiences, wanting to remind the Johnny-come-lately crowds that Nirvana hadn't sprung into existence only when MTV paid attention. The audience in Australia confirmed Nirvana was attracting a pop clientele who knew nothing of the underground but all too much about "in" trends.

PAUL BROCKHOFF: I had been living in the forest in a swag for six weeks prior to the gig and had trouble adjusting. I remember not being allowed to stay in the band room and hating the crowd . . . I remember being offended at seeing such a large and young crowd that weren't into us and were all wearing Dayglo orange and white. Such were the fickle fashions of the time.

The shows were packed, with one show in Canberra, at the Australian National University, even involving a riot.

RICHARD LEWIS: It was sold out and there were just as many people outside as there were inside. The walls at the ANU are glass and some of the people outside smashed the glass wall to get inside, there was blood everywhere backstage, we were slipping around on it . . . My favorite was the Phoenician Club show in Sydney. It was the first show and it was a great venue. It had three levels all looking over the stage. People were diving from the upper levels, there was just this incredible energy in the room, the sound in there was huge, I remember the sound check: Kurt sat on the drum riser for about twenty minutes playing one note over and over, staring out from under pink hair. I thought it was interesting that Kurt's guitar was patched through an effect rack backstage and that the guitar sounds from *Nevermind* were programmed into it and controlled by his guitar tech. It sounded just like the record, only louder and wilder.

SHAUN BUTCHER: Selinas was an old '20s biggish hotel/motel venue just south of Sydney CBD [Central Business District] on Coogee Beach. It had balconies where you could watch bands from if you didn't wanna fight the mosh. I saw heaps of overseas bands there and thought it was a great choice by Steve Pav.

MICHAEL McMANUS: The Palace . . . It was a low, squat chunk of a building near the beach in St. Kilda built in the '70s I think . . . The room itself was quite square, with a balcony above the back half. There was a glassed-in VIP area on the first floor between the balcony and the stage, three bars, and another slightly smaller room at one side. It didn't have the greatest air-conditioning . . . They'd brought in a big PA for the night, I remember getting there and being impressed by the size of it . . . Even arriving at the Palace in the afternoon was intense; there were a lot of people outside hoping to get tickets, or even a glimpse of the band. Tickets were well and truly sold out, but I did hear of a few folk that managed to get in at the last minute. Our guest list had been full for a long time, and I'd had to knock back many friends who called in hope of getting on it . . . [there was] a real frenzy in the air.

The band snatched whatever rest or amusement they could amid the rigmarole of anonymous hotel life.

YOURI LENQUETTE: One night in Sydney [Kurt] had problems sleeping and noticed I was up late. He knocked on my door, asked me if I was sleeping and what I was doing. I replied I was listening to music so he asked, "Can I come in?" He was intrigued by all this music. He knew the Sonics, the great '60s Tacoma band, but I could play him dozens he hadn't heard of before. That's something that maybe gets forgotten sometimes with Kurt Cobain. He was a huge music fan, he loved music! It's not always the case with all musicians, but he loved listening to music . . . I had all these tapes of '60s garage music. He was really interested in that period, in that sound, but he didn't have a deep knowledge of it. I was a real specialist on that era and had all these compilation tapes I was carrying around when traveling . . . That's how we got to know each other, not because I was a photographer, but through a common love for music and the fact he wished to discover it.

RICHARD LEWIS: We shared a dressing room with the Cosmic Psychos or the Meanies—Lenny, our guitarist, had his twenty-first birthday at the Melbourne show; our manager got him a cake and Krist and Dave came to our room, sang "Happy Birthday," dug their hands into the cake with us, and had a drink to celebrate. Kurt was quiet, didn't see him much, I remember I had a chat about kangaroos and cricket and the usual first Australian experience stuff with him in Canberra . . . I think they went to a wildlife park to see some Australian animals. I saw Krist taking lots of photos, not of the gigs but of Australia, and I think they had a good time. Dave watched a lot of our shows and then when we played in Seattle later in the year he rocked up to our show at the Crocodile so I assume he liked us.

Once sound checks were done, activity would ramp up throughout the day of a performance, as the assorted memories of the bands that accompanied Nirvana on this tour make clear.

SHAUN BUTCHER: They opened the doors early, as it was getting unsafe outside, and thousands of kids rushed to the stage to be met with us onstage and our "'roo-in-the-headlights" look.

CHRIS van de GEER, Second Child: I remember at one stage Damien's amp fell over backward; I was looking at the side-of-stage roadie and indicating to him to put it back up and him just staring at me basically refusing to do it.

DAMIEN BINDER: I learned a valuable lesson that night: Don't ever, if you are supporting a big band, say "This is our last song!" I think that got us the biggest cheer. I, in turn, promptly told the crowd to fuck off, serious young man that I was. I hadn't yet developed my inimitable stage banter.

PAUL BROCKHOFF: There was condensation dripping from the ceiling, so people were yelling, "It's raining it's raining!"

MARK HURST: It was completely packed that evening. Very hot and humid.

MICHAEL McMANUS: Looking up at the VIP area and the glass was completely steamed up. I could see some minor celebrities trying to peer through the bits where the condensation was running down and found that extremely amusing.

All the background distractions were forgotten when the switch was hit: lights, action.

PETER FENTON: The rest of the night was defined by a sort of dark energy—I'm not really sure how else to define it. Suddenly it was showtime for Nirvana and we went into this caged mezzanine area and watched the show. They were an incredibly tight and powerful unit. One of my clearest recollections was that Kurt's voice was mountainous. It was everything that you heard on record and more. He had a quality to his voice that was quite primal.

MICHAEL McMANUS: They hit the stage with gusto . . . I remember thinking it was one of the best rhythm sections I'd ever seen. So intense. Kurt seemed more fragile, but still swayed and flung himself about the stage at times. It was hard to tell if that was just his persona or if it was other factors . . . I vividly remember the first few chords; they started playing "Aneurysm" and the room exploded. I was standing at one of the smaller bars about twenty-five meters from the stage on one side, and was immediately thrown back against the bar. The entire front half of the room was a surging mosh of at least six hundred or seven hundred people . . . I ended up watching about half of the show from behind the monitor desk on Kurt's side. I could hear his voice really well there, and it was enormous. I could see through to Krist on the other side and got a clear view of his lurching and bouncing 'round . . . There is a special something that bands get when they've played together for a while, and they had that and more. They were probably feeding from the electric energy in the room, and they were definitely sending it back in spades . . . Kurt laid his guitar against his amp stack after the last song and walked off while it fed back and the crowd went nuts . . . It's funny, the most vivid memory I have of Nirvana is heading back into our dressing room to grab a drink, and peeking out through the stage door at the rear. It was right near the drums, and I watched Dave scream and belt into his drum kit . . . It wasn't until then that I realized exactly how good a drummer he was, and how good his voice was.

SHAUN BUTCHER: A blur of bodies, sweat, flannies, distortion, and this little blond-haired bloke onstage screaming into the mike with a voice that seemed to come from another being. Actually, I was transfixed by Kurt probably because with the giant bass player on the other side of the stage he looked even smaller . . . I seem to remember Kurt stopping and jumping in the crowd at one point to rescue a girl getting manhandled by security . . . they looked like they could've been any young band from the suburbs, in any city in the world . . . They jammed for a bit between songs just like we did. Dave Grohl was an incredible drummer and Krist hurled his bass around like a toy. Never saw anyone play bass that low on a body before either . . . Kurt . . . his playing, his persona . . . played like a mongrel possessed and had a real connection to the crowd. He was just like any one of us punters watching, but he seemed to be purging himself of all the messed-up shit inside him by playing the way he did . . . Kurt attacked his guitars making sounds I never knew a Fender could make!

RICHARD LEWIS: Watching Dave Grohl playing drums at the Palace one night, he was like an H. R. Giger machine: an orb of energy and perspiration surrounded him, every muscle and tendon like pistons, he hit the drums so hard, they were on fire—they were wild, volatile! And Kurt was truly amazing, great sound, incredible voice, weird, wacky, irreverent, funny and he just put everything into it, it was amazing. Then when they pulled out "Something in the Way" it was pins and needles and goose bumps up the back of your neck type of stuff, hauntingly sweet and beautiful . . . Courtney came to Melbourne. Kurt came out onstage and declared, "Courtney Love is the best fuck in the world." . . . There was definitely a buzz backstage, maybe a bit of fear; she had a reputation for speaking her mind and being a little crazy . . .

In the aftermath of each show it would be a while before the venue cleared, the gear was packed away, and the bands could leave; the musicians, adrenalized and exhausted, simply had to kill time until they were finally set free.

SHAUN BUTCHER: Dave Grohl was at the side of the stage after we finished and gave me a thumbs-up, a nod, and something like "great show." I passed by Kurt backstage and initially thought he was someone's kid running around, but when he faced me I realized my mistake and blurted "G'day!" but he scurried off without acknowledging.

MICHAEL McMANUS: They went to their dressing room for a while, then Krist and Dave came back out onto the stage to chat to the backstage folk . . . once the curtains were drawn. I met Dave and Krist really briefly; they were easygoing and down to earth. It was pretty brief; as I said, there was a lot of folk around backstage, so it was all group conversation. I don't remember seeing Kurt then; he may have still been in their dressing room . . . I said something to Krist about his bass sound, and hanging the bass low 'cause we both did it. I said something to Dave about his vocals sounding great too. It's pretty hazy from there; we hung about drinking the rider and talking to a lot of friends. I do remember taking a peek in their dressing room at the end. I was a bit jealous about the food platters they'd had; there was one of various meats and sandwiches . . . and one with fruit. A few large bins full of drinks, too, most of which had probably been swiped by the band and crew for drinks back at the hotel.

RICHARD LEWIS: Kurt was charismatically quiet; he seemed almost meek until he hit the stage and was instantly transformed. There was a sense that anything could happen at any time; he was very unpredictable, he had a charm, a quick wit, he was wild and funny, self-deprecating, and a little cynical—he was really a big music fan and from the conversation I had with him seemed as though he was kind of nervous of people. Dave was the kid, the newest member in the band, an incredible drummer and very professional. He was approachable and easy to talk to, he was loving every moment. I spoke to him a lot, great drummer, great dude. Krist was solid, he was cool, he was hanging with his girlfriend, taking photos, having a laugh.

MARK HURST: The whole show was disappointing to me and a bit of a circus and I felt sorry for them, to be honest. They were in the eye of a hurricane, which did not look like fun.

By the time they reached New Zealand, a month on the road enduring the new pressures placed on the band meant they were visibly worn out.

CHRIS van de GEER: We watched sound check and yeah, they were pretty subdued and exhausted . . . I think the NZ show was on the tail end of their tour . . . We were possibly the last stop in Nowheresville . . . I think they did one or two songs as an encore and got the hell out of there. Kurt especially looked tired and depleted.

DAMIEN BINDER: At their sound check . . . I recall Kurt said, "I want CD-quality sound" over the mike to the sound person. He seemed a little annoyed at what he was hearing back through the monitors. I don't recall much, if any, interaction with them. It lingered with me that he/they seemed rather sullen and exhausted and played that way too . . . Their performance was workmanlike but lacking any great enthusiasm. As I said, they looked like they weren't that thrilled to be there.

THEO JACKSON, Second Child: Kurt looked very cool and seemed totally unapproachable or interested in any goings-on around him. I was really struck by how upright all of Dave Grohl's drum kit was and how high he set his hi-hats . . . Krist gave me a smile and hello prior to the show and got on with a conversation with a lady who was part of their crew. I thought they played fine and didn't seem tired to me. Just doing the business. They were certainly committed at sound check to getting things right for the punters. The other thing was how good their light show was! Plain color behind them changing from time to time, red and blue, I remember. It's always been my benchmark for lights since.

JULES BARNETT: I remember watching them sound checking "Drain You" when we walked in, across the main floor with our gear. Kurt was wearing a super-cool pair of shades . . . lime-green frames . . . Their set was OK enough, however not very energetic . . . Krist jumped around in his bare feet while Kurt was much more subdued . . . After the show I went upstairs anyway to look around. Nirvana's dressing room door was open and I saw Dave sitting on the floor, back against the wall. He looked at me for a second and then back to whoever was talking in there . . .

Just one month into their first tour as globetrotting superstars, their lingering impression was of a band standing on the edge of the world looking over with trepidation. Yet it didn't mean things weren't going reasonably well.

NAOKO YAMANO: On February 13, 1992, they came to Osaka. On the day that they arrived, we took them to a restaurant and ate dinner. Kurt looked to be having a good time in Japan. The next day, Nirvana played a big venue and we also had a show at a club. Their showtime was earlier. The drummer Dave said that the band would come to our show after their show onstage. Much of the audience followed the band and came to our club! The neighbors of the club claimed many people were hanging out on the street.

All Nirvana had to do now was await DGC's plan for what to do with Nirvana's accidental rise to global domination.

16.0

Festival Season
June to September 1992

In the aftermath of the Asia/Pacific tour, DGC Records could now begin treating Nirvana as a multimillion-dollar revenue stream. They set twenty-two US dates for April and booked European festivals for the summer. It was a chance to establish Nirvana as one of the handful of megastars with the power to pick and choose top billing at the world's most revenue-rich events . . . Except Nirvana was exhausted. They'd toured ceaselessly since August, so DGC had to accept the US tour being canceled. The band mates went their separate ways and began finding their own methods of dealing with having suddenly become unbelievably famous.

GEORGE SMITH: The pinnacle of fame was when "Weird Al" Yankovic did a Nirvana song! It sounds kinda trite, but it's true: when you've gotten to the point where you are a cultural icon to the point that people can make money by making fun of you, that's the top. They had risen to a cultural peak where [Kurt] was worth making fun of.

ABE BRENNAN: Krist lived in Tacoma, the town My Name ended up living in, so I'd see him around; really nice guy. I remember one time after *Nevermind* came out and went to number one, I was at a show in Seattle, I saw him outside and I wasn't going to say anything to him because I'm sure everyone bothered him all the time, but as I was walking by he called my name and we talked for a bit. The success didn't seem to have changed him; still a really nice guy.

DANA HATCH: Krist Novoselic came to see us at Rock Candy but passed out with his head on a table before we went on (we were the first band) and stayed there until he was awakened and politely asked to leave as the club was closing.

SCOTT VANDERPOOL: I remember Krist being fairly drunk most of the time—of course, so was I . . . My fave Novoselic story was at the Neil Young/Sonic Youth show at the Seattle Center Coliseum . . . Sonic Youth had invited half of Seattle to their dressing room . . . The promoter decided the party was getting out of hand and sent someone in to take all the beer away, which they loaded on a cart . . . I was out in the hall hitting on some chick or something, and all of a sudden Krist comes running out of the door as the cart is going down the hall . . . "Nooooo!" He ran and jumped/flew onto it Superman-style, yanking it out of the hands of the guy pushing it, and by the time it crashed into some double doors at the end of the hall, he'd drained a beer.

JOSH SINDER, Tad: I first met Krist Novoselic at his new house at the time in Greenlake. He was having a party the day after Nirvana played on *Saturday Night Live*. Kurt and Dave were not there, but Matt Lukin, Dan Peters, and Mark Arm, whom I met for the first time at this party, were all there. Tad brought me over . . . "This is our new drummer, Josh," to which Mark replied, "Ha, hope you can cut it!"

RYAN von BARGEN: Saw Dave Grohl at a Shriekback/Sky Cries Mary show at the Moore Theater in 1992. I saw him in the lobby surrounded by a bunch of people. I started to head his way, then thought, Man, he has enough people hassling him already. As I started to turn away I hear him say "Ryan!" as he came through the semicircle of people that had him surrounded. We ended up walking off and chatting. After the show, we met back up backstage and then ended up going to a club called the Vogue on Second Avenue, which was nearby.

ABE BRENNAN: At another show in Seattle, Chad and I commiserated for a time, because we'd both been kicked out of our bands; I ended up getting back in My Name before we started putting stuff out with C/Z Records, but Chad never made it back in Nirvana.

Cobain, however, no longer had a home in the Northwest. Instead, he and his new bride were ghosting around L.A. rental properties, hotels, and rehabs while evading crowds.

JOSH HADEN: I was working at the Rhino Records store (no longer exists) in L.A. with the drummer of Treacherous Jaywalkers and one night around closing time Kurt and Courtney came in to shop.

JON WAHL: The next time I bumped into Kurt was stepping over his passed-out self, leaning up against Courtney on a couch backstage at the Hollywood Palladium at a Mudhoney/Claw Hammer gig. Not an entirely talkative fella.

GERARD LOVE: We met up with Kurt and Courtney after our show in Los Angeles. They invited us over for lunch the next day, but we had to travel on to Vancouver. In Seattle, Krist and Shelli offered to do some laundry for us, which was very kind.

Nirvana regrouped in April to record for a single with the Jesus Lizard.

DAVID YOW, The Jesus Lizard: [We] opened for Nirvana at Maxwell's in Hoboken—a full-on fucking blast! They kicked ass. We kicked ass. And it was our first meeting, so we'd made new acquaintances, which is always exciting. Kurt and I were talking about stuff and kind of mutual back-patting each other when I suggested we do a split single much like Sonic Youth had done with Mudhoney, but instead of releasing it through Sub Pop, we would put it out via Touch and Go. Kurt loved the idea and we started working on making it happen . . . The next time I saw Kurt was in Denver at the Gothic Theatre and he came up to our van to make sure that we were still doing the seven-inch. We were.

Cobain's persistence of vision never faltered; these shows were a year apart, April 1990 to June 1991. It was a further year until the song was recorded and almost another year until the single emerged.

DAVID YOW: They signed to Geffen, and that slowed the process somewhat. Kurt was insistent with the label, but the label limited the number of copies to be released: 50,000 for the USA and 50,000 for the rest of the world . . . When it was first proposed, Nirvana was just a band on an indie label. There was no kind of commercial thinking at all when the thought was an infant. Once Nirvana became the biggest band in the world, we all just sort of figured, "Cool, that can't hurt."

Nirvana didn't need the money; they wanted to reconnect with the underground and took genuine pleasure in shoving the spotlight onto bands they loved.

STEVE DIGGLE, The Buzzcocks: We were on a two-month tour of America—we had a lot of old secondhand TVs behind us showing soaps, films, bit of politics, bit of porn, nine of them every night. Drove the roadies mad! . . . We're playing in Boston, we do the show and at the end there's a great bit where we get to smash the screens so they implode, smoke. Did that in Boston, came off, it was around the time "Teen Spirit" was number one and the *Nevermind* album was number one. I came off a bit breathless and someone said, "Nirvana are here." [And I'm like] "Oh, bring 'em in!" So, stepped out of the dressing room and straight in front of me is Kurt. We started talking—he loved the way I smashed the televisions. "I smashed a television once!" he said, so we went on discussing how to smash televisions because I told him how I'd gotten an electric shock in Germany—was using an old steel mike stand, probably last used by Bill Haley! Hit the wrong bit but luckily thanks to my adrenaline I managed to get my hands off and after that I thought I needed to treat these with some respect. So I discovered that when you throw it at the screen, the base of the mike stand, if you flick the screen, the screen will implode and smoke'll come out. It took me a while to learn it but I perfected it! Kurt loved it! Dave and Krist were there, they were fans of the band—nice to meet us, they said they had our records, we said we'd heard their records. We got on really well, had a drink, they said, "Come and do a tour with us!" . . . We told them to stay in touch and that when they were in Europe we'd do something there. We met again in Japan but we were all pretty exhausted and out of it. It was straight after a show— we said there'd be another time.

Cobain forgot nothing; having last seen the Buzzcocks in February 1992 the call came in late 1993 to tour in 1994.

His artistic drive was aimed in directions other than playing with Nirvana; in 1992 Cobain worked with director Kevin Kerslake on four music videos then posited a lengthier endeavor.

KEVIN KERSLAKE: We talked a bit about it in L.A., then I went up to Seattle and spent a week at Kurt's house just going over tapes every day—that was also when we shot "Sliver." But that wasn't the first session we'd done—we'd gone over tapes in L.A. too. I can't remember if I pressed them to shoot the "Sliver" video or it was scheduled . . . but it may just have been convenient to shoot it while I was up there. I had a Super 8 camera with me and all three guys were around so we ended up shooting it in Kurt's basement . . . As the band started to recover from *Nevermind,* and started setting their sights on the future, a lot of different things came into our conversations. Obviously there were a lot of B-sides and various singles that were going to find their way onto an album, and they'd started doing *In Utero*, but we started talking about the film . . . We never got into real deep detail about what the film was going to be because when you're going to do a long form like that and there's a lot of different material, you just start by gathering things, putting things together. You don't say, "I know exactly what this will look like in the end." Kurt probably appreciated this more than anybody—definitely more than any record executive—that when you're making music, when you're making films or doing anything like that, it's a process. You go into a studio and start putting chords together—you don't preconceive what chords you're going to put together until you pick up the guitar and you do it. In the same way, for a film, you just start gathering all this material and you start putting it together.

Nirvana met up in June ready for ten of the biggest shows they would ever play.

GERALD LOVE: The shows were either arenas or festivals . . . I would have imagined that their appearances at the festivals would have been in front of 30,000-plus on average. Maybe more. The arena shows were in Ireland, France, and Spain . . . I would guess the average attendances at being around 10,000 per night. There was the palpable sense of the band breaking through on a massive scale. We had already played at the Reading Festival the previous year and had done a few supports in big rooms, so we were accustomed to the different experience of playing a large stage in front of a sea of people, sometimes in broad daylight . . . The first few shows with Nirvana, in Dublin, Belfast, and Paris, were indoor and with the four walls and the roof they were all loud and powerful affairs. At times the sound of the room can overwhelm the stage in big cavernous halls, so at the beginning I found it difficult to hear what was happening on the stage, especially vocals. We were playing pretty loud at this time and our original setup was to be pretty far apart on larger stages. We soon learned that it was better to set up close and to turn down just a little. At outdoor festivals, the sound escapes into the air and it can give you the feeling of being weak and exposed, as if nothing is coming out of the PA. With the experience you learn to get on with it, to do your best, and have faith that the sound man is doing his stuff. The buzz is definitely dispersed at a larger gig, and it can feel nonexistent at a festival in daylight, but a great band can make it happen anywhere and Nirvana were at the top of their game . . . Kurt seemed to be with Courtney most of the time on the tour, which was completely natural as they were a young couple expecting their first baby, and Dave and Krist mostly hung around within the general entourage. I remember Krist's partner, Shelli, being aboard for a section of the tour . . . A few of their crew were Scots and this probably had the effect of making their touring party feel a lot closer and familiar to us. Nirvana had obviously made a quantum leap in popularity so security between band and audience was naturally tighter, but that's the way it goes with success. Backstage, as I remember it, was an ego-free zone, very friendly, efficient, and calm . . . The first time I met them [in 1991] . . . I spent most of the time we spent together chatting with Kurt, and what struck me most was how unlike he was of the image I had in my mind of the stereotypical North American. His physical size and his demeanor felt more Glaswegian to me, more European; he was small-framed and wiry. I remember him as being warm and friendly; the chat was mostly about our respective home lives. During the tour [in 1992], it was obvious that something had changed; he was more distant but still friendly whenever he engaged. On the tour, Krist was super-friendly, wisecracking, and alert, Dave, from what I remember, was a little quieter than Krist but smiled a lot and liked to joke around with the crew . . . They were a great team, the band and the crew, and there appeared to be no hierarchy.

All was well, given that one key issue wasn't in plain sight, thanks to a little careful management.

GERARD LOVE: There was a doctor in the touring party, and Kurt had been taken to hospital with a suspected overdose in the hours after the Belfast show, so everyone was aware of the situation early on. On a social level, we didn't see Kurt around a whole lot on the tour, but he did make the effort to hang out a couple of times. When you're aware of the reality of someone's condition it's easy to spot the symptoms but if I hadn't known that Kurt had a drug problem I don't know if I would have spotted anything particularly unusual, especially in the performances where he seemed completely engaged.

The band took another six-week breather before the now-legendary Reading performance.

GERARD LOVE: It was a stormy night and Reading was dark and muddy . . .

ROD STEPHEN, Björn Again: We were doing a concert in Melbourne and Nirvana were playing down the road. They were looking for something to do afterward and stumbled upon our gig. We didn't know they were there; we were onstage. Then after, our guy who was selling the T-shirts—I don't know how many we had, twenty-five or something—and the guys from Nirvana bought the whole lot and told him how much they loved the gig before they left. Our guy ran upstairs saying, "You'll never believe who just bought all our T-shirts!" . . . Next thing we know, there's a phone call through promoters and agents saying we've been asked to play at the Reading Festival. We knew the nature of it and though Björn Again had always had this Spiñal Tap–meets–ABBA vibe in some regards, we were nervous if we were right for the festival. Ultimately, though, we understood it was more or less on Kurt Cobain's insistence that we were being asked, so we thought,

Let's do it! . . . I positioned "Smells Like Teen Spirit" at about the twenty-minute mark just to establish Björn Again and our identity . . . I thought we needed something to nail the last ten minutes of the show and that guitar riff was the perfect thing. We launched into it and the crowd moshed like you wouldn't believe—going mental. Absolute candy . . . Prior to the gig I'd spoken to Dave Grohl about us doing our version . . . Ordinarily you wouldn't dream of doing a song when the main act is going to do it later on: He said, "No, no! You've got to do it! It'll be great!" So we went ahead and it really capped off the performance. Krist was down in the pit with his camera, people could see him taking photos of us. In context, it was great light and shade for the day . . . the crowd made the connection to the three guys from Nirvana who, by the end, were almost onstage with us showing it was all right and they were having fun here. I was pleased to see Kurt doing that because before the gig when I went up to talk to them it was noticeable that Kurt was in the dressing room but there was this sense that he didn't want to talk—nothing was said, but I didn't wade on in there. Dave and Krist came out and I think they were kind of putting a bit of a protective layer between anyone else and Kurt. They were chatty, told us they wanted us to be there, but it wasn't Kurt bouncing out. I didn't ask about it, but I got that feeling things were going on. To me it felt like shyness. I know that he wanted Björn Again to be there but maybe he would have felt a bit uncomfortable chatting. He must have been bombarded with people just wanting to talk, people wanting information. Maybe part of the problem, he felt he had to be on full form to deal with people at all hours of the day . . . Kurt mentioned us on the liner notes of *Incesticide*; he says something about how he realized he'd reached "wunderkind" status when he had the power to bring Björn Again to Reading.

Hurt by the UK media's intrusive speculation on his drug problem, Cobain choreographed Nirvana's show as a parody of his supposed frailty.

ROD STEPHEN: Kurt was wheeled out in the wheelchair with the blond wig—I've always speculated what the wig was about, part of me thinks it was about the blond singer in ABBA—wearing the wig . . . it made sense, "the blond singer in the band." Iconically, Agnetha is the standout in ABBA with her blond hair. Kurt is perhaps usurping that; that blond wig is a statement, what else was it meant to be?

He moaned a riff of "The Rose"—the title theme of a film about a star self-destructing under the impact of fame—before mock-collapsing. Most journalists sang praise for the festival performance without seeing that Cobain had made a sarcastic attack on their negative coverage of his personal life. Meanwhile, some observers saw nothing special.

IAN PROWSE, Pele: When you're actually near someone, though, you realize how prosaic it all is. Unfortunately when stuff is filtered through the lens of the gutter media it takes on a certain sick glamour that isn't actually there. When you see them walking across a muddy field backstage they are simply Walking. Through. A. Muddy. Field. It's so dull . . . Our show was a bit of a nightmare too; the bad weather curtailed our gig so we didn't manage to explode . . . I watched them for thirty minutes, yes. They were truly awful . . . Our roadie Nick Leech was a notoriously bad-tempered drunk (we called him Killer as a nickname). He went straight up to Kurt after the show and told him they were rubbish before being bundled off out of the enclosure.

Nirvana broke again from the corporate plan, canceling their November US tour. Instead, they were motivated to make their first mainland US appearances since the New Year by their opposition to an anti-gay-rights ballot measure in Oregon and to the Erotic Music Law in Washington. Neither was a topic that endeared them to mainstream audiences, but Nirvana saw fame as valuable only if it stood for something.

JON GINOLI: The only communication we had with Nirvana at the time was through Jello Biafra, who was a fan of ours. He was at the No On 9 benefit that Nirvana played in Portland against an anti-gay measure on the Oregon state ballot. I thought, Wow, how cool! Guns N' Roses would never do that—a popular rock band had never taken such a pro-gay stand at that point in time. Jello told us he was going to emcee the show, and I asked him to ask Nirvana if they minded us doing a gay version of their song as "Smells Like Queer Spirit." He said he spoke with all three of them together, and said they were cool with it . . . We did the song the way we did it for several reasons. *Nevermind* did not come with a lyric sheet; we couldn't tell what half the lyrics were. We thought, what if the lyrics were slurred and indecipherable because they were all about being gay? That's when I came up with the title "Smells Like Queer Spirit" . . . One reason we wanted to do the song was that even though we *loved* it, it was so ubiquitous that we were getting sick of it.

Cobain spoke of the Pansy Division cover as a real pleasure; his band had been baiting homophobes all year.

JELLO BIAFRA: Jon wasn't sure they were going to release that song because they were afraid of being sued by Nirvana—or, more likely, Nirvana's management or record company . . . The bill was set and they added me as emcee and "rantologist"—for all the bands involved it was a very important issue, but Nirvana knew full well that they were such a huge band and so many of their fans were jocks by then that it was a great opportunity to wake people up and educate them about tolerance and gay rights, against this kind of attempt at back-door coups by religious-right bigots. I heard grumbling in the crowd throughout that they had no idea this was a "pro-faggot" concert, but I'm really glad that those people may have woken up a few months later realizing we were right. I mean, a lot of the pre-hardcore punk

bands in San Francisco, L.A., and New York, among other places—
there were many of them, many people in them, who were gay and
out and people didn't bat an eye. It was just people we knew . . .
Finally I'm introduced to Kurt and I could tell he seemed shell-
shocked, very. Not knowing when the next shoe was going to drop . . .
I couldn't resist anyway asking him why he didn't name his baby after me—I used to use that as a joke way of congratulating people on
their family, but he couldn't tell I was joking. He may be the only
person I've ever asked who thought I was serious—it was real evidence that he was just in shock at the position he'd gotten himself in.
Later on he warmed up; all of a sudden he lit up like a Christmas
tree telling me about this photo he had of a Republican headquarters
in Southern California on fire—we had a good laugh about that and
I chased for ages wanting it for an album cover until I realized they'd
used it as part of the collage inside *In Utero* . . .

Cobain and Nirvana made repeated statements, whether subtle or otherwise,
regarding the issue of gay rights; Cobain appeared on MTV in a ballroom gown, Novoselic French-kissed him on *Saturday Night Live*, the "In Bloom" video dissolved
into cross-dressing hilarity, and Cobain accused Axl Rose of sexism, homophobia,
and racism . . . Nirvana helped to bring a downplayed strand of the underground to
the fore.

JON GINOLI: People noticed all right. It was a big middle finger to
hard-rock stupidity. Rock stars were not supposed to make fun of themselves and not take their image seriously. They got away with it because they were *huge*. I remember too when they wore dresses for the
"In Bloom" video—that was a gesture that had major impact, to so
blatantly fuck with gender. It wasn't about rock-star cool . . . Kurt sang,
"God is gay" and "Everyone is gay." Axl sang "Immigrants and faggots, they make no sense to me," and that they "spread some fucking
disease" . . . I don't think much pro-gay sentiment was happening in

rock until the '90s—punk rock got more macho as times went on. Originally punk could be aggressive without being macho. Part of the homophobia stemmed from the idea that people thought gays weren't making or listening to that kind of music, because almost no one playing it was out of the closet. Part of the reason I formed Pansy Division was that I knew that wasn't true. Our mere presence (along with queer peers like Tribe 8 and Team Dresch) forced the issue out into the open the same way that Bikini Kill did for women and feminism . . . Someone told me that *Maximum Rocknroll* magazine were afraid to give us bad reviews because they didn't want to look homophobic, but because they were the home of hardcore they were never too enthusiastic, either.

GARY FLOYD: If I had just been singing about gay issues only, I would have been pegged as more of a "gay singer" than I am. I think I was more "a singer that was gay" than "a gay singer." My songs were multi-issue . . . I'm happy Kurt felt gay topics were part of what was going on. I loved him for that. However, most punks could not care less that Bad Brains did some despicable homophobic bullshit . . . Never apologized . . . Never said "We are sorry," anti-"bloodclot faggot," crap . . . They do not care a fucking thing; maybe Kurt did . . . Most so-called punks don't give a shit. I didn't get shit because I didn't take shit.

While Nirvana dedicated time to their political commitments, the whirlwind of attention that had followed *Nevermind* was now lashing the Northwest scene from whence they'd come.

BEAU FREDERICKS: Things changed a lot for sure. Before, no money. Afterward, big money—in Seattle, at least . . . Once the money hit, then the Seattle attitudes changed and there wasn't as much of just playing music for fun anymore.

LEIGHTON BEEZER: We actually had some major label approach my band Stomach Pump . . . The A&R person told us we would be big stars and would have total creative control. I said our band was totally improvisational, and he held his finger up to his lips and said, "Shhhh. I don't give a shit. You guys are from Seattle and you play loud grunge. You'll sell and become huge. So whaddya say?" I smiled, shook his hand, and said, "Yes!" He told me to get my band into the studio . . . he would fly us down to L.A. and advance us a bunch of money to make a record. So, I asked the guys from the Thrown Ups: Mark, Steve, and Ed, to join me as a hoot. We showed up at the L.A. studio two weeks later wearing our old flower costumes. The A&R guy called us motherfuckers and kicked us out of the studio, and that was the end of that deal . . . It did get pretty ugly, but funny at the same time. I remember Mark saying, "But we have a great cover of 'San Francisco'" while the A&R guy shouted obscenities . . .

DUANE LANCE BODENHEIMER: The music scene was great, always something to do every night of the week . . . Not much attitude—not really. Everyone happy to play, not trying to be famous or doing it to become a rock star; they were just doing what they did—that's what I really appreciated about Seattle. It changed after the whole Nirvana thing; it seemed like this band and that band were just there to try and get a record deal.

ROBIN PERINGER: People saw Nirvana make it big and wanted that as well. As a result, everyone thought they could achieve it, even the labels. It seemed to me that every little shitty band that got a small blurb in the *Rocket* started to believe that they were hot shit. I don't know, it somehow created a competition that hadn't really been there before.

Thanks to the ludicrous hype surrounding Seattle, what had been a close-knit community of musicians, venues, and labels found itself drowning under a wave of out-of-town wannabes.

RYAN LOISELLE: Everyone hated the popularity. C/Z Records would get boxes of demo tapes in the mail and I'd hang out with the guys running the label. They had a tape deck and they're on the fifth floor of some building in Seattle and they'd put in a tape and within the first three seconds just: All right. Yoink! Boom! They'd throw it right out the window. Everything. Three seconds—if it wasn't amazing right now they'd throw it right out the window and it'd hit the streets out on the avenue. But there seriously were boxes of tapes being sent to labels in Seattle.

JOHN PURKEY: I was given the box of demo tapes sent to the Central Tavern—people were sending tapes into clubs—so 1993, they asked, "Anybody want these?" I took it. There were some good demos in there, I went through everything myself and found some good bands . . . There was a huge number of bands came in, a lot of clubs opening—there were bands moving to the Northwest to try and get a record deal. Two bands from Hawaii lived in Tacoma—they moved *here*? From Hawaii?!

TIM KERR: When Nirvana "hit" in '91, it broke the dam and you had the industry machine come in full force plastering their template and guidelines for the future generations, through mainstream magazines, to follow so they could be successful in this "new industry." This, of course, led and always leads to another generation of smaller pockets digging deeper into the real DIY ethic, which still happens to this day . . . the scene at the time was more a community that was having to deal with a big influx of "fans" now showing up. They all had a great sense of humor and reality about it, which I thought was a healthy attitude and I respected them for it. I still do.

BEN MUNAT: That's what made the Nirvana happening so extraordinary; the pop commercial world cracked into the "Fuck you we don't need your money" world and there was a crazy period of swirling opportunism and confusion; some people got hurt . . . With the unexpected smash success of Nirvana, many labels of all stripes swooped down on Portland looking for the next big thing.

DANIEL RIDDLE: Portland . . . changed radically once Nirvana broke nationally with a hit record and all of a sudden, like most musical towns at that time, became a hypercompetitive snake pit filled with money-hungry vampires representing the record labels and many so-called musicians who could barely conceal the fact that they were plagiaristic chimps looking to prostitute themselves.

For most bands there was no revolution; the mainstream wasn't buying punk, it was buying a version that didn't need a parental advisory sticker.

RICK SIMS: The biz didn't change for us. We were still on the same label (Touch and Go) as we'd always been and getting the same push/support as we always had. I kind of doubt we were going to fit into that mainstream punk rock world anyway. We were too crude and our attitude was a little too fuck-you to all of a sudden start dealing with some major-label schmo. I think most bands still had to fight hard, as in having to schlep around in a van for two months playing one-night stands and sleeping on friends' floors.

JOE KEITHLEY: Punk rock was still an obscure art form that never really got its due—no complaining, but that's the way it was. It was too political, too offensive, and it wasn't safe for kids . . . The punk rock movement is akin to the hippie movement, but 1 percent of the size because with the hippies you did have bands who were big and were saying stuff—even the Beatles and the Stones, the giants, they got into that culture. You never had those big bands in punk. The biggest was the Dead Kennedys, who might draw a thousand people when the MC5 had been drawing fifteen thousand and preaching revolution.

PETER IRVINE: The idea of a genre called "alternative" was new, and not yet mainstream. It started as an actual alternative that was not popular. So it was strange and mystifying to watch "alternative" catch on as a genre term, become "Alternative," and then become mainstream . . . Touring actually became more difficult after *Nevermind* . . . there were suddenly a lot more bands trying to play the same venues, with the result that it became economically more challenging to tour. We were suddenly competing for gigs with bands that had label tour support and booking agents. They weren't necessarily drawing bigger crowds at first, but they were able to get booked places we couldn't. With tour support, those bands could afford to play gigs for little money, while we had to turn more to the folk scene for gigs that would pay enough for us to survive.

KEVIN RUTMANIS: Grunge as a label and a genre was always repellent to me—that stuff was all so conservative musically. Like nostalgia. I was really hoping music was gonna progress more. It looked good there for a second. Until grunge. We referred to Nirvana as "the N word" in the Cows . . . it just seemed more and more like they were shitting on bands like ours and what we thought we were trying to accomplish. The whole "corporate rock sucks" thing seemed like total BS, as they were behaving exactly how corporate bands always behaved. If they really were against corporate rock, they wouldn't need to say it on the cover of *Rolling Stone*. It looks like they were saying that they themselves sucked, which within that context they did! They had this amazing chance to do something really creative and different. But they just did what everyone does. Played big giant boring arena shows at any price. I have no problem with "corporate" rock. I have a problem with lazy, half-baked complaining, however . . .

Nirvana's effect wasn't entirely negative: the flood of media attention, record-label attention, new audiences, and sales meant that the dream of surviving solely on music did become reality for many musicians.

DANA HATCH: All the old musical barriers seemed to collapse . . . More people developed wide-ranging musical tastes rather than living and dying for one particular genre. Nirvana's success brought indie rock into the mainstream and made it easier for low-budget indie bands to record and tour. Record labels, caught unawares, starting throwing a lot of money around. We got a development deal with Warners that probably wouldn't have happened otherwise. It also gave mainstream rock fans a point of reference for weirder music.

MARIA MABRA: [It was] literally the biggest music scene in the world, it was awesome being in the middle of it . . . from one day listening to your fellow musicians playing bars and clubs, then it seemed like overnight they got that one sweet deal and they were gone. That's awesome because that's kind of the dream—as punk as I can be, I don't give a shit what anyone says when something like that is offered to you, a chance to take off, then you're going to do it—I don't care how punk-rock you are. What they did changed music forever, just these Northwest boys . . . Washington is a huge state, it's largely barren, it's redneck, it's hillbilly, it's got these few big towns they call cities, then other than that it's coal-mining towns. Those guys, Nirvana, were small-town . . . these small-town boys getting a chance to be huge . . . And it's awesome. It gave us all a chance, it cleared the playing fields and made us all think, Yes! We can do this! That we could be artists and do great things.

Sub Pop was in the best financial shape it had ever been in, given a percentage from *Nevermind* as well as Warner Bros. Records' buying a stake in the label. This didn't, however, mean a lavish lifestyle just yet.

STEVE MORIARTY: They tried to have this businesslike facade about how brilliant they were, but they were fans and just about to go out of business when Nirvana signed to DGC and kept them going . . . They had some strange firings—there was a lot of controversy there for a while, then Bruce quit and Poneman sold part of it to Warner Brothers and now they're living large.

KURT DANIELSON: It became necessary for us to leave Sub Pop in order to preserve our friendships with Jon and Bruce, as well as to protect our relations with the label as a whole. The situation had become just too untenable in terms of financial security . . . had we known how soon *Nevermind* was going to go gold and then platinum, saving Sub Pop's fortunes, we would never have left . . . Considering the circumstances, there were no wrong moves, just moves with unknown consequences. All too soon we would find out what those consequences would be: the most poignant one being how we would miss the intimate, supportive, always-creative contact with Jon and Bruce—something we never found elsewhere.

MARK PICKEREL: Sub Pop wasn't exactly "broke" at the time . . . I should know, I was working there. We just mismanaged our money as we tried to manage our passion and appetite for so much music, and with commerce and economics, that can prove to be a difficult juggling act! . . . You hear about how the band Kiss used to show up to their first shows in a limousine that they would have to wait to pay for till after they collected from ticket sales? That's exactly how Sub Pop appeared on the scene! It's also why they almost went bankrupt right before the success of Nirvana's *Nevermind*. Nirvana's huge breakthrough helped put Sub Pop back on the map with sales of *Bleach* entering the pop charts for the first time. It didn't hurt that Soundgarden and Pearl Jam were having the best sales of their careers at the same time, leading to a new interest in their earlier titles associated with Sub Pop.

RICK SIMS: My friend and collaborator suggested I give them a call and solicit them to be in the singles club . . . I think the deal was $500 and the money to produce the record and a split of the profits. Nothing very sexy about the arrangement business-wise. Great to be a part of that series, though.

JOSH SINDER: We recorded the *Salem/Leper/Welt* EP as a final obligation to Sub Pop. I don't think Sub Pop had much money, and they were not really supporting Tad, although we did do one last tour under the Sub Pop banner . . . The band drove in a 1993 Lincoln Town Car and the gear traveled in a Ryder truck that ended up smashing through a Taco Bell. I don't think Nirvana's success brought more music to Sub Pop; it brought more bands to Seattle and probably annoyed Jon and Bruce to no end with them all begging to be on the label.

Meanwhile, Nirvana was still barely performing—there'd been just thirteen shows since the Asia/Pacific tour; only two of them in the mainland United States. They were all over the news at the time but barely anyone had seen them play. Keeping with the trend, the two remaining US shows they would play in 1992 were both secret gigs.

BEAU FREDERICKS: Bellingham is about one and a half hours north of Seattle . . . There was the rumor that Nirvana was going to play that started a few weeks before the show. I didn't believe it and ignored it, focusing on getting ready for our big show. I think that Nirvana was going to play from the beginning and I think it was booked as such. Carver Gym [at Western Washington University] was only used for the biggest campus shows . . . Nirvana played great that night and was used to big shows obviously. We were just scared.

CHRIS QUINN: It was a secret performance at a Mudhoney show. I'd lost interest in them after they went to Seattle and became really popular . . . all they played was stuff from *Bleach* and odd singles and stuff—they didn't do any of the big hits. And that was the perfect show for me—nostalgia only a few years in.

FRED STEUBEN, Saucer: Megan Boyce, who booked the gig, told us she had a surprise for us but didn't tell us what it was . . . I watched Mudhoney and Medelicious sound check and noticed a big, black drum kit sitting off to the side of the stage. I figured it out right away that Nirvana was in the house. I'll never forget Megan walking us down the hallway and leading us up to the stage in a bright silver dress. It was like, Holy shit, here we go!

HENRY SZANKIEWICZ: It was mostly obscure stuff and it took about two songs in for the crowd to realize who was onstage. A slow roar built up from the crowd. I don't know if it was shock, Kurt's shorter hair, or what . . . I cannot gauge time after all that has passed. Maybe twenty minutes . . . Not much moving about by Kurt. Dave was an animal, though . . . What stands out was that they were the biggest band in the world at the time and we were lucky to be so close on the side of the stage to take it all in. More like an event to witness than anything musical at that point . . . What was most amazing was that three kids about ten years old went up onstage and took over bass, drums, and guitar. Just banging away on it. People started chanting, *"Smash it! Smash it!"*

CHRIS QUINN: I was standing on the side of the stage with Matt Lukin and they sent these kids out to strum their instruments and me and Matt were trying to get this kid to smash Krist's bass! He whacked it on the ground; one of the control knobs went spinning out across the stage but he didn't break it.

SCOTT HARBINE, Saucer: We tried to have fun playing but had no idea how to deal with the natural slap-back reverb from the gymnasium. We played very reserved and were pretty conscious of the poor sound . . . Nirvana seemed pretty solid and unconcerned. They sounded very good. Kurt seemed a little bored from my vantage at the side of the stage. I talked briefly to an old friend who was their guitar tech, Ernie, and he mentioned that Kurt was pretty "wiped out" from touring.

FRED STEUBEN: Most of the people backstage were scenesters, friends, and local press . . . I remember Kurt and Courtney sitting on a bench in front of the lockers and the local press surrounding Krist with cameras and notepads. A huge entourage had come up from Seattle. There were people in the showers .I heard someone had put a fucking kayak in the pool, pretty nuts. I didn't meet anyone from Nirvana that night; the backstage party was pretty chaotic and none of them seemed approachable.

HENRY SZANKIEWICZ: They did not look too cheerful. A friend offered to take a photograph of me with them but I declined. Didn't want to bug them. That is the vibe I got. I do remember Courtney Love smoking inside the gymnasium behind the stage. First of all, no smoking allowed and secondly, don't put your cigarettes out on the carpet. Western Washington University's varsity football team were security that night and were about to throw her out. I had to explain to them who she was . . . I also remember her staring at my wife with a mean look. Just a glare. I guess she didn't like the skinny blond competition. Of the three, Kurt seemed very distant, Dave and Krist the most cheerful—if you could call it that. I think they were tired of all the fans and hanger-ons by then.

SCOTT HARBINE: We had heard that Mudhoney stole our beer, so we went to the Mudhoney/Nirvana locker room to steal some back . . . I saw a friend named Michelle, who knew Cobain and was good friends with Steve Turner. She told me she wanted to introduce me to Cobain and I followed her into the shower area. We overheard an argument between Cobain and Love and I saw him sitting down under a shower. Love was telling him he was a "fucking baby" and he was staring down at the floor. When Courtney saw Michelle and [me], she told us to "get fucking lost." We turned around and left as she continued to yell at him . . . He looked pretty depressed and defeated to me.

17.0

Politics, Pressure, and South America
October 1992 to January 1993

While a rarities compilation—*Incesticide*—was readied to capitalize on Nirvana's unexpected fame and the Christmas sales bonanza, Nirvana was dispatched abroad once more. Sound commercial planning had gone into the show in Buenos Aires on October 30, 1992. An audience of 45,000 promised significant money, which, along with the strong attention from Argentine media, would create a major boost to local sales. It was also the first show to indicate the scale Nirvana could now play on regularly if they so wished; this wasn't a festival, this was a stadium-filling audience just for Nirvana.

GABRIEL GUERRISI, Los Brujos: In the middle of the *Cannibal* tour we were invited to play with Nirvana. I must make it clear that at that moment we felt worried because the B-52's were coming and they were the ones who we wanted to play with, but we couldn't; we felt happy either way.

This is a telling point; at home, Nirvana still claimed to be an underground band that just happened to be on a major label. In South America, however, there was no knowledge of the US underground, and the band existed only as a mainstream phe-nomenon.

As a well-established Argentine favorite, Los Brujos was chosen to add local fla-vor. With two gold albums they were, in local terms, bigger than Nirvana at the time—part of a new wave emerging.

GABRIEL GUERRISI: The scars and blows of very aggressive military governments gave way, after the well-known War of Malvinas, to a new democratic period . . . The "democratic spring" generated an op-timistic environment that, in the music field, made the protest groups of the '70s obsolete and began to usher in "strange new hairstyles," groups of optimistic pop . . . bringing in punk and New Wave that could only be listened to if smuggled in during the military period . . .

Nirvana chose who would play right before them.

GILLY ANN HANNER: I got home from work, my roommate says, "There's a message from Kurt Cobain on the answer machine." He was saying, "Hey, this is Kurt, I wanted to know if you wanted to come play a show with us in Argentina—give me a call." I was shocked, ex-cited, wow . . . I called him back, he said, "Here's the manager you need to contact to set up how much you want to get paid—call him, or if you've got a manager get them to call him." We didn't have a manager so I spoke to the people at the booking agency. I didn't know what to ask for because we'd never played a big show or been trans-ported anywhere—we'd only played shows we'd booked ourselves and driven to in our van. It was a little daunting. I didn't really know what I was doing but I wanted to play along so I threw out a number: "We want $5,000, plus all of our travel expenses." They said, "Sure, that's fine." We were in the middle of a tour that I'd booked, so half-way through the tour—we were in New Mexico—we got on an air-plane, marked up our equipment and shipped it, then flew down to

Argentina. Crazy. We'd never done that before. We did it all ourselves, no management, no booking agent . . . they had a handler come meet us at the airport, got us to the hotel and told us where we were supposed to go and all that stuff [and we were all] "Wow, we have our own rooms, and a person showing us around! Exciting!" It was fun!

There were good vibes all around. These were happy people lost in one of the world's great cities.

GILLY ANN HANNER: We went and partied; Kurt wasn't really hanging out—he was feeling really ill so he wasn't going out at night with everybody, he was just in his room and not out there. Frances [Kurt and Courtney's daughter] was there when we played in Portland with Nirvana a month prior; they had a motor home they were traveling in but they didn't have her in Argentina—maybe back in the room or home with a nanny. But Courtney, Krist, Dave, they were all going out—and the crew—we went out to bars, did karaoke and fun stuff the night before.

ELIAS ZIEDE, Pirata Industrial: Well, well . . . I remember the magic and mysterious night when Novoselic, Grohl, Courtney, and two of Calamity Jane played with Pirata Industrial in La Cueva—a hard-rock club downtown in Buenos Aires! These nice rock people, we're all onstage together with motorcycle gas tanks playing "Blue Monday"! Punk! New Wave! It's just our fans, friends, groupies! Wild energy—hell of a party, there's Pampa cocaine for anyone who wanted, there's so many drinks we could keep going all night long!

Buenos Aires started well enough, with the audience responding brightly to Los Brujos—the local heroes.

GILLY ANN HANNER: They had a following there; they struck me as carnival music, Red Hot Chili Peppers a bit—party. They had big puppets on the stage with them, things you'd see at a parade . . . everyone got riled up for them. Then it was our turn to go on.

GABRIEL GUERRISI: What happened was a combination of things; Los Brujos were at the peak of our climb and the 45,000 people knew our band very well so expected much of our performance . . . Our show was really good and, as we say in Argentina, "The stage was left on fire." Then it was the turn of Calamity Jane, an unknown band with a more quiet intensity; people had been excited to see Los Brujos, then there was the anxious desire to see Nirvana—they wanted everything to occur *now*! It had nothing to do with Calamity Jane being women, it was because they were in between two acts who were very heavily promoted in Argentina . . . The scale of the intolerant audience was minimal but enough to be a major rejection . . . it was exceptional behavior and had nothing to do with manly stereotypes.

GILLY ANN HANNER: We maybe got through one song before we realized the crowd's reaction—it seemed possible—"might" be negative. There were things flying at us! Chunks of dirt! Ice! Coins! A lot of spit coming up on the stage! I started taking it in. Up there you usually take in the crowd a little bit but mainly focus on what you're doing, singing, hitting the right notes but then it was really obvious—I thought, Oh my God, they hate us! They're booing us off the stage! Throwing shit at us! I just stopped, looked around, looked at my band mates and I think I walked over to the side—Courtney was over there. She said, "Go back out there! They love you!" They clearly did *not* love us! She's like, "Come on, it's punk rock, get out there!" So I went back out, started playing again, and made it partway through a song . . . My sister [Megan] and I had been on a US tour and played a lot for weird crowds, but we were completely bowled over. I can't imagine what the new members were feeling. Marci [Beesecker] was hiding behind her drums trying not to get hit by stuff. Megan was just walking around the stage ignoring it and doing a pretty good job of it too, not really reacting. But we were like, What?! They're being assholes!

They're flipping us off! Look—there's people actually pulling their pants down, taking their penises out! All kinds of stuff, it was unbelievable, all kinds of crazy shit . . . Also, I've come from a place where there was a lot of stage diving and slam-dancing at shows and throwing things, bottles, hitting people. I'd taken to stopping the shows and saying, "Guys, you need to calm down or we're not going to play—people are getting hurt." I really wanted women to be able to come up and be in the audience without getting pummeled by some big huge punk-rocker punching people—trying to see a band when someone's elbow is hitting you in the eye, it sucks. I'd done that throughout the tour and the shows that year. On this scale though, I wasn't used to it. Everyone is flipping out partly because we keep stopping—it's fueling the fire. So my band mates are like, "Don't stop playing! Just keep playing! Don't talk to them! Go, go!" I thought No, not cool, so I yelled obscenities through the microphone at the end—don't remember what I said but I was very angry, shocked. My sister and I ended up smashing our guitars on the stage and letting them feed back. We left the stage—we might have played two and a half songs.

Nirvana decided to retaliate.

GILLY ANN HANNER: We went off, we're all really upset. The crowd is booing and yelling. There was a big gap . . . partially because we didn't complete the set and partly because Nirvana stalled after that; they were upset and didn't like how we'd been treated. So they stalled as long as they could. Then it was time, they had to. Courtney came and told us, "Hey, they were going to not play because of how you got treated but they're getting $250,000 for this show—they can't really not play . . ." I totally understood, I didn't expect them to not play just because of us. They went up, played, Kurt was . . . he never engaged with the audience anyway, but he was real standoffish even for him during that show—they didn't play their hit song, they pretended to play "Teen Spirit" but never did, they did a big noise jam, they really dragged it out.

Cobain plainly stated his intentions in that warm-up jam, announcing, "I can shit on the stage; I promise to shit on your head . . ." As well as teasing "Teen Spirit," they killed the clock by starting songs with weak runs then restarting. Cobain replaced a verse of "Come as You Are" with "Hey-hey-HEY-hey!," barely mumbled "Beeswax," then walked off, leaving Grohl to hammer on toy drums while Novoselic deadpanned, "We're one of the most exciting bands on the face of the planet, as you can see . . ." At another point Krist roared, "Tu me gusto TECHNO!" and impersonated techno over Grohl's improvising . . . This was music as mockery.

The locals weren't aware it was deliberate; all they saw was a famous junkie putting on a bad show.

GABRIEL GUERRISI: It was not seen as a band being annoying; but everything did seem to be going without direction, Kurt not knowing the lyrics or the riffs, sometimes he walked off to the backstage and seemed absent from the show, a lot of things were said about it. People read the performance as a little bit crazy rather than seeing it as an angry one . . . It was known that Kurt was in rehab, so anything could be expected. Nobody related the tone of the show with the incident involving Calamity Jane until *Incesticide* came up . . . It was not one of the best; I was a little bit lost among the jams and songs that I didn't know. I don't like stadiums either, where the sound comes and goes with the wind.

The bands waited for the audience to disperse.

GABRIEL GUERRISI: There were food stains on the wall as if they had made some jokes. Kurt looked like a zombie, like somebody lost floating to some other place, no relevant attitude, like a person in suspension . . . Courtney Love was in a bridal dress . . . After the show, some of Los Brujos went to greet them. Dave and Krist came in a good mood, made some photos for the press, and left.

GILLY ANN HANNER: After the show, my band mates got slaughtered, drank a lot—got ill. We were stressed out . . . the next day we had to go back home and were faced with this large hotel bill from having eaten snacks out [of] the minibar. I think anyone who isn't used to big hotels has done that: "Look at all this free stuff!" We had no money, we were in trouble, the minder, this woman who had been so nice to us the day before, wasn't nice to us at all and told us, "You shouldn't have done that, it was really ugly when you yelled at the crowd, women don't do that." She really got on my case . . . So, we went back to our broken-down van, our broken guitars, all our crap in New Mexico . . . Then our band imploded once we tried to go back on tour. We'd lost heart . . . our guitars were broken, we couldn't get the money we were supposed to get because we didn't have a bank account in the name Calamity Jane and that's who the check was made out to—it took us three months to get the money. We were broke, bummed out . . . Argentina was our last show.

Until Buenos Aires, the two October shows had been the only times in 1992 Nirvana declined to play "Smells Like Teen Spirit." From its debut, from 150 known sets, the song was excluded only 11 times. Four of those times (Pukkelpop; October 3–4, 1992; the Mia Zapata benefit) were when Nirvana was a substitute or secret guest. Without the pressure to please, they would drop it. Sometimes it was done in anger, as in Buenos Aires, or in Chicago on the *In Utero* tour when the gig went so badly the audience booed and Cobain yelled at them for throwing wet T-shirts onto his pedals. MTV's ever-despised management was also a factor; having refused to play it at the MTV Video Music Awards, Nirvana pointedly sliced it from *MTV Live and Loud*. In November 1993, when negotiating *MTV Unplugged*, the band skipped the song at two performances before hauling the support bands onstage to demolish the tune as a jam. In a non-coincidence, the final two times the song was evicted from the set list were Nirvana's last-ever shows. Cobain was a musician; he voiced his dissatisfaction through music by killing his most famous song—a vengeance running to his last days.

January 1993; Nirvana headed to Brazil for their first shows since the Buenos Aires debacle. This was the Hollywood Rock Festival, an event named after a cigarette brand, Hollywood, that was itself named after one of the grand symbols of American mainstream culture. It was apt, given the local audience were aware of Nirvana only as part of the larger wave of US culture sold into the market.

CASTOR DAUDT, Defalla: MTV Brazil has just started to air, and everybody was waiting for the "next big thing." Turned out that it was us, and from the States, it was Nirvana . . . When MTV Brazil opened, in 1990, that was the starting point for every good Brazilian rock band of that time.

EDU K, Defalla: By then we were not living under the dark clouds of the dictatorship that shredded the country apart in the '60s; we were free to enjoy our Coca-Colas, MTV, and rock concerts.

BRUNO CASTRO GOUVEIA, Biquini Cavadão: Until 1990, all the music production was brought by the five major record companies: EMI, RCA, WEA, CBS, and PolyGram. Most of the records were released here, but sometimes it took nearly a year to have new albums, especially from minor labels and [the] punk movement.

Nirvanamania had already hit Brazil.

IVAN BUSIC, Dr. Sin: Nirvana were already taking control and becoming the number one band on the planet.

EDU K: They were, for sure, a huge crossover band here; pop heads as well as rockers and metal heads loved them. It's like, we, the cool people, were aware of them a long time before the "Smells Like Teen Spirit" video set the world on fire, but after they took MTV by assault, there was no resisting their power and panache!

ANDRÉ STELLA: The first time I heard Nirvana was in 1991, on

MTV . . . I tell you, it was a punch to the face. I couldn't believe what I was hearing . . . The next day, in college, my friends were all asking me, "Did you hear that band Nirvana on MTV last night, did you hear that song? The song kicks ass and the singer looks like you!"

The audiences didn't view Nirvana as unique. They were only one among many world-class American cultural invaders.

CASTOR DAUDT: There was a kind of "Nirvanamania," but there were other bands considered just as important like the Red Hot Chili Peppers, Metallica, Soundgarden, Pearl Jam, Alice in Chains, Extreme . . . Like I said, MTV Brazil was our connection with the "music world" and we saw all these great bands on a daily basis and listened to them on the radio.

The Brazilian bands chosen to play the festival were all significant regional stars.

EDU K: We were traveling by bus to a city for a gig, an' we opened up the newspaper an' learned that we were voted by public choice to play the festival!

CASTOR DAUDT: It was the perfect festival for us to be in, because we were the Brazilian band that had most in common with these bands and we had just released a very well-received album . . . Apparently the people who were producing that festival thought the same, Defalla was the perfect band to open the festival and represent the new Brazilian sound.

IVAN BUSIC: Dr. Sin was new, but we were already very popular among the rock scene in Brazil because of many other bands we played with before, such as, Platina, Taffo, A Chave do Sol, Anjos da Noite . . . We are still a reference when talking about technical musicians and so in the beginning it sounded kind of weird to put our band on the same day as Nirvana, a very straight rock band.

BRUNO CASTRO GOUVEIA: The show was in the Morumbi Stadium (aka Estádio Cícero Pompeu de Toledo), a soccer stadium adapted for the concerts. It was complete[ly] filled with nearly 60,000 people. I think that there was a ten-meter gap between band and audience . . . Biquini Cavadão opened for Alice in Chains and Red Hot Chili Peppers. After my show and Alice's, I was hidden at the back of the stage to see RHCP performing . . . Suddenly, Layne Staley from Alice in Chains arrived . . . When I looked back again, Kurt and Courtney were also there, just behind me! I spoke only a few words with Layne, the usual thing: "How was the gig?" And I thought, Look at this calm guy with his big wife, a bit shy and quiet: he's Kurt Cobain! Then security arrived. A big guy asking us in English to move from there. Kurt didn't like this and started arguing with him, so did Courtney. I was predicting a fight between them and decided to leave the place . . . I believe we were not allowed to stay because the RHCP show had special effects—they used helmets with flames throwing from the top of their heads, for instance. I believe the security was not only a question of keeping the place clean. I left them discussing and arguing with Kurt and Courtney . . . Kurt was serious, not smiling as I recall, but didn't seem angry or upset, or even uncomfortable. Just a quiet guy.

The next evening, however, was close to a reprise of Buenos Aires—this time with no gallant justifications.

IVAN BUSIC: I guess that for that concert Kurt was a little bit crazier and he couldn't sing or play guitar very well . . . The studio album with "Smells like Teen Spirit" had such a great sound that we were really shocked; Dave played the drums very well and the bass sounded OK, but Kurt was on another planet . . . I remember Flea from Red Hot Chili Peppers going onstage with them to play trumpet—oh my God . . . That's OK. It's only rock 'n' roll.

At its nadir, Novoselic threw his bass at Cobain and stormed off, only to be hustled back on once reminded of legal obligations—he didn't bother re-tuning. Cobain, meanwhile, mashed cantaloupe melon over his guitar.

EDU K: Kurt couldn't get those harmonic notes he did in "Teen Spirit" right anytime they played it. I thought it was hilarious!

Nirvana capitulated, swapped instruments, and ran the clock down jamming old pop songs. In an echo of Buenos Aires Cobain mauled "We Will Rock You," singing to the audience, "We will fuck you" instead.

EDU K: I'd never expected Nirvana to do to a "tight" show an' they lived up to their legend. The Chili Peppers, on the other hand, did their "tight" an' bored usual end-of-the-tour show. They lacked energy and danger an' I was disgusted by that an' threw all my Pepper records an' T-shirts in the bin when I came back home . . . Lemme tell you, when Nirvana swapped instruments an' played Duran Duran's "Rio" I literally creamed my pants, ha-ha! It was incredible. It's not your usual daily thing that you'd see a band falling apart and being so careless an' wild onstage . . . It seems to me that some people in the press or in the crowd were a li'l pissed off in a sense because, fuck, they've waited that long for this? It was really mixed, in fact. I myself think the ones that didn't get it missed the point of it all and I absolutely loved both shows an' thought they were real genius!

Edu K's positivity is matched by a very clear-sighted assessment of what was witnessed.

EDU K: It was pretty clear that they were collapsing but, crowds are like Romans at the Coliseum, are we not? Who doesn't like to see public figures falling apart in public? I mean, Nirvana was . . . this gigantic wounded animal, raw an' alive an' bleeding in front of everybody: if that's not what legends are made of, I don't know what is! To me, at that moment in time, Nirvana was scratching their names with broken an' bloody fingernails in the Rock 'N' Roll Badass Blackboard. It was the stuff of nightmares an' forever unforgettable . . . They had a lotta guts to do what they did an' also, a show is not only about goin' onstage an' reproducing your hits: these guys were the real deal an' like the Pistols in their heyday, they were def floggin' a dead horse in front of thousands.

CASTOR DAUDT: It was Nirvana. They had a sort of "free pass" to do that kind of stuff.

Darker rumors circulated about the reasons for the poor show.

IVAN BUSIC: We had the chance to talk a bit with Dave before the concert and, of course, he was a very nice guy. Unfortunately, Kurt was kind of "too fast" to talk to anyone, if you know what I mean . . . After a bit we saw him backstage very, *very* slow, if you know what I mean . . . Still, he shook our hands and was nice to us right before our sound check.

CASTOR DAUDT: I remember people talking backstage, and back in the hotel, saying that Kurt had taken a lot of pills, like Valium and stuff . . . the media saw it as funny and punk. We all had listened to Nirvana stories. I think nobody saw it as sad or bad.

BRUNO CASTRO GOUVEIA: Brazilians believed that Nirvana was uncomfortable with the fact that the festival was sponsored by a famous brand of cigarettes. Therefore, they did a non-show, played with anger, spite, ironically changing instruments, asking Flea to play trumpet . . . The critics loved it! It was all against the system! The public didn't understand at all. There were some boos.

ANDRÉ STELLA: The festival was sponsored by a brand of cigarette and Kurt said he didn't know that when he came to Brazil to do the shows. And he didn't like it. I think his attitude on the show was because of that.

Given that Nirvana had been sold as hell-raising pranksters, everyone simply thought what they wished, whether that meant Cobain's demons were on display, it was a protest gesture, or it was just rock 'n' roll. Heedless of what people had made of his performance, Cobain simply retreated into seclusion and would be seen only fleetingly before it was time for the Rio de Janeiro gig.

JARDEL SEBBA, *Fan*: On the Tuesday before I had the chance to meet [Kurt] and Courtney (and Frances). They were the only act in this festival who were not in Copacabana (they were in São Conrado, which was a much more isolated neighborhood), but they used to hang out with the other bands, and I had the chance to meet them leaving this hotel. I was seventeen years old and had a fanzine . . . The curious part is that he was wearing the exact same clothes he was then wearing at the gig four days later.

ANDRÉ STELLA: We met Kurt a couple days before the show. My friends and I went to the front of the hotel where Kurt was staying and we waited there for him for a long time until he finally appeared . . . He was lovable, pleasant, and attentive with me and my friends. He talked with us a little bit and said they would play new songs at the show. He really paid attention to us.

Kurt may have been cordial to fans but this didn't mean he had undergone a full recuperation.

EDU K: I saw Kurt stretched out on a sofa in the common backstage area with Frances and Courtney; he looked worse for wear and rather sick.

CASTOR DAUDT: Kurt was always with his wife and had a large group of people around him. Very inaccessible.

EDU K: Krist seemed to me like a very relaxed guy riding the eye of a hurricane thunderstorm. He was just hanging around backstage an' came to our dressing room to share a J. We had a good laugh because I told him, "Man, Kurt looks so much like a fucked-up version of Shaun Cassidy!" He said, "Fuck yeah, that's what we've nicknamed him in the band!"

CASTOR DAUDT: Krist was very kind and seemed happy to be there. He came to me in our dressing room and asked me who I was and which band we were. I explained that we were from southern Brazil, that we had opened the festival and were big fans of Nirvana . . . We had big laughs comparing Kurt with Shaun Cassidy and I presented him with very good southern Brazilian marijuana.

The relatively orderly show disappointed some, given Nirvana's burgeoning reputation for chaos.

JARDEL SEBBA: Based on the news that was coming from São Paulo, everybody was a bit frustrated, as they did not change instruments nor break any of their equipment.

There was still enough fire, however, for one further defacement of rock as TV-friendly product for family consumption . . .

BRUNO CASTRO GOUVEIA: Simulating masturbation in front of the cameras of Globo TV (the major TV network in Brazil).

EDU K: Kurt took his cock out an' did a mocksturbation scene in front of TV Globo's (the biggest TV conglomerate in Brazil) cameras and it was all the rage all over the country. That moment in time, to me, was probably the last stand of punk-rock antics and teenage angst and alienation ever in the history of pop music . . . One thing is really funny, though: when we played São Paulo, there was a moment onstage where I was butt naked except for a sock on my cock—yeah, it was a Chili Peppers dark-humor pun. We were always the ones to pull that kind of party trick outta our hats an' it caused a real commotion in the media. So, if you check Nirvana [and] L7's performance in Rio you can tell that they were influenced by that.

South America brought Nirvana face-to-face with a choice: they could embrace a future as a stadium-filling Guns N' Roses style carnival, or they could walk away. These shows were Nirvana's window into a world where they were known not as interlopers from the underground but simply as one more bunch of American celebrities, kith and kin of bands they would never keep company with by choice. Nirvana made their call and would never play for such large audiences again. These three shows formed a bloody-toothed demonstration of Nirvana's refusal to be packaged like Hollywood cigarettes or sold as light entertainment for primetime TV while, simultaneously, being a visible display of Cobain's drug-frayed state. Regardless, it still thrilled those lucky enough to share it.

GABRIEL GUERRISI: In Argentina it remains a legendary show.

EDU K: It still resonates in my heart till these days.

CASTOR DAUDT: I'll never forget that moment in my life! It was a very happy moment for us.

IVAN BUSIC: We felt very honored to be sharing the same stage with such a huge band as Nirvana . . . We had a lot of respect for them and Hollywood Rock is still in everyone's memories. Such a great festival.

18.0

In Utero
February to September 1993

Between February 1992 and October 1993—the peak of Nirvanamania—Nirvana played only twenty-one shows, with just nine in the United States. Media hype, however, focused instead on the good news that a new album was imminent. Tentatively entitled *I Hate Myself and I Want to Die*, renamed the equally sardonic *Verse Chorus Verse*, it was ultimately to emerge as *In Utero* in September. Of the fifteen-day recording session, the band played together for only three or four days with half the songs having been written before *Nevermind* back in 1991. It was hard to tell if Nirvana, as a creative unit, still existed.

At least the band made a clear statement by choosing to record with a man with impeccable underground credentials, an ally in Nirvana's retreat from the mainstream: Steve Albini.

RICK SIMS: Steve was an invaluable friend and accomplice to the band . . . He gave us the money to record our second record, agreed to release it on Ruthless (although he convinced Touch and Go to release it instead), produced and engineered the *Que Sirhan Sirhan* record for a dollar! We fought and argued like crazy a couple of times during *Que Sirhan Sirhan* sessions about guitar levels or some shit . . .

but that dude was/is great. But be warned: if you hang or collaborate with him he won't couch his opinion. Bottom line is yes I trusted him yet sometimes needed to sort my own direction from what he thought it should be. Plus it was cool recording with him because [you] could hang out at his house, where he made great-sounding records, brewed Café Bustelo, and cooked orzo for us.

TED CARROLL: Albini was perhaps one of the best people I ever met in the world of music. Opinionated. Absolutely, but at the same time . . . he came out to L.A., stayed in our shithole of a house, recorded our first album, cooked us dinner (he is an excellent chef) and was a fun, actually sweet, guy. He even offered for us to stay at his mom's house when we were in Missoula, Montana. We stayed at his place in Chicago several times—he had a BBQ for us—and *In Utero* seemed to be all the rage the second time we were there and recording our second (and last) album. Steve pretty obviously *hates* major labels, and I think he was offended by major-label interference with the record . . . not with Nirvana at all . . . He liked the album and said quite emphatically it was the record they wanted to make. Not him or his influence. But I never got the impression that he was upset or mad about anything. He was pretty detached from the stuff he did in that he saw it as the band's baby . . . not his.

Wrangling over the album continued all summer, with Albini taking heat for Nirvana's choices. The presence of older Cobain compositions—"Dumb," "All Apologies," "Pennyroyal Tea"—disguised how noisy his newer material was, a continuation of the style of songs recorded the previous April; the new sound wasn't just the result of production decisions.

BLAG DAHLIA: The follow-up proves they were already on their way down. "Scentless Apprentice"? "Heart-Shaped Box"? Give me a fucking break. Sorry, kids, but rumors of this band's "Beatletude" were grossly exaggerated. A one-trick pony, but hey, it was a good trick.

CHRIS QUINN: I think the Melvins have been the kind of band that Nirvana wanted to be—they've maintained credibility, they've maintained creativity, they make a living . . . The Melvins have released thirtysomething records, Nirvana's got three real records—and the last one, whether you love it or you don't, it's still a transitional record—it's not the statement *Nevermind* or even *Bleach* was. It's just a record made by a guy with drug problems. When you "make it," there seems to be a lot of stuff that has nothing to do with music, but there are people who are impressed by all that stuff and confuse that with what makes the music.

The album succeeded in reconnecting Nirvana to the underground community by virtue of simply trying to be no big deal.

Cobain was still paying a lot more attention to visual concepts—every Nirvana single or LP after "Smells Like Teen Spirit" would feature either his art or would interpret his ideas. He also poured energy into the videos.

KEVIN KERSLAKE: With *Live! Tonight! Sold Out!* Kurt and I spoke about a much more evolved film than what it ended up being in the end. It was going to include more of an interior sense of what it was like to be in the band. Obviously we never got to the point where that part was shot. What ended up coming out was sort of frozen in time—very much a one-note film, which shows a certain frustration about being stuck in the limelight, and is expressed in a charming sort of brattiness. This frustration was a common topic at the time in my conversations with Kurt, but the film wasn't supposed to just be about that, alone.

The video as it emerged is therefore a fair indicator of Cobain's mood in early 1993 even as he had others executing the vision.

KEVIN KERSLAKE: Source-wise, this was all VHS tapes. Keep in mind this was all pre-DVD, so we're looking at Hi-8 tapes and VHS. Crap quality, but charming for sure, and hoping that at one point we'd contact the sources to get as close to the master footage as possible. But the early stages were just going over those tapes in the TV room . . . What would happen is Kurt and I would get together, we'd go through a batch of tapes, and that would typically happen over one or two days. I'd take all the tapes back and then Steve McCorkle (the editor) and I would just start editing them together . . . So, you notice where you start seeing a song in one setting and then it cuts across to another setting? Those decisions just happened to come about because there was a great show in Buenos Aires, there was a great show in Dallas, a great show on some TV show in England . . . So do we use fragments or do we just choose which of those is the best? It was just throwing ideas against the wall and seeing what stuck. Steve had his ideas, Kurt had his ideas, I had mine, and hopefully we all arrived at the same conclusions. We weren't working for a deadline—as far as I remember— that was any more dramatic than we typically were under, but I do know that we never ended up shooting some of the other stuff that we had intended to. Whether I was going to travel with them on the road or shoot in Seattle, we just never got to it . . . Kurt knew what was on his shelves, so handing those off to somebody—I'm sure I did notes at the time—but I could have asked him, "What's on these?"— basically, if he liked a particular song on a certain tape, to flag that. But it's our job, mine and the editor's, to look at everything in their entirety—you do your homework. Kurt probably did his homework too . . . When it was time to start shooting and adding some of the other things, *In Utero* was coming out, and the scheduling got tight, and they had to do the press for it. Lots of other things were going on that competed for time.

Cobain had one other studio engagement that spring.

JONATHAN BURNSIDE, *producer:* It's not easy reminiscing about making the album *Houdini* with Kurt Cobain and the Melvins. Bad

communication, drugs, major-label profiteering, rehab, schedule blow-
outs, backstabbing, and album miscrediting . . . it was a devil's album.
I hadn't worked with Nirvana in a studio, but I had mixed live versions
of "About a Girl," "Spank Thru," and "Molly's Lips" for them. [These
tracks appear on the "Sliver/Diver" single and elsewhere.] Kurt was
coming to San Francisco, ostensibly to produce the Melvins' major-
label debut, *Houdini*, for Atlantic Records, with me engineering and
mixing and Billy Anderson assisting on some of the sessions. *Houdini*
was the fourth album I had recorded and mixed for the Melvins.
Kurt, Courtney, Frances Bean, and an au pair showed up in a white
Volvo and parked in front of the graffitied doors of my studio, Razor's
Edge Recording. Kurt told me later he hated that car. It shined con-
spicuously amongst the rust piles lined up along Divisadero Street.
Like a lot of San Francisco, the street gentrified during the dot-com
boom, but in the early '90s, it was Cocaine Alley, crack dealers slouch-
ing in front of the BBQ joint and storefront gospel church. I saw men
shot dead on that block. My studio was near the corner, in the same
three-story Victorian where Anne Rice wrote and set *Interview with
the Vampire*.

What played out in San Francisco was a tragicomedy.

JONATHAN BURNSIDE: Kurt was a sweet, gently-spoken guy to be
around. The surrounds didn't bother him and he seemed like he'd
be more comfortable in an edgy neighborhood than in an upscale
one. He never had a dime in his pocket and he still owes me pizza
money. Most days at Razor's Edge, he'd sink into the couch and stare
wistfully at the covers of the albums that adorned the studio's walls.
Like Nirvana's earlier label, Sub Pop, they were small to medium-sized
companies: Boner, AmRep, Nettwerk, Sympathy, 4AD, Rough Trade.
The records had all been recorded without label oversight and with

little hype. Sadly, Kurt was out of it. He would take long trips to the restroom, clutching his embroidered Mexican pouch. He'd emerge wobbly, his pupils pinpricks. Then he'd have a nap on the couch. A week into the recording, we were throwing around overdubs and the Melvins asked Kurt to play guitar on the song "Sky Pup." Until then, I wasn't aware he was going to play on the album, and a left-handed guitar wasn't around. Worried about Kurt changing his mind, I quickly handed him the Fender Mustang I had been given by Helios Creed, guitarist from the acid-metal band Chrome. It was charred from a meth-lab fire on Ashbury Street and smelled bad, but it tuned up. He noodled around on the upside-down guitar and I twisted the knobs on stomp boxes. At the end of take one, he shrugged and handed me back the Mustang . . . At times, the sessions were a dog-and-pony show, with the record company and press attending. Evelyn McDonnell from the *L.A. Times* joined us while we were tracking the songs "Hooch," "Joan of Arc," and "Sky Pup." "The session moves quickly because Crover, Osborne, and Burnside have worked together for so long they can step into each other's heads," she wrote. "Cobain is the somnambulant lord of this strange manor. He sleeps, he hardly says a word, he misses whole songs and lets Burnside run the show." As the three weeks of tracking drew to a close, sometime in March, April '93, I became dissatisfied with Kurt being credited as producer of the album and broached the subject with the Atlantic Records A&R rep. He said in a conspiratorial whisper, "I've been at the sessions. I understand how you feel, but he's *Kurt Cobain*!" Kurt was there in name, and that was obviously the important thing for the marketing department. Never mind if his head, heart, or soul weren't anywhere present. Never mind that he seemed very depressed. At that point, I saw where things were coming from and where they were going. After tracking seven of the album's songs, I mixed them, mainly on my own. Melvins drummer Dale Crover sat in the most. During the fine adjustment stage, I'd call in Kurt, the Melvins, and whoever else was around. When Kurt heard the studio reverb I had automated to blast out the already huge sound I had captured on the double snare hits of "Hooch," he made his only comment on a mix: "Wow! That sounds awesome!" Objecting to the album credits had made me persona non grata, and when the album came out in September '93, I didn't receive a production credit. Worse, Kurt and the Melvins were credited for all my mixes, without my name listed. I don't believe Kurt was party to this. His name was just brand recognition, and he knew it. He seemed pretty over caring about the machinations of a sleazy industry. But I took this major-label con-job hard. Before this, I had believed in albums I recorded and in the people I worked with. Getting my mixing credits stolen felt hubristic and vindictive. I couldn't believe that a band I had worked so hard with would do that. Now I realize that it's nothing unusual. Lesson of the day: don't piss on the hype parade. And get credits in writing before you twist a dial. *Houdini* had a relationship body count for everyone involved. I guess no one looks back on that time too fondly. A talented, lovely guy was spinning down and there were those spinning right with him, getting strung out with him, abetting him, profiting from him. But over the years, you have to let go. Life's too fucking short. I hope everyone involved in *Houdini* has made their peace with it.

Cobain would make one more visit to a studio session in 1993, popping in at Hole's sessions for their debut on DGC Records.

ERIC ERLANDSON: It wasn't a day in the park. It all came with a scenario that I was hoping to keep out of the studio. But it was a lot of fooling around, and nothing serious. I personally did not want him on our record, and I'm sure he didn't want to be on it either. Luckily he just mumbled over two tracks and none of it was usable. We had some fun jamming, though.

While Sub Pop was becoming a major-label subsidiary and the last big names of the grunge explosion had moved on, the rest of the Seattle scene had a chance to retrench and laugh at their recent history.

TERRY LEE HALE: The only ones having the impression that the "scene" had been hollowed out were the music-business sharks trolling the clubs looking for another clone Nirvana/Alice in Chains/Pearl Jam/Screaming Trees band. There seemed an overabundance of those kinds of bands actually, but the real bread-and-butter bands (i.e., Chemistry Set . . .) that made Seattle such a great and diverse place to live in were at least working in a city suddenly loaded with venues and receptive audiences.

RYAN LOISELLE: *Nevermind* and all that, Mudhoney being popular—everyone here, 99.9 percent of people thought it was hilarious. They were making fun of grunge—everyone thought that was the most stupid term ever and we were laughing at it so big: "Oh my God, are you effing serious? This is the stupidest thing we've ever heard!" . . . Everyone here in the Northwest hated it so much they made fun of it. Everyone hated that term—it was really annoying.

JOHN PURKEY: It's embarrassing—people in the city just trying to make money off it. There was a level of embarrassment. A lot of bands deserved more attention than they got or a lot of bands would get a little record deal or something and it would destroy the band because they were all getting picked up but very few of them would end up putting out records—it would end up destroying the band . . . A lot of small labels started—some of them very shifty: they'd get a ton of money and throw it at bands, and the bands would not be realistic.

JAIME ROBERT JOHNSON: Things didn't feel that different for me until around 1991 or so, when the whole world seemed like they were kind of losing their minds over the grunge thing . . . After a while it became a total circus and I became somewhat suspicious of newcomers . . . I personally lived hand-to-mouth and ignored the absurdities I witnessed (the guys moving to Seattle to "make it") and distanced myself from people like that because they usually turn out to be soulless clowns and I have better things to do with my time.

MARIA MABRA: That cesspool of major-label guys coming around trying to sign bands—just signing what was poppiest. They don't sign the most hardcore or what people are listening to. They take a genre of music and just regurgitate it over and over again . . . Especially after the movie *Singles* came out, Seattle was full of label guys. I remember all the guys—Tad and everyone—all down at the OK Hotel doing some stuff, filming it. Some of it was shot across from the house I was in at the time, but they just wanted grunge bands. We were like, "What's a grunge band?!" That's what was funnier. It was a big laugh—oh please. No, we don't hang out with grunge bands. You could imagine every fucker wanted to be in a grunge band—here came the influx of long-haired rock 'n' roll metal dudes trying to sound like Soundgarden and Nirvana—it was so bad . . . All of a sudden the frumpy look, the long beards, that Northwest thing became a fashion—we all looked frumpy! It's the fashion that comes from it being really cold and raining a lot and we're musicians and we need to walk our gear to band practice, so yeah, we have on boots because it's raining. Then all of a sudden it's a fashion? I think it was a constant joke, to be honest with you—a constant joke but also a constant reality. That's what it's like when you're in a music scene and it suddenly becomes famous. I remember when *Vogue* did the slang thing, their grunge layout—I just laughed my ass off. Dr. Martens, some gaunt-looking chick with a flannel tied around her waist—it was ridiculous and funny and kinda cool all at the same time.

TY WILLMAN: A&R representatives were up here and different people actually would give you their card—Gary Gersh literally cornered me in a room just to give me his card—I had a bunch of cards from people. These people would come up, take you out, hang out. If you were somewhat good you could get a deal, everybody did.

When you have three hundred record execs coming here to seek out bands, then the chances are pretty good.

There was certainly not a lot of commercial ambition visible in Nirvana's stuttering live performances. Nirvana's return to the New Music Seminar was a true low; Cobain had overdosed beforehand but still took the stage with his friends shepherding him on.

DAVID YOW: The Roseland show was pretty sad. Kurt was very fucked up and Krist was playing the role of babysitter/handler/dad. I don't recall if we were any good that night, but Nirvana certainly wasn't—they phoned that one in.

There was no plan anymore, just ad-hoc events. What was still present, however, was their genuine zeal for pro-female causes; their April show was a benefit supporting rape victims in the Yugoslav conflict while later Cobain would join Courtney Love for a Rock Against Rape performance.

Then, in July, while Cobain and Love were sheltering in a rented apartment in Seattle, something happened to stun the entire music community in Seattle. Mia Zapata, lead singer of the Gits, was murdered on July 7, 1993.

STEVE MORIARTY: It was a small scene in a small city and we all hung out in the same areas. Tad lived nearby and would come by for barbecues and there was a rehearsal space right next door to the bar we hung out at, so we'd all comingle. Mia was a waitress at this dive bar all the bands would go to, so she knew a lot of people. I knew people because I booked bands at the OK Hotel, which was a major all-ages place where Nirvana did their last show before they got in the van and headed down to record *Nevermind*—they needed gas money . . . we had plans to go to Europe and tour with Dead Moon . . . We'd also had a US tour with L7 and Seven Year Bitch going from New York back to Seattle from up the West Coast, same cities that the pope was going to be visiting . . . We were going to be on an antipope tour, like the Damned song, because they were talking about abortion rights, so that was going to be really cool. All set up. We were finishing our second album, Mia wanted to recut a couple of different vocal tracks, so we got back after playing for Atlantic and this guy wanted to sign us so we were considering them . . . For the first time we could have [made] a living playing music, we wouldn't have to work other jobs—what a concept! So that day we went into the studio, two days later we were going to leave on tour, she was murdered the night before she was going to finish her vocal tracks. Couldn't find her to go to the studio, so we looked and looked and eventually about two in the morning we called the morgue.

MARIA MABRA: Mia's death was . . . I remember it like it was yesterday. That sounds like a cliché, the opening to an epic movie, but I really do. I remember it and it was a very crazy time and for me that was the essence of confusion. In a murder situation there's not only confusion among you and your friends, but we were all musicians too so all of a sudden all of your band mates are, if they're male, all under suspicion of murder. So not only do we have this music scene filled with all these people we had played with—we were tight—suddenly all of the guys in our group and in our scene are being investigated. It was unreal.

STEVE MORIARTY: The process when it comes to suspects is you start with the boyfriend, then look at the band, then go up from there. It was crazy—a dark time for a few years . . . Nirvana kinda bookended the Gits' short career in Seattle—our second show was with them and then the first benefit to find the killer. We needed money to hire a private investigator. I was sitting in my house bummed out thinking, What the fuck can I do? Then I get a call on the phone and it's Courtney Love: "Hey, this is Courtney, me and Kurt are here and we heard that you were doing this benefit and we were really sorry to hear what happened—so we were thinking, maybe we could get some more people out if Nirvana played? They haven't played in a while, they need to practice and they'll all do it." Then Kurt got on the phone and was like, "Yeah, it really sucks what happened, we've been listening to the band, it's really good—I remember you guys—anything we can do to help . . ." They said they'd do it but were clear we couldn't do an announcement to the press until after four p.m. and they wanted to go on at eight p.m. I think he was really going downhill—but when he was really bummed out he was still able to reach out and help someone and I think that's admirable. I was moved. A guy Tad knew called Mike Nicholls was really responsible for calling the venue and setting it all up. He was the tour manager for a lot of the bands back then, great guy. We got down to the show, hung out, talked—he was the same sort of Kurt, kept himself to himself, and Courtney was like a whirlwind around him. Nirvana went on, did "Kashmir" by Led Zeppelin to start—they did it like a rehearsal or a jam, like they were playing a basement party. People were still filing in—it was really casual and really cool. They didn't go nuts or break stuff, they just played. Krist sang a couple of songs, they had a good time—then they gave us a lot of money.

MARIA MABRA: She and I played music together in several things outside the Gits—like Hell Smells. I was also one of her vocal teachers, so not only were we best [friends] but we were inseparable—we would always sing together . . . When people die they put them into these strange states of angelic being. She was my best friend. I had no problem telling her, "Fuck off, you're full of shit"; she was my sister, we fought a lot—we might be in a corner at a party fist-fighting and rolling around on the ground then we'd make up twenty minutes later. Sisters, inseparable. She meant everything to me . . . That show in 1993, I was really glad Nirvana wanted to do the show—as much as they inspired everyone else at that time I was glad they looked back at us and recognized one of their own and were willing to help. That made me love them more too. Thanks, guys, I'm glad you did that.

They honored where they came from because we all came out [of] the same scene.

JOSH SINDER: That show was absolutely the most insane oversold-out show I've ever played. We in Tad knew that Nirvana was going to announce their playing the show at the last minute on the radio (I think it was KISW), but no one else knew. Anyway, there was like two hundred people at the King Cat Theater before anyone knew Nirvana was playing and after they announced it on the radio, it seemed like the entire city swarmed the building. There were probably a couple thousand people flooding the streets. It was mind-blowing. Dave Grohl borrowed my drum kit and when I got it back all the drumheads were beat to a bloody pulp.

LARRY SCHEMEL: Everyone was really having a good time that night despite the reason we were all there. It felt like we tried to go back to our little scene for a night; it was for a good cause and really cool to see the community come together for Mia . . . [Nirvana] seemed to be having a good time, very loose and I think maybe relieved to not be playing an arena show or festival. It also seemed like it was sort of a homecoming for them even though it was a solemn occasion . . . The covers stand out because they seemed to be having fun with them.

STEVE MORIARTY: Mia . . . she was funny, gregarious, but also an introspective artist, [a] poet like Patti Smith. She had a fighting spirit, didn't take shit. Completely honest and direct . . . We organized about two hundred benefits all over the country, all over the world—every band from Sonic Youth to Hootie and the Blowfish played at one of those shows. Home Alive, they formed to teach self-defense to women in Seattle so it wouldn't happen again as it did to Mia. They did a load of compilations—everyone got in line to be part of that—X, Soundgarden, William S. Burroughs, Pearl Jam—it's just insane. Nirvana, too. They talk about the bands in the '60s, Jefferson Airplane living next door to the Grateful Dead next to Janis Joplin—it was like that except we were all around the Comet. All in houses on Capitol

Hill—similar . . . Kathleen Hanna was really wonderful when Mia was murdered; she was the one who turned Joan Jett on to the Gits and they both loved Mia's voice and singing, so that's what led to the album with Joan doing Gits songs. I still have gratitude to them.

Despite the tragedy, it was time for Nirvana to return to business. The pace ratcheted up—DGC released "Heart-Shaped Box," the band played *Saturday Night Live,* and the media rounds commenced.

YOURI LENQUETTE: When they were promoting *In Utero,* I went to Seattle for a photo session. The idea was to go over there with this young kid who won a Nirvana competition with the prize being to meet the band in Seattle. So it was me and this young sixteen-, seventeen-year-old, we got there in late August and spent maybe three days in Seattle. The photos I shot for *Best* were mostly taken . . . in the garden of Dave's house, in front of a car. At some point Kurt sees this little toy M16—it's a lot smaller than the real thing—he grabs it, puts it in his mouth. We do three photos—click-click-click—he puts it down and we finish the photo session . . . It was just some toy, it could have been a clown nose—he would have put it on. It was the spirit; that photo session was very happy, I remember we went to do some go-karting. We were hanging out at Dave's place, the weather was good, we were happy to see each other, all making jokes. A happy moment . . . Kurt wasn't the guy who'd say, "Yeah, let's go out, get a drink, have fun . . ." It just wasn't him. It meant he could look like someone who was closed, someone sad. But that wasn't all he was. The way he ended makes it hard to recognize that he had this other side, that his music was fed by his enthusiasm, that he could be a very funny guy, witty—very funny jokes. You don't imagine that of him, but he could if he was in the right atmosphere. The reality is, though, that touring is very stressful, very tiring, and on top of that he was a sick man and simply not a very social person.

Meanwhile the planning went on for the upcoming tour but already there were rumblings of discontent.

JOSH SINDER: We were confirmed to be the opening act for Nirvana on the *In Utero* USA tour. We were so excited; the first show was Seattle, I think, and we were even hearing the ads for the Seattle show on the radio. So anyway like a week before the tour was to start we got news that we were kicked off. What happened was Tad was doing interviews in New York weeks earlier and a journalist from *Melody Maker* was pressing him about what he thought about Courtney Love or something like that. I think he said something that Kurt didn't like and we were off the tour.

KURT DANIELSON: Kurt always tended to be a quiet, withdrawn, soft-spoken person; but back when Tad used to tour with Nirvana, there were many times when he would open up, and his sense of humor would emerge, making it possible to achieve a closeness with him that was impossible later due to how isolated he eventually became due to Courtney's interference and also his drug use.

19.0

Creaking: The *In Utero* Tour
October 1993 to January 1994

When Nirvana ended their US touring for 1991 they had been lined up along-side Pearl Jam and Red Hot Chili Peppers—mainstream talents. By contrast, when planning their first full US tour since becoming superstars, Nirvana ignored the mainstream entirely and plucked comrades from the underground. They were the world's biggest band but were making decisions the way Sonic Youth had in 1990. They had no desire to emulate lucrative superstar follies like the Metallica/Guns N' Roses tour.

JAD FAIR, Half Japanese: It was funny how I found out about Nirvana wanting Half Japanese to open for them. I had a show in Toronto and picked up a copy of *Spin* magazine at the airport. There was an interview with Kurt, and Kurt said that Half Japanese would do the tour with them. That's the first I'd heard of it. I called my booking agent and she told me she was just contacted by Nirvana's manager.

CRIS KIRKWOOD, Meat Puppets: A request came in through the management—maybe they'd realized that we were still alive or something—it was cool realizing the guys liked us, that they wanted to ask us to go out with them on tour . . . It was amazing seeing these bands who dressed like us, who name-checked us, suddenly on the radio and MTV. Scruffy hair, jeans, T-shirts—that we could relate to. The '80s, there were some extreme hairdos and there's me thinking I was lucky if I remembered to put some gloop under my arms so I don't stink.

Old favorites alternated with up-and-comers, Nirvana doing for them what others had done for Nirvana scant years earlier.

THALIA ZEDEK, Come: Come had played with Hole a few times early on, before Kurt and Courtney became involved. And Come's manager at the time, Tom Johnston, was friends with Janet Billig, who managed both Hole and Nirvana (I believe?). We had heard through the grapevine that they (Kurt and Courtney) were both Come fans and really into *11:11*, so probably both that and our managers being friends were factors in us being asked. I think we ended up with the Southern leg of the tour simply because that was what was available; we weren't given a choice in that.

TROY VON BALTHAZAR, Chokebore: They heard our music through some friends, I think. They asked us personally, not through any managers or anything, very low-key. I remember seeing Krist Novoselic at a few Chokebore shows the year before and I heard that Kurt liked our music. They just asked and we said "YES!" . . . There were no contracts or legal junk, from what I can remember . . . I think the second time we played in Seattle, Krist was there. Just a tall, dark figure standing in the back. I didn't think anything would come of it. But somehow he got the CD to the band, or maybe it went through their friend Cali. The next thing we knew they just asked us to do some shows. It was all very casual.

This was how the underground had always worked, right back to the days of wearing each other's T-shirts at local shows. Cobain's attitude toward the trappings of his newfound fame are summed up by a private moment.

TROY VON BALTHAZAR: When we were on tour he would let us stay at his place if we didn't have anywhere to sleep that night. We would stay there between shows. The house was usually empty when we got there because Nirvana was also on tour. It was nice of him to lend us a place to sleep. (We were tired boys . . .) I remember using the bathroom one time and seeing an MTV Music Award on the floor sitting there holding the door open. Awesome.

The rock-star insouciance of using the award as a doorstop matches their unwillingness to place success on a pedestal.

STEVE DIGGLE: [Kurt] was into a load of bands from the punk era—and a lot of little-known bands too. It was great that he was in that position, then, of doing the big gigs but fishing out people that were playing in very tiny places and bringing them. He felt real.

As with Calamity Jane back in Argentina, there was a bad side to these invitations—a lot of these bands had never been anywhere near shows on this scale.

CHRIS BROKAW, Come: Our understanding was that the invite came from the band. None of us knew anyone in Nirvana, so, it came somewhat out of left field. We were excited and a little bit scared at the prospect—it was a very, very high profile tour, playing bigger places than we'd ever played before. Arthur [Johnson], our drummer, was particularly freaked out at the prospect of playing at the Omni in Atlanta, where he had seen Loverboy, et cetera, when he was in high school. When we were asked to do the shows he exclaimed, "I can't play my $150 garage-sale drum set onstage at the Omni!"—which was in fact the drum set he had been using up till that point (first with BBQ Killers and then with Come). We promised him we'd buy him a new drum set and he mopily said OK. I think he was really nervous about playing the Omni.

TROY VON BALTHAZAR: Backstage [Nirvana] seemed really nice and would always try to talk and comfort us because we were a little out of our league going from playing in front of 50 people one night to 20,000 the next opening for them.

MARK ROBINSON: We were asked to open for them at a few 20,000-seat arena shows in and around Florida and we politely said no, since we had done our share of opening gigs at big shows. Never this big, of course, but the bigger the show, the less interested folks are in watching the opening band. We had also just finished a long nationwide tour with Stereolab and were a bit tired. Our booking agent was perplexed by our refusal and wondered what we were trying to accomplish with our band.

Nirvana carried their own fears. Despite having played 244 shows since dispensing with Jason Everman, Cobain now felt he needed a second guitarist to share the burden; Pat Smear from the L.A. punk band the Germs came on board.

CHRIS BROKAW: I wasn't a big fan of Nirvana, but I was a huge Germs fan, and really excited at the prospect of meeting and touring with Pat Smear! Prior to our touring with them, I actually thought that Nirvana was sort of mainstream hard rock . . . By the end of the tour, I'd become a fan; I liked the songs, and I liked Dave Grohl's drumming a lot. What's funny now is that I hear a band like Alice in Chains, and I think they sound *a lot* like Nirvana . . . and maybe vice versa . . . I understand the differences between the two, and they're vast; but they also sound *a lot* alike . . . and they are viewed now in such different ways.

Choosing to bring a punk veteran into Nirvana was another sign of the urge to hold tight to what Nirvana had been, changing as an act of resistance.

The other fear was about what Cobain could, or would, endure. While Metallica racked up 272 shows from 1992 to 1994 and Guns N' Roses hit 202 on the *Use Your*

Illusion tours, Nirvana had managed a threadbare 105, and at its peak, the *In Utero* tour saw just 16 shows per month.

STEVE TURNER: The *In Utero* tour seemed very chaotic, unorganized, and kind of a bummer all around . . . Their team seemed confused as to what to do and when to do it. They were walking on eggshells afraid of being fired. It wasn't much of a team, I guess— every man or woman for themselves . . . Except when Nirvana was onstage. They were pretty awesome most nights. Krist and Dave would come hang out some, it was cool to meet Pat, and I rarely saw Kurt. We just did our thing and watched how chaotic it all was.

CHRIS BROKAW: We had heard that Kurt Cobain had a bad drug habit, and that they were thinking of canceling the tour; the shows weren't confirmed until very soon before they happened . . . At any rate, it was no secret that both Kurt and his wife had a lot of drug problems that were causing unrest in the band. No one was sure if the shows were going to happen . . . no one knew what shape Kurt would be in . . . I honestly don't know whether he was "on" or not during the tour. It wasn't my business and I didn't ask.

The venue choices showed a nervousness also.

THALIA ZEDEK: They were big, but not humongous? Definitely stadiums, but basketball/hockey stadiums not baseball or football ones (thank God) . . . We did things a bit differently than for a normal Come tour: we hired a tour manager who had a cell phone (a rare and expensive thing in those days). Nirvana's management kind of insisted on that, if I remember correctly. And we brought along a friend (Curtis Harvey from Rex) to be a general roadie, string-changer. Because when you're playing in front of 40,000 people you really can't ask everyone to wait while you change a string! And we brought along our own and favorite sound person, Carl Plaster. But besides that we traveled in our van and stayed at the same shitty motels we would have otherwise. We didn't travel with Nirvana, and their management team didn't make our travel arrangements.

JAD FAIR: I'm not good at guessing audience size, but yes, it probably was in the three- to ten-thousand range.

These shows were deliberately a fraction of the size of the South American events or the summer festivals.

For all the caution, Nirvana onstage could still be an awe-inspiring spectacle.

CHRIS BROKAW: The thing to remember is that this was the first big tour they did after becoming successful—about two years after *Nevermind* came out and sold ten million copies. So people had been waiting a long time to see them and everything around them was sort of a constant soap opera with the press . . . The audiences were wild . . . crazy, just really excited that they were finally seeing Nirvana. And yes, every night people constantly threw clothing onstage. A lot of shoes. Hundreds of shoes! It was insane. The crowds were cool to us. One fascinating thing: when the tour was happening, the Breeders' song "Cannonball" was the number-one song on MTV's *BuzzBin*—and every night that song got the biggest response of the whole night, more than anything Nirvana played. Just total pandemonium. It really showed how powerful MTV was then.

THALIA ZEDEK: The audiences were absolutely incredible to the opening bands, which was so cool. We were the first band on and they cheered the second we walked onstage, even though I doubt hardly any of them had any idea who we were. No one was shouting "Nirvana" or "Get off the stage!" They were incredibly receptive! I remember there was a strange shoe-tossing thing that was going on at the time, where kids would express their devotion to the band by tossing just one of their shoes onstage, meaning that they had to walk home half-shod. We didn't inspire that level of emotion, but the Breeders did, and they didn't appreciate it.

TROY VON BALTHAZAR: I remember standing on the side of the stage one night while [Nirvana] were playing and thinking, This is a damn good band. They were an exciting band. The fame around them was also exciting to watch, but seemed a little heavy. I looked out that same night from the side of the stage and realized I couldn't even see anyone's face. The audience was too far away. It's like they were playing to an imaginary crowd a million miles away. I remember thinking they must be phenomenal in a small club. That's where I wish I could have seen them . . . Playing ten shows with Nirvana on their final American tour was really a thrill. Something I'll remember for the rest of my life.

NAOKO YAMANO: I enjoyed the shows in front of the big audiences. It was easy for us because we were a front act and the set time was just thirty minutes. It seemed that the audiences liked Shonen Knife because we were all female and came from a faraway country and the audiences knew we were invited by Nirvana . . . [Kurt] looked tired but performed very hard onstage . . . I was impressed by Kurt's attitude toward music. He always performed as hard as he could for shows and had a pure mind for music.

JAD FAIR: The set time for us was tight, but we knew it was going to be. I didn't notice bouncers. I'm sure there were some, I just didn't feel their presence. It was pretty relaxed . . . Nirvana was such a great live band. I enjoyed every show . . . Kurt was a great performer at all of the shows I saw. He certainly could perform.

STEVE TURNER: I was really happy for those guys, and all the success they were having. The crowds were pretty mainstream, I suppose, and opening up for a hit band like that isn't the greatest thing, since the crowd was unfamiliar with us. But we had a good time, as we usually did.

Some bands learned crucial rules of the big band experience.

JAD FAIR: It was mostly playing to college venues. I was expecting that it would be a college-age audience, but most of the audience was younger than that. At the first show we played some fast songs and some slow ones. Every fast song got a great response and every slow one bombed. For all of the other shows we only played fast ones.

TROY VON BALTHAZAR: Another lesson I learned came on the night of the first show. We got to the venue and the first thing we saw: the catering tables. Rows of delicious sandwiches and cakes, soups and puddings, sausages, and fish. Chokebore had been starving, sleeping on couches for the past two months barely surviving, and the sight of all that food flew me into an eating frenzy. I tried it all. It was heaven. Vitamins finally, after so long. When I went out onstage it was amazing. Twenty-five thousand people standing in front of us going crazy. We played that show and it all seemed like a dream. But all I was concentrating on was trying not to poop my pants the whole time. All that rich food and then the terror of playing in front of so many people . . . not a good combination. I learned that night never to eat right before a show, not worth it. Even for all those vitamins.

CRIS KIRKWOOD: It's ass-whipping to stomp through a PA that size—a great experience, the gear's bigger but they hold a lot of things back for the headliners—like, they have tons of lights but they hold a lot back. You don't get to play with much of the gear. Bigger shows are huge productions—you adhere to a schedule, multiple setups ready, there are people off setting up the next gig ready.

For Novoselic and Grohl, at least, the tolerant freedom afforded musicians on tour still meant embracing and enjoying the experience of being out.

TROY VON BALTHAZAR: [I] remember that Krist loved red wine. He would roar through the backstage areas jumping over sofas, smashing through doors, throwing food and laughing, and this wasn't at the end of the night . . . it was on his way to the stage. He seemed like a pretty jolly guy . . . and after all that, still solid on the bass.

THALIA ZEDEK: We hung out with the Breeders a lot and with Krist and Dave, who were both really friendly. One night in Miami I remember we all hung out together after the show and went swimming in the sea. The next day we found out that the water was full of sharks. I remember Nirvana's management being really angry at us because Krist was really hungover the next day.

PAUL LEARY, Butthole Surfers: It seemed like [Kurt's] wife wanted to keep him away from us as much as possible. But for the few times we got to hang out, he seemed pretty mellow and normal. And their shows were great . . . As far as "normal," I really didn't know Kurt well. The times we hung out before and after shows, I didn't notice anything "unusual" about him.

TROY VON BALTHAZAR: It felt to us that they were just a good small band surrounded by a whirlwind. When they played, it was like all the shows we went to at home in the small clubs—strong and natural.

The tour paused for the *MTV Unplugged* performance that has since defined Nirvana to many. At the time, however, it wasn't clear it would go on to such lasting renown. MTV sulked over the absence of hits, the presence of so many covers, the choice of guests who weren't on their mainstream A-list, and Cobain's refusal to play an encore.

CRIS KIRKWOOD: There was this open desire to share that with bands like us, bands who were in the same place in terms of attitude. I mean, they were the biggest band in the world, could do whatever he wanted and what does he choose to do with that? To take somebody on MTV with them and play some of our stuff that he really digs. Knowing full well that we weren't making management happy—the guys at MTV didn't want him to have us do it. He *made* them, for real. The idea came up on the tour with them: we got to know him, we were hanging out somewhat. He came up with it somewhere along the way—at first he wanted to do some of our old songs on the show . . . So, Curt, my brother, was going to teach him how to play [them]. Somewhere in there it just became having us go on and we'd play with them. It came 'round that quick . . . We were not on MTV at the time, we'd been around a long time and deemed unworthy, so it was like Kurt asking them to let him bring on a turd. MTV were surprised, not that into it, but he got his way.

The band didn't celebrate the MTV performance; the rehearsals and recording had been tacked on at the end of a solid month of near nightly concerts, so they all went their separate ways to enjoy a week off from touring. It would take a year of MTV rotation, one death, and a posthumous LP to cement its subsequent reputation.

JAD FAIR: I was at the *MTV Unplugged* show. The band seemed to be in good spirit and did a great job.

CRIS KIRKWOOD: It was just this little performance—but it was nice to get some notice and for little things to pop up that let us make music. After he passed away, they came to us about getting our permission to release it. They'd played the living fuck out of it on MTV and then they decided to release it.

THALIA ZEDEK: There definitely was a sense that something really incredible had happened. I didn't hear it from the band, but the crew was talking about it . . . We really didn't understand what they were going on about until much later.

In December, MTV were again involved as Nirvana played the *Live and Loud* show.

B-REAL, Cypress Hill: We had done some MTV shows in the past starting with *Yo MTV Raps, Daytona Spring Break* and our reputation for live shows had been growing—we'd done Lollapalooza and stuff like that, so MTV now and then, depending on the event, would call upon us to be a part of it . . . getting a chance to share the stage with Nirvana, who were pretty much the biggest thing at the time, it was a great experience . . . [We] had to get there early—it was in one of the docks that MTV rented out for this particular show—and it was three bands to play. It was a pretty hectic day; MTV was trying to get everything together and get everyone's sound checks rolling through. We actually did a sound check with Pearl Jam because we'd just done a song with them for the movie soundtrack to the film *Judgment Night* so we had planned to play that with them. So we played our sound check, they played their sound check, and then we ran through that song. The main tension that was going on that day was that nobody could get hold of Eddie Vedder—nobody knew where he was at and people were skeptical that he was going to show up. Everyone was on edge about that. He never turned up—there was no reason given, he just didn't . . . They're very much about being on time and keeping everything rolling and moving, so they don't fall behind schedule because it was to go out live—realistically, they were pre-recording it for one part of the nation but it's going live to the other part. They're always nervous about getting it off on time but they're very pleasant when they're pushing you to hurry up! . . . That particular day we were floating around hanging out with everybody—we got to meet Krist and Dave, and Pat, they befriended us, it was very cool—we're friends to this day, always great when we see each other. We got to interact with Flea and Anthony Kiedis because I believe they were the hosts that day, which was funny because I never felt like Anthony liked me so it was probably funny for him to be actually cool with me, just on camera, for once in his life.

Cobain ended *MTV Live and Loud* by sarcastically clapping along with the audience, a manic glint in his eye, before returning to chasing cameramen around the stage; he could tell that regardless of what he did the crowd would applaud like performing seals. He'd been less than merry toward audiences all tour, but without the camera present his approach was usually to withdraw; with MTV there he ratcheted up the aggression far more than usual.

RICK SIMS: I saw them when they played the Aragon Ballroom in Chicago . . . I got ferociously drunk with Dan (Peters), the Mudhoney drummer, and remember watching both bands from the side of the stage. They were a good live band, but honestly they occupied the same level of showmanship and musicianship that a lot of the upper-tier bands of that time shared . . . I also liked to move onstage, probably a nod to my Kiss and Plasmatics influences. And then there were the FUCK THE PIGS signs which we handed out to the audience before shows—they usually ended up beating each other over the head with them. The optic was great, though! I would also put on a confrontational air, and this is what audiences came to expect. I had a chip on my shoulder and a resentfulness of "punk rock" pretentiousness. In other words, I didn't like it when people didn't respond favorably to our band and would get belligerent. Audiences seemed to really enjoy that after a while and would cheer favorably when I told them to go fuck themselves and their shitty little town. Nirvana was *nothing* like this when I saw them. They did their show and got off stage. No antics. No fuck-yous. I don't think that was their style. Ha!

No one thought negatively of Kurt's MTV antics; it just cemented Nirvana's reputation as rock thrills for TV audiences. On the road, however, the sense that there were issues circling Cobain became unavoidable.

NAOKO YAMANO: It was an arena tour. The distance from the main act and a support act became so large. Our dressing rooms were usually far from Nirvana's. We didn't have much time to talk with the members. There were many people around Kurt at the dressing room at any time . . . From the 1993 tour, I don't have a clear memory about Kurt.

B-REAL: Kurt might have been around or he might have showed up right before they went onstage—nobody was worried whether he would show up or not, so I think he must have been there, secluded by himself away from everybody, because he struck me as the type who didn't like being around the lights and the glitz . . . You know, we never ended up meeting him—after the show he was whisked off, like I said; we ended up hanging out with Dave, Pat, and Krist and developed friendships with them but we never met Kurt Cobain.

CHRIS BROKAW: The vibe was just sort of . . . high drama. I think everyone was sort of afraid of Kurt and afraid of what he might do. But a lot of that drama surrounded his wife . . . When she left the tour, in Atlanta, the whole mood of the tour became instantly more relaxed.

PAUL LEARY: His wife was always doing her best to make sure he didn't hang out with us. She had been a concert promoter in Minneapolis, Minnesota, a few years earlier, and had booked us to play a show in Minneapolis. We drove for two days to get there, played our show, and then she stiffed us . . . We didn't get along after that. She was extremely unpleasant during our shows with Nirvana. I remember once talking with Kurt, and his wife literally grabbed him by the ear and pulled him away. I have to admit, in my thirty-plus years of being in music, I have gotten along well with every musician I have ever met, except for Kurt's wife. So I don't really consider her a musician.

CRIS KIRKWOOD: He was so famous by then and dealing with so much stuff, it was at the point they'd have to put signs up backstage telling people not to molest the guy—where even seasoned show hands are stopping you to try to get their photo taken with you, certainly you could tell that was something. He was just withdrawn, sheltered in a way—but we still had fun, things like that MTV practice session was trippy . . . We'd take them to parties at an old friend's house and it'd feel like we'd brought this little Northwest guy with us but he's really fucking famous and everyone was aware and that changed things. And he was such a newly minted star—but then it's not like he was a plumber who suddenly became famous.

Cobain was notably withdrawn and lonely. He was barely visible when he wasn't onstage.

CHRIS BROKAW: I was walking down the hallway and Kurt came up and was saying how we should come to their backstage room more often. He was saying, "You guys should come and hang out with us before shows . . . it gets so lonely back there." When he said that, he was looking into my eyes. He looked so sad, and suddenly a group of people came rushing down the hall at us and mobbed him screaming for autographs and trying to touch him. There was this circle of people swarming around him and he was still just looking into my eyes. He looked so alone, so small and lost. He was a sweet person but his fame seemed overwhelming. I just backed up slowly. It was a scary moment. He was surrounded.

THALIA ZEDEK: My impression of him was pretty fleeting. He didn't hang out much with us or with the rest of his band and he was pretty quiet. I think he enjoyed our performance, but he was pretty reserved. He seemed pretty overwhelmed and not comfortable, either physically or mentally. I didn't get the impression that he was enjoying the tour or their success very much. He was traveling in a separate bus with Frances, if I remember correctly, and he seemed really devoted to her.

JAD FAIR: I saw a lot more of Dave and Krist than I did of Kurt. Krist and Dave seemed to spend time together. Kurt didn't . . . We didn't see much of Kurt at the shows.

YAMANTAKA EYE, Boredoms: Kurt seemed like he already had angel wings—his steps across the stage were uncertain and it looked so pitiful you could almost see his heart bleeding with a deep self-pity that I thought was very dangerous indeed.

KEVIN WHITWORTH: The next time I saw him was walking off the huge stage at some enormo-dome . . . I was stage left. We'd just played the punk-rock club down the street and were let in the back door. And he looked so tired, walking out of a room full of thousands of adoring fans, like he'd just left a coal mine after a twelve-hour shift.

No one felt more than a vague unease. This was Kurt Cobain, after all, a man everyone knew had a few problems. There wasn't anything to suggest that his moodiness was anything more than "Kurt being Kurt."

CHRIS BROKAW: They seemed like any other band to me. All bands fight and get over it. They are together because for some reason when they make music together it sounds good, and they know that is worth something to them even if they argue in the van. Every band goes through it. I think they were like everyone else in that respect.

THALIA ZEDEK: I remember that Kurt always had this huge fan blowing air directed right at his head while he was playing. I guess that's the image in my mind of that tour. I don't know, I definitely got the feeling that something was wrong, everyone was just kind of uptight. But they played really good every night and treated us very well and with respect

PAUL LEARY: Those shows were a blast. I remember on New Year's Eve sitting in the audience watching Nirvana put on a really great show. Nine shows didn't seem like enough, I wanted more . . . I never saw his mood drop. He seemed to be in a good mood backstage after the last show.

In contrast to late 1991, when he had been writing on tour and the band sound-checked new material, it seems Cobain had written only one song since January

1993. Fans place hope in the supposed "lost song" jammed onstage on November 12 and December 29, but it barely registered at the time.

TROY VON BALTHAZAR: I think they might have been writing a bit and jamming at sound check, but everyone does that on tour. It's usually the only chance to work on anything new. I don't recall the particular piece you are talking about though.

THALIA ZEDEK: I don't remember hearing any jamming or new material at sound checks. But they *did* always sound check. But they didn't spend hours noodling around or anything. The sets were slightly different every night if I recall correctly, but there wasn't a huge variation.

Fans claim the piece may have been demoed in 1994, but producer Adam Kasper can only say, having listened to the live track, "Sounds familiar but I would have to hear it re: the demo again to know for sure." That didn't mean there was nothing there, but it certainly hadn't gone so far as to become a true song.

JAD FAIR: Kurt was always friendly to me. He told me that he would be starting a label and wanted to release albums by Half Japanese and my solo albums. Yes, he made it clear that he liked my music.

TROY VON BALTHAZAR: I know Kurt was considering starting his own record label. I do wish that would have happened. There would have been some good music on it. He was a huge music fan.

The cessation of creativity had become a deep malaise stretching back two years. At first everyone could shrug it off, but there'd been less than a dozen songs written since Nevermind. The band made it into the studio in January but Cobain only showed up for one day.

ADAM KASPER, *producer*: Not sure how long we spent, but Cobain was present all day and after dinner break. Cobain was the creative genius behind Nirvana and we all knew things were not right, as far as the well-documented problems Kurt was having . . . So we just got to work. The studio and band is sometimes the last refuge for someone thrust into that kind of whirlwind and incredible fame . . . Everyone seemed to be getting along good. Kurt was like a brother to Novoselic and Grohl. So there was love, there was concern—there was the hope that the music would be the healer . . . The thing that stood out for me was the fun we had—all those guys are incredibly funny and smart . . . He had a song ready to go, minus some final lyrics, which became "You Know You're Right," and we got to it. I had the studio all set up in terms of amps, guitars, and drums . . . Cobain arrived and we began his song in earnest. Cobain gave no direction or input on sounds. He had the song and the arrangement complete and Dave and Krist jumped right in. When it came to vocals we did some takes, listened back, and punched in some spots and did a few more parts. I made some rough mixes that only the band and myself had for all those years . . . I was blown away by Cobain's raw talent. He was completely self-contained and what you hear in terms of songwriting and performance is just so real. I've worked with many talented people, but few can get up to the mike and in one performance be so transcendent . . . It was a complete song that Cobain brought in. We attempted to get the best version of it we could. There was no discussion of future releases or any business-related conversations that I was aware of . . . Can't recall future bookings. But there was definite talk of doing more when they got back from tour in Europe.

There was no talk of a Lollapalooza EP, or of further Nirvana releases; the future of the band, and any aim for that last recording, remained veiled.

20.0

One More Solo? The Curtain Falls
February to April 1994

The January session was to be the last time Nirvana worked together in studio. While there was only the scantest evidence of artistic activity from Cobain—he was too busy switching homes again—Grohl and Novoselic still presented compositions for Cobain's perusal as potential material for Nirvana. Even now—as late as January 30, 1994—no one could see that the end to Nirvana was within touching distance. The future was vague, but not preordained. There was no forewarning of the spiraling events that led to Cobain's death.

ADAM KASPER: I was struck by Grohl's songs and the demos we made that week. At the time I offhandedly made the remark that he should do a solo album someday . . . There was talk of the guys wanting a chance to include some of their songs on the new album work. Cobain listened to a few tracks and it seemed he was open to considering other material, but not much time or energy was spent on this.

STEVE DIGGLE: I sat with Dave at the end of the tour and said, "We're gonna miss you guys, y'know?" because we got on really well on the road—all in [it] together. We were sat at the table and he said he had some songs he wanted to do when he got back. I have to be honest, I thought, I bet they're pretty good but . . . the drummer? You're not sure what he's got but . . .

Having spent part of 1993 on a reunion tour with Scream, Grohl joined other musicians in early 1994 for the soundtrack to the film *Backbeat*.

DON FLEMING: Thurston [Moore] put the lineup together and told Don Was we would do it but only if we could do it without any rehearsal and if we could do it in two days. That helped everyone with their busy schedules; we literally flew out there, learned the songs on the spot one-by-one . . . There are certain drummers, especially from producing, I've worked out are such a key element of the band. They can take a band that are great and make them a step above—that's what [Dave] did with Nirvana. There were great songs, great front man; the drums took it a step up, and that's why they were so successful . . . He brought so much energy to the songs and never fucked up. I don't remember about where they were at as a band at that point. They'd become very popular but I don't remember him talking about it at all. I think he was just there to have a good time.

While Cobain was increasingly absent as a creative artist, Nirvana as a performing entity rolled on and arrived in Cascais, Portugal, in February to play their first European shows since 1992. Cobain, Novoselic, Grohl, and Pat Smear had performed these songs so many times that whatever was occurring behind the scenes, their well-drilled onstage chemistry was still there.

STEVE DIGGLE: I remember those shows, standing at the side of the stage, hearing Dave Grohl's drums and just thinking, Jesus! It's like John Bonham! This guy can play! Krist was an amazing bass player and Kurt was sometimes quiet but suddenly this roar of a vocal and this intensity. Pat Smear—great guy and great guitarist, he blended in well. It was amazing to see, I'd heard the records but I was blown away by the live thing . . . I'd heard *Bleach* and I'd heard the *Nevermind* album, but the first time I saw their show I thought, Wow, I've got it now. Watching Dave Grohl just a few yards away banging the fuck out the drums, Krist to one side, Kurt in the middle belting it out, the intensity rocketing up and down . . . I saw what it was all about. Kurt was a great guitarist in his idiosyncratic way—using your limitations. A lot of people in punk are like that; it's not like you're some virtuoso muso guy, you never got that sense off him, but it was just the right thing—right on the button. It's the noise, the inflections. I was a big fan of Neil Young and the way he works the noise as well as the notes—that's passion, feeling, a lot of artistry.

Cobain's band mates had long since developed immunity to the roller coaster of his moods. For years he swung between spells of shyness, sullenness, or whatever.

STEVE DIGGLE: He was up and down on the tour—one day he'd be quiet, other times he'd be animated. Everyone gets like that on tours—you didn't detect anything heavy. There's a bit of video somewhere: I'm walking to the stage, he walks out [of] his dressing room and walks with me all the way to the stage—together. He was such a lovely guy, like they all were. All of them had learned something from punk rock and he'd taken it into this era—and he was true to it. There's a lot of inspiring things about the heaviness of what he was saying. They weren't there to be fucking bought. I thought he was sticking to his beliefs—heavy-duty, real things. Maybe dark and intense but real—we couldn't see where it was ending. As well as Kurt, Dave, Krist—incredible musicians and very thoughtful. Krist is very thoughtful! A big part of that band . . . There's the serious side, the intensity—I did get that from the way the band played. It was like thunder coming—but just in the dressing rooms, we knew about this, that we all deal with our own stuff when out on the road. But we did connect in a lot of ways with those guys. I could sympathize with that awkwardness.

Likewise, the drugs had been an issue for over three years now. There was only so long anyone could worry or cushion someone from their own actions. Plus the reality was that Cobain may have been unwell but he wasn't completely wrecked. One kind soul was sweet enough to share their own drug experience—quite a contrast to Cobain's private indulgence, which included a cushion of cash, professional minders, and a regular supply.

ANONYMOUS: We got into heroin and started making daily trips up to Seattle to go get it to keep from getting sick. That lasted for a couple years and then [we] . . . moved to New York . . . thinking we would get clean there. So, we got an apartment in Hell's Kitchen and found that, Wow! There's drugs on every street corner! It's fucking Christmas! So, you can see where that went. It took until 1995 before I got clean and ended up back in Olympia again. Yep, my parents kidnapped me from New York at the age of twenty-seven; humbling, isn't it? I was pissed, so I showed them and moved back to New York on my own and used for a couple more years, until I ended up temporarily blind from shooting up heroin traced with rat poison. Next thing I knew I woke up in a hospital and they transferred me to the medical rehab portion for a few weeks. Then I decided I didn't want to live anymore and kept threatening to kill myself, so they transferred me to the Beth Israel psych ward for a month. From there, a friend and my parents chipped in and paid for my rehab in Washington State, so I went directly there from New York. Let's see . . . That was my tenth detox and third rehab and hopefully my last.

Regardless of his physical condition, the *In Utero* tour had commenced in Europe as scheduled on February 4 with a TV appearance in Paris. The band returned to the city two weeks later with Cobain ducking out to visit an old friend.

YOURI LENQUETTE: Kurt often came by my place and he'd spend the afternoon playing the guitar or just sitting on the sofa not saying a word, just being there. Then one afternoon he said, "Youri, I'd like to do a photo session with the band tonight, would you like that? Around seven or eight?" I was like, "Well, Kurt, are you sure?" I didn't really believe it, but he was positive—I had to ask him because he hated photo sessions. More often than not, rather than me using our relationship to get more out of him, he'd use the fact we had a friendship to avoid them! My assistant was meant to be off work that evening and I told him, "Go, they're not going to come. He says he is but he's not going to come." I didn't have a makeup artist either because she asked me straight, "Do you think it'll happen?" When I said no she confirmed she was heading off; she had something else to do that night. I went back home about eight thirty, had dinner, a bit later I got the call telling me, "We're coming in twenty minutes." They arrived around ten.

It wasn't the best time for a photo shoot; Cobain's face was pockmarked and damaged.

YOURI LENQUETTE: He ended up wearing a lot of makeup because he had things on his skin as a result of his bad health and his bad habits. I told him straight, "It's going to look really bad." He agreed but I had to tell him I didn't have any makeup in the studio. My girlfriend happened to be a mixed-race girl, so he asked, "Can she lend it to me?" So he went into the makeup room, started putting it on without an assistant and, after a while, I go in. He's looking like Al Jolson! My girlfriend's skin was a light chocolate color; he has all this makeup made for her skin tone all over his face. I had to say it: "Come on Kurt, it looks ridiculous, we can't use it." So, I'm thinking this photo session isn't going to happen; it's late, I've got no assistant, we've got no makeup. I'm thinking it's best not to do it. Then this guy, who is always avoiding photo sessions even when there was a good reason to have one, he insists, "Don't you have someone you know who would have some white-skin makeup?" So I remember one friend who was OK to come out even though it was eleven now, [and I said] "Come right now, bring your girlfriend and her makeup." We just waited for him to arrive. Kurt did the makeup himself and it's all over the place but it was his idea and basically this whole session was happening because he wanted it. I wasn't commissioned by anyone except, I'd say, by Kurt himself. I wasn't ready to do such an important session—I didn't even have the films I liked to use; I just had to use others I had in the fridge from another shoot. The whole business was done with whatever we had. Artistically it wasn't my best session even if, looking back, it was the most important session of my career.

Unfortunately, Cobain does resemble a doll in some of the photos.

During this break in Paris, Cobain's well-honed sense of the pointedly mischievous was on display.

STEVE DIGGLE: He had a gun at the French gig—was pointing it out the window at the journalists. I was up in the dressing room thinking, What's he doing? Didn't know if it was a plastic gun or a real gun, to be honest. There was a whole bunch of stairs up to the dressing room at the Zenith—I'd been meeting some friends of mine so I'm milling around where the journalists were and I looked up and thought, Fuck, he's got a gun up there! He was pointing down at them. I headed upstairs and he was kneeling down by the window. I enjoyed that—it was great, funny.

YOURI LENQUETTE: The thing of holding the gun, playing with it—he brought it with him and it was his idea. Eventually I said, "OK, Kurt, let's do something else other than the gun." He's all like, "OK!

So let's try this, oh, and what if I put this hat like this?" I had this ceremonial hat made with ostrich feathers I bought in Zimbabwe and he's trying it on. The others were waiting at the back of the photo studio until it was time do some of the whole band together. First it was just three of them because Pat Smear arrived a bit later. We finished around two in the morning, chilled a bit, drank a bit, he saw photos I'd shot in Cambodia in the temples of Angkor—he loved the place. So I said, "Look, Kurt, if you're so tired, if you're so fed up with everybody, just have a break. If you like that place I can take you there, we'll relax, I'll shoot a few photos of you so that'll cover expenses and you'll get to spend two weeks in someplace really different . . ." He was really into it: "How can we get the visas in the US?" Talking, talking, "Yeah, I'll call you to organize it when I'm back in the US." Maybe his last words were "Let's get organized for the Cambodia trip, great! Wow . . ." I took them down to their taxi and that was the last time I saw him . . . In 1994 everyone could see he wasn't happy. Some things still made him really happy—like having a baby, finding good music that sparked him—but I would still say he wasn't in the best mental shape. In all areas of life—whether his role as a rock star, his relationship with the band, his drug problems—this was not a happy spell he was enduring. He told me openly, "I'm fed up with everything." Looking at my photos of the Angkor Wat temple—remember, this was the early '90s and there were no tourists, you'd maybe see a bus or an adventurous Australian tourist . . . maybe a few monks but no tourists, nothing—he really liked the place and the fact it was deserted attracted him. He really thought that nobody liked him and that everyone was against him. He was deep into this very negative way of thinking. Plus there were the drugs. I told him to take a break, "You're huge, take a holiday. You can go away a few months, a few weeks at least—break out of this and when you've recovered you can come back fresh." That's where the Cambodia idea came in.

Even at this late date, Cobain still spoke of new ideas he might try, whether it was escapes like Cambodia or new techniques he might add to his music.

STEVE DIGGLE: We spent a lot of time walking 'round these big arenas, me and him, and a lot of time on that bus. He told me he really loved the vocal of "Harmony in my Head"—I told him I smoked twenty cigarettes before I sang that to get the roughness in the voice. I said the reason I did that was that I read John Lennon did it before he did "Twist and Shout." Kurt loved that—said he'd try it out himself; he wanted that gravelly voice. He said that was his favorite song by the Buzzcocks. He was very down-to-earth, a bit of a fan, but we were fans of what he was doing. We went from there. We went through a lot of things like that—he asked me how we survived when we were locked in the tour buses. He said that in the vans from the early days you developed a sense of humor. I told him, "Sense of humor? Listen Kurt, coming from Manchester you grow up with it!" But it does help in those intense atmospheres . . . We also spoke about that shark that Damien Hirst did; he liked that—mentioned it to me, he seemed very favorable toward it. I was thinking, How does he know about *that*? I didn't think he'd be mentioning something like that—I thought we'd be talking about Neil Young more or stuff like that . . . There was one day we were all staying in the same hotel, waiting for the tour bus, Kurt said, "I wanna go with you guys." His tour manager said, "No, Kurt, we've got to do this an' that—you've got to come with us." He was insisting he wanted to come with us. That was nice—his heart was in the right place but he had a lot of interviews to do so didn't come with us in the end. It was a very natural thing with us, all of them, we'd hang out—no awkward moments. But we'd be walking 'round the stadium and there'd be fifty people chasing after him saying he had to do things—he'd say, "Steve, I just wanna walk here with you." I got what he was saying . . . Ironically we spoke about guns and stuff like that—not knowing what was to come. Now I put that together with him asking me how we survived and it feels like a profile of what was to come, something building up. But the great thing is we spent all that tour with Nirvana and I liked the record but I was turned on a lot more by them live.

The warm moments rarely lasted; the band was existing in well-catered tedium.

STEVE DIGGLE: You've got to remember, big gigs meant hours of hanging around. They had a couple of acoustics in the dressing rooms but that was it. The thing about those stadium gigs is you get a lot of traffic, so you've got to get there a bit earlier. You don't want to be hanging around too long—I like the spontaneity of turning up still feeling fresh, having a drink then getting on a stage—not hanging around for hours in a dressing room staring at the walls . . . Plus a lot of traveling involved—it wears you down, gets to you. I don't even know how many sound checks they did . . . Plus there was all this food and people coming up asking if you wanted to order your meal for after the gig. We went to look at the food for the rider before the show—fucking hell, there was everything! Meal upon meal upon meal—then they're asking us what we want for dinner! A table the length of a street you could help yourself to all day. On that tour you had to watch yourself—you could just eat all afternoon! Must have put on a couple of pounds on that one! People coming 'round saying they had to take down my meal for afterward but there's already everything there we could want. It's par for the course because it's also for the road crew—there's a lot of staff—twenty, fifty guys—a lot of people working so needing that food there. You can't just pop to the shops—not in a stadium. At the front there's a big car park, at the back there's a big car park full of tour buses—a lot of people working on those tours.

By March 1, the mood of the tour was at a perilous low as Nirvana strolled through virtually the same ninety-minute sets they'd played every night for sixty shows over five months and Cobain complained of illness—"bored and old" indeed.

YOURI LENQUETTE: There was some kind of destructive logic in him at the time. He believed the people around him didn't like him— which totally wasn't the case! From being on tour with Nirvana, seeing how they acted with him, they were really good people . . . The fact that he couldn't connect to these people anymore was a sign of depression . . . I have good memories of that session—I didn't feel there was any tension. It was just friends having drinks and shooting photos. It wasn't tense. But with depression you feel good some moments, then the very next day you're back to a negative way of thinking—it's not all one or the other. He didn't hate them, it wasn't a conflict, but my impression was he was brooding on this idea that nobody loved him, building up something not based in reality. It was just him; his whole way of seeing things was very dark . . . He didn't look well, he was in bad health mainly fueled by the use of drugs.

The tour crossed into Italy and up-and-coming Sicilian favorites Flor de Mal joined the tour.

MARCELLO CUNSOLO, Flor de Mal: We were already huge fans of Nirvana . . . I had read all about him, about Kurt, I knew almost everything that was known at the time . . . It turned out Nirvana really appreciated our music, so my recollection is that the most beautiful thing for me was to stand in the same place as Kurt would onstage and to hear them live at such close range, playing just a couple of feet away from me . . .

It's a telling point. Cobain had become a media entity. In the early days the band had played to crowds of fellow musicians, often to clusters of friends. Fame had dragged Cobain into the spotlight, isolating him (partly through his own choices) while making him ever more real in the minds of complete strangers—he'd become a modern-day ghost.

MARCELLO CUNSOLO: All I remember is that once I saw Kurt, I could see a great malaise in his eyes. A darkness . . . Kurt didn't seem very good and to see it with my own eyes, it was very sad . . . The lineup commenced with the Melvins opening, then after that we played. Flor de Mal were the solo opening act for the concert in Modena because the Melvins noted that Flor de Mal were more appreciated than they had been. The audience wanted more and so we continued until Nirvana came on . . . During our sound check, Krist and Dave of Nirvana were behind the stage and danced (I even have a record of their dancing on video somewhere) . . . I remember that Kurt was always standing aside, aloof and usually stood with his eyes closed. The rest of the band would be together and were joking with each other, as I told you, during our sound check they were there with us all the time dancing to our music . . . After the sound check, I went to look for Kurt to give him a bottle of Sicilian wine. He was in the hallway outside, that's where I found him, behind the stage standing against the wall as if he was going to puke. He still took the bottle and took the time to say "thank you" and to bow to me kindly.

YOURI LENQUETTE: Like most people who take drugs, at some point they lie to you because they know what you're going to say . . . It was obvious, I could see what was going on, I had proof of what was going on, but it was difficult to have a real discussion because he'd never tell me the reality of things. In 1994 he lied about having an addiction when, at that time, he really was addicted . . . You couldn't have a real discussion—he really was in denial. It's hard dealing with people when they just don't want to tell you. If I asked him he didn't even try to deny it but it was always the same: "Yeah, well, but just these last three days." He would tell you he was doing good in some sense even when you knew that wasn't the case—it's a key symptom in a way, someone trying to tell you not to worry and that they know what they're doing.

As Cobain's last weeks disintegrated, only fleeting contacts remained.

YOURI LENQUETTE: He called me once from Germany—Munich— early one morning, maybe nine o'clock. He said he wasn't feeling good there and asked me if I wanted to come join them on the tour. I had to say no, I was really busy, I told him I couldn't just up and go to Germany. It showed me things were getting worse while he was there. That last phone call was very brief, I heard no more news from him. After that I just got it like everybody else, Rome, then that final news.

LISA SMITH: The last time I saw him he was trying to get in my apartment building to see if Courtney was at Eric Erlandson's apartment. I went downstairs to let him in the building—he looked like shit. Apparently they were having one of their many tiffs.

ERIC ERLANDSON: It seemed like he wanted to play with other people and just have fun. No pressure. I believe he was working on ideas for something, who knows what, but he was not really in the head space to accomplish much of anything at that point.

PAUL LEARY: Shortly before Kurt's death, Gibby [Haynes] called me from rehab and told me that Kurt had checked in and was assigned to be Gibby's roommate. Kurt refused to be his roommate, and declared he wanted to escape over the back wall. Gibby told him that all he needed to do was walk out the front door, but Kurt insisted on going over the wall.

That was Friday, April 1.

On Tuesday, April 5, Mazzy Star—one of Cobain's favorite acts—played Seattle's Moore Theater. Cobain didn't make it, but Krist Novoselic did.

JOHN PURKEY: I ran into Krist at the show and with all the bad news going around I asked him straight whether it was all true. He just told me, "John, don't believe anything you hear right now. Kurt is fine." Krist seemed like he honestly felt like Kurt was fine.

Just nine weeks had passed since Cobain had stepped off the plane in Europe.

YOURI LENQUETTE: I was trying to call him because he'd said this Cambodia thing with enough certainty that I thought I needed to know yes or no because I couldn't put a two-week trip to Cambodia in the middle of my schedule without organizing. I was trying to call his home, he gave me a number, his home number, I called . . . There was no answer. I told my girlfriend, "Look, I don't know what's going on with this Cambodia trip with Kurt, I can't speak to him . . ." She called me on the Friday night to tell me, "You've got your answer if he's going to come or not. The news just broke. He was found dead at his house . . ."

PAUL LEARY: Dark days that I do not miss . . . I remember the day I heard on the news that Kurt had died. I was with Daniel Johnston [founder of K Records] in the living room of his parents' house watching the news. When it was announced, I said, "Oh my God." Daniel's mother asked who that was, and Daniel said, "That's the guy who wore my [HI, HOW ARE YOU] T-shirt."

STEVE DIGGLE: We were brothers for those weeks. When I got back and saw the news that he was gone—I couldn't believe it. You don't expect it. Seeing him on the TV all I could think is he was still alive, that it was just days ago I'd seen him.

The long-form video that emerged under the sneering title *Live! Tonight! Sold Out!* was the final project executed under Cobain's guidance.

KEVIN KERSLAKE: The team that finished the film was the same team that started it . . . With a lot of the videos that I did with Nirvana, you could say that stream of consciousness played a role . . . We wanted something that just washed over you rather than simply taking you on some sort of narrative ride. Even the stuff that we were going to shoot for it was supposed to have that sense that you were stuck in a bubble—but it wasn't supposed to just be the one bubble it ended up being. It was supposed to be a few different takes on the experience of being him, of being in the band . . . This was just the stuff that was under his bed, on his shelves and on the floor throughout the house. We hadn't yet gone on a big hunt for other footage that existed. We were just sort of forming the "base coat," if you will, for the movie that was going to be painted over with many different brushstrokes. It ended up being, to me personally, something that still feels just like a base layer . . . because the appearance and likeness rights hadn't yet been obtained for various people who were in certain shots or scenes—because those people couldn't be found or didn't want to be in the movie—we ended up cutting a lot.

Nothing was left but archival footage and latter-day sainthood.

Cobain's death was not just a Hollywood spectacular, a morality tale of rise and fall. A high school dropout from an isolated corner of the United States had, less than eight years after leaving Aberdeen, connected with people the world over. His death was all the more powerful because he died as one of the rare souls to win fame and great fortune only to declare celebrity to be null and void; something to despise and to leave behind.

YOURI LENQUETTE: What I think of is not Kurt as the big rock star. It's just Kurt, this really young guy I knew, this very talented young kid, who lost his life and all the promise he had.

Grief at his death bonded his band mates, his family, and his friends with teenagers and fans in every country of the world. This was a man, however, who had little beyond disdain for what came with the spotlight—he would have been dismayed to learn that death itself served to elevate him even further above his community. In a book about that community, it seems only right to remember the many who were lost alongside him.

DAVID YAMMER: Many friends, colleagues, and acquaintances have passed away in the last twenty-some-odd years . . . What I do like to dwell on is the many more people from the scene who survived, straightened up a bit, or even kicked real danger out of their lives altogether. I am very proud of my scene. We were family and still are: Northside punx rule!!

GLEN LOGAN: Faces of folks no longer with us come to mind. These thoughts make me smile a bit, then a wave of loss follows. It makes me once again appreciate the human side of all this. To many, grunge is a big musical movement or genre. To me it is more about the diverse and incredible folks that sought an emotional outlet in the form of the music they created and the lifestyle they lived. Some of these folks didn't make it through but they are not forgotten, even the ones who may not be the big names that many outside Seattle have come to know.

There are sadnesses scattered throughout the bands interviewed in this work. Kai Davidson of the Joyriders also took his own life:

MURDO MacLEOD: [Kai] was a good example in most things. Hardworking, compassionate, funny, wild, very smart, very loving, and an enthusiast . . . That's been my experience of people in bands over a long time—those are the sort of people they are, in general, and I'm friends with many of them to this day. They've enriched my life. They enrich everyone's life.

Colin Allin of Skin Barn was shot dead while being robbed for his laptop in Nicaragua; Sean McDonnell of Surgery sank into a coma after an asthmatic attack.

JOHN LEAMY: [Sean] was one of the funniest, driest guys, who could also wash up real nice and meet your parents and charm the pants off of them. And then he would write a song about some unmentionable whore or something. I miss that fucker.

Jeff Wood of Forgotten Apostles was taken by brain cancer; Scott F. Eakin of Knife Dance, brother of Tom Dark, died of a heart attack at age thirty-eight, while drummer David N. Araca was taken by a brain aneurysm at twenty-six; Ian McKinnon of Lush overdosed in 1990.

SLIM MOON: We all still miss [Ian]; he was a really cool funny guy—very, very popular in Olympia.

Drugs killed Rich Rosemus and Dale Moore of Oily Bloodmen; Slater Awn of Lonely Moans died a month prior to Kurt Cobain's demise.

J. M. DOBIE: Slater's attraction to heroin was similar to Kurt's in that he also suffered from a great deal of physical pain—he was fixing a friend's car and got crushed underneath it. When his doctor suddenly cut off his prescription pain meds, he turned to street drugs to numb his pain.

This book serves as a celebration of Nirvana, but it is as much about the many musicians who made the underground into the home that the superstars never wished to leave. This book is a tribute to what was created and to the people who are still making it what it is.

PAUL KIMBALL: There are so few artists of any sort that you can talk about a time pre- and post- and have it be meaningful. Nirvana was one, and they were just some guys up the street at one point. That someone from our midst went on to make this massive global and cultural impact is a crazy thing, but it's not *the* thing. It felt, at times, after Nirvana reached the levels they did, like the rest of us from the Olympia music scene were standing next to a massive explosion that shook everything around us, took some of us out, launched some of us to new places, and then re-formed the landscape completely afterward. But after the noise recedes and the smoke clears, you look at the smoldering crater for a while, scratch your head, and then go about your business.

TIMELINE

Over the course of my research for this work in 2013–2014, I interviewed members of 170 bands who performed alongside Nirvana at a full 275 of the approximately 380 shows that Nirvana performed. The timeline that follows is intended to allow you, the reader, to see the shows at which the witnesses in this book performed and where they were able to provide insight.

In order to provide greater visibility of the rhythm of Nirvana's career, its major peaks and troughs, this data has been combined with information on when/where the band performed on TV or on the radio, when/where they were engaged in major studio recording work, or where Nirvana material was being released (US dates only unless a release was only released in another region of the world). Dates listed in italics refer to occasions at which no witness within this work performed (even if someone interviewed for this book could confirm that they were physically present as an audience member or fellow party attendee).

Crucially, I would like to salute the extraordinary work of both the Nirvana Live Guide (and of Mike Ziegler and Kris Sproul, specifically) and of the LiveNirvana fan community. The hard work and deep wisdom of the individuals concerned with these two resources made this book possible. In among the wide mix of resources and personal testimonies used to construct this book and chronology I wanted to acknowledge them. For deeper information on the events in the timeline below I recommend that you visit either of these two resources.

1987

March, Raymond, WA (Nirvana play without yet possessing a definite name. Ryan Aigner: "I actually don't recall that they or myself referred to them as any particular name at that show . . ." Tony Poukkula: "They were running through different ideas for names at the time.")—Black Ice

March/April—Skid Row plays one undated house party in Aberdeen, WA

April 18, Tacoma, WA (as Skid Row)—Nisqually Delta Podunk Nightmare, Soylent Green and Yellow Snow

May 1, Olympia, WA (as Skid Row)—Dangermouse, Lansdat Blister, Nisqually Delta Podunk Nightmare

May 6, Olympia, WA (as Skid Row)—Nirvana's first radio session takes place at KAOS Radio

May 27, Tacoma, WA (as Pen Cap Chew)—Hell's Kitchen, Soylent Green

August 9, Tacoma, WA (as Bliss)—Inspector Luv and the Ride Me Babies, Sons of Ishmael

1988

January 23—Kurt Cobain and Krist Novoselic joined by Dale Crover on drums for their first recording session with Jack Endino at Reciprocal Recording in Seattle, WA

January 23, Tacoma, WA (as Ted Ed Fred)—Moral Crux

January 24—Nirvana records a first video at the Radio Shack store in Aberdeen, WA

March—Dave Foster plays the Caddyshack house in Olympia, WA, as the band's drummer

March 19, Tacoma, WA (as Nirvana)—Lush, Vampire Lezbos

March/April—One show at the Witch House, Olympia, WA, plus Nirvana's first Seattle show

April 24, Seattle, WA—Blood Circus

May 14, Olympia, WA—Nirvana plays Gilly Ann Hanner's birthday party at the Glass House with Lansdat Blister and Sister Skelter

May 21, Olympia, WA, K Dorm at the Evergreen State College—Herd of Turtles, Lansdat Blister

May 28, Olympia, WA—Nirvana plays Chris Quinn's birthday party at the Glass House with Sister Skelter

May—In time for an undated Seattle show Chad Channing joins on drums

June 2, Seattle, WA—Chemistry Set

June 11—Nirvana enters Reciprocal Recording to start recording for their first single

June 17, Ellensburg, WA—King Krab, Lush

June 30—Continued work on the single

July 3, Seattle, WA—Blood Circus, the Fluid

July 16—Sub Pop sends Cobain to re-take the "Love Buzz" vocals

July 23, Seattle, WA—Leaving Trains

July 30, Seattle, WA—Skin Yard

August 20, Olympia, WA—My Name, Swallow

August 29, Seattle, WA—Treacherous Jaywalkers

September 27—mixing session for the "Love Buzz"/"Big Cheese" single

October, Bainbridge Island, WA, undated house party

October 28, Seattle, WA—Blood Circus, Butthole Surfers

October 30, Olympia, WA, K Dorm at the Evergreen State College; Cobain smashes a guitar for the first time—Lansdat Blister and Lush

The "Love Buzz"/"Big Cheese" single is released in November

November 23, Bellingham, WA—Coffin Break, Skin Yard

The *Sub Pop 200* compilation featuring the Nirvana song "Spank Thru" is released in December

December 1, Seattle, WA—Coffin Break, D.O.A.

December 21, Hoquiam, WA—Attica, Psychlodds

December 24, 29–31, Seattle, WA—Nirvana records *Bleach* at Reciprocal Recording

December 28, Seattle, WA—Blood Circus, Swallow, Tad, the Thrown Ups all play the *Sub Pop 200* record release party

1989

January 6, Portland, OR—Mudhoney

January 14, 24—Nirvana concludes the recording of *Bleach*

January 21, Portland, OR

February, Olympia, WA, K Dorm—Helltrout and Psychlodds
February 10, San Francisco, CA
February 11, San Jose, CA—Mudhoney, Vomit Launch
February 25, Seattle, WA—the Fluid, Skin Yard
April 1, Olympia, WA—Helltrout, S.G.M., Treehouse
April 7, Seattle, WA—Love Battery
April 14, Ellensburg, WA—King Krab
April 21—Cobain joins the Go Team and records guitar for the songs "Scratch
    It Out" and "Bikini Twilight," released on seven-inch single in July
April 26, Seattle, WA—Steel Pole Bath Tub
May 26, Auburn, WA—Bible Stud, Skin Yard
June 9, Seattle, WA—Mudhoney, Tad
June 10, Portland, OR—Grind
The *Bleach* album is released on June 15
June 16, Olympia, WA (as Industrial Nirvana)—Lush
June 21, Seattle, WA
June 22, San Francisco, CA—Bad Mutha Goose
June 23, Los Angeles, CA
June 24, Los Angeles, CA—Claw Hammer, Stone by Stone
June 25, Tempe, AZ—Crash Worship, Sun City Girls
June 27, Sante Fe, NM—27 Devils Joking, Monkeyshines
June 30, San Antonio, TX—Happy Dogs, Swaziland White Band
July 1, Houston, TX—Bayou Pigs, David Von Ohlerking
July 2, Fort Worth, TX
July 3, Dallas, TX
July 5, Iowa City, IA—Blood Circus
July 6, Minneapolis, MN
July 7, Madison, WI
July 8, Chicago, IL
July 9, Wilkinsburg, PA
July 12, Philadelphia, PA—Napalm Sunday
July 13, Hoboken, NJ—Tad
July 15, Jamaica Plain, MA—Cheater Slicks, Death of Samantha
July 18, New York, NY—Cows, God Bullies, Lonely Moans, Surgery
**The *Teriyaki Asthma* compilation is released in August, featuring the Nirvana
    song "Mexican Seafood"**
August 20, 28—Cobain and Novoselic take part in *The Jury* recording sessions
August 26, Seattle, WA—Cat Butt, Mudhoney

September—Nirvana records B-sides for the *Blew* EP European tour release

September 26, Seattle, WA—Dickless, Knife Dance

September 28, Minneapolis, MN

September 30, Chicago, IL—Eleventh Day Dream

October 1, Champaign, IL—Steel Pole Bath Tub

October 2, Kalamazoo, MI—Steel Pole Bath Tub

October 3, Ann Arbor, MI—Steel Pole Bath Tub

October 4 or 5, Toledo, OH—Steel Pole Bath Tub

October 6, Cincinnati, OH—Grinch

October 7, Lawrence, KS—24-7 Spyz

October 8, Omaha, NE—Mousetrap

October 11, Denver, CO—the Fluid

October 13, Boulder, CO

October 23, Newcastle, UK—the Cateran, Tad

October 24, Manchester, UK—the Cateran, Tad

October 25, Leeds, UK—the Cateran, Tad

October 26—Nirvana records a radio session at the BBC Maida Vale Studios, London, UK for the John Peel show

October 27, London, UK—the Cateran, Tad

October 28, Portsmouth, UK—the Cateran, Tad

October 29, Birmingham, UK—Tad

October 30, Norwich, UK—Tad

November 1—Nirvana records a radio session at the Villa 65 studio, Hilversum, the Netherlands, for the *Nozems-a-Gogo* show

November 1, Rotterdam, the Netherlands—Tad

November 2, Groningen, the Netherlands—Tad

November 3, Utrecht, the Netherlands—Tad

November 4, Apeldoorn, the Netherlands—Tad

November 5, Amsterdam, the Netherlands—Tad

November 7, Mönchengladbach, West Germany—Tad

November 8, Cologne, West Germany—Tad

November 9, Hanover, West Germany—Tad

November 10, Enger, West Germany—Tad

November 11, Berlin, West Germany—Tad

November 12, Oldenburg, West Germany—Tad

November 13, Hamburg, West Germany—Tad

November 15, Heidelberg, West Germany—Tad

November 16, Nuremberg, West Germany—Tad

November 17, Gammelsdorf, West Germany—Tad
November 18, Hanau, West Germany—Tad
November 20, Linz, Austria—Tad
November 21, Budapest, Hungary—Tad
November 22, Vienna, Austria—Tad
November 23, Graz, Austria—Tad
November 24, Hohenems, Austria—Tad
November 25, Fribourg, Switzerland—Tad
November 26, Mezzago, Italy—Tad
November 27, Rome, Italy—Tad
November 29, Geneva, Switzerland—Tad
November 30, Zurich, Switzerland—Tad
December 1, Isy-Les-Moulineaux, France—Tad
December 2, Ghent, Belgium—Tad
December 3, London, UK—Mudhoney, Tad
The *Blew* EP is released in the UK in early December

1990

January 2–3—Nirvana enters Reciprocal Recording to record new song "Sappy"
January 6, Seattle, WA—Crunchbird, the Gits, Tad
January 12, Portland, OR—Oily Bloodmen
January 19, Olympia, WA
January 20, Tacoma, WA—Machine, Rhino Humpers
February 9, Portland, OR—Rawhead Rex, Screaming Trees, Tad
February 11, San Jose, CA—Tad, Vegas Voodoo
February 12, Sacramento, CA—Tad, Thornucopia
February 14, San Francisco, CA—Dickless, Tad (two performances took place
   on this date)
February 15, Los Angeles, CA—Distorted Pony, Tad
February 16, Long Beach, CA—Haywire, Tad
February 17, Tijuana, Mexico—Tad
February 19, Phoenix, AZ—Tad
February 21, Chico, CA—Tad
March 12, Vancouver, BC—the Bombshells, Tad
March 20, Nirvana records their attempt at a formal video at the Evergreen State
   College

April 1, Chicago, IL—God's Acre, Bhang Revival

April 2–6—Nirvana record demos for their (aborted) second Sub Pop album provisionally entitled *Sheep* at Smart Studios, Madison, WI

April 6, Madison, WI—Tad, Victim's Family

April 8, Milwaukee, WI

April 9, Minneapolis, MN—Tad, Victim's Family

April 10, Ann Arbor, MI—Tad, Victim's Family

April 14, Cincinnati, OH—(Peter Prescott, Volcano Suns: "The show that never happened—think we were to play with them in Cincinnati and they canceled, so we never ran into them.")

April 16, Toronto, Canada

April 17, Montréal, Canada

April 18, Cambridge, MA—the Bags

April 20, Swarthmore, PA

April 21, Cambridge, MA—Slaughter Shack

April 26, New York, NY—Rat at Rat R

April 27, Amherst, MA—3 Merry Widows, Cordelia's Dad, Gobblehoof, New Radiant Storm King, Sweet Lickin' Honey Babes

April 28, Hoboken, NJ—the Jesus Lizard

April 29, Washington, DC—Loop

April 30, Philadelphia, PA

May 1, Chapel Hill, NC

May 2, Charlotte, NC

May 4, Tampa, FL

May 5, Jacksonville Beach, FL

May 6, Atlanta, GA

May 9, Columbus, OH—Barbed Wire Dolls

May 10, Cincinnati, OH—Coffin Break

May 11, Tulsa, OK

May 13, Lincoln, NE

May 14, Denver, CO—Jux County

May 17, Boise, ID—24-7 Spyz

July 11, 24—Nirvana records the "Sliver" single

The *Hard to Believe* compilation is released in August, featuring Nirvana covering the song "Do You Love Me?" by Kiss

August 16, Las Vegas, NV

August 17, Hollywood, CA

August 19, San Diego, CA—Chemical People

August 20, Sacramento, CA

August 21, San Francisco, CA

August 23, Portland

August 24, Seattle

August 25, Vancouver, BC

The "Sliver"/"Dive" single is released in September

September 22, Seattle—the Derelicts, the Dwarves

September 25—Grohl is given an audition at the Dutchman rehearsal rooms in Seattle, then Cobain records a radio session for KAOS Radio, Olympia, on Calvin Johnson's *Boy Meets Girl* show where he announces Grohl has joined Nirvana

The *Heaven and Hell* compilation is released in October, featuring Nirvana covering the song "Here She Comes Now" by the Velvet Underground

October—Cobain joins friends Earth at Smegma Studios, Portland, to record vocals for the songs "Bureaucratic Desire for Revenge" and "Divine and Bright"

October 11, Olympia, WA—Witchypoo

October 17, Olympia, WA—Unrest

October 21—Nirvana records a radio session at the BBC Maida Vale Studios, London, UK, for the John Peel show

October 23, Birmingham, UK

October 24, London, UK—Godflesh

October 25, Leeds, UK—Arm, Victim's Family

October 26, Edinburgh, UK—Shonen Knife, the Vaselines

October 27, Nottingham, UK—Shonen Knife

October 29, Norwich, UK—Jacob's Mouse

November 25, Seattle—Heavy into Jeff, Holy Rollers

December 31, Portland—Caustic Soda, Hitting Birth, Roger Nusic, Thrillhammer

1991

Nirvana's live cover of the Vaselines' song "Molly's Lips" is released on a split single with the Fluid in January

January 1—Nirvana enters the Music Source Studio, Seattle, to record demos

January 18, Olympia, WA—Fitz of Depression, Helltrout, Nubbin

March 2, Boise, ID—Anxiety Prophets, Blank Frank and the Tattooed Gods

March 4, Calgary, Canada

March 5, Edmonton, Canada

March 8, Vancouver, BC—Doughboys, Mudhoney, Screaming Trees, the Wongs

March 9, Victoria, Canada

April 13, Olympia, WA (Cobain/Grohl with Witchypoo)—Giant Henry, Witchypoo

April 17, Seattle, WA—Fitz of Depression

May 2–28—Nirvana enters Sound City Studios, Burbank, CA, to record *Nevermind*

May 29, Los Angeles, CA—Fitz of Depression, I Own the Sky

The *Grunge Years* compilation is released in June, featuring the Nirvana song "Dive"

June 1, Olympia, WA (Cobain, Grohl with Witchypoo)—Giant Henry, Witchypoo

June 8, Olympia

June 10, Englewood, CA—the Jesus Lizard

June 11, Salt Lake City, UT

June 13, San Francisco, CA

June 14, Los Angeles, CA—Hole

June 15, Tijuana, Mexico

June 17, Sacramento, CA—Kai Kln

June 18, Santa Cruz, CA

June 20, Portland, OR

The *Kill Rock Stars* compilation is released in August, featuring the Nirvana song "Beeswax"

August 15, Los Angeles, CA—Wool

August 20, Cork, Ireland

August 21, Dun Laoghaire, Ireland—Mexican Pets, Power of Dreams

August 23, Reading, UK—Power of Dreams, Teenage Fanclub

August 24, Cologne, Germany

August 25, Hasselt, Belgium

August 27, Bremen, Germany—Didjits, Gumball

August 28, Halle, Germany

August 29, Stuttgart, Germany

August 30, Nuremberg, Germany

September 1, Rotterdam, the Netherlands—Charmin' Children, Mudhoney, Paradogs, Son of Bazerk

September 3—Nirvana records a radio session at the BBC Maida Vale Studios, London, UK, for the John Peel show

The "Smells Like Teen Spirit" single is released on September 10

September 16, Seattle, WA

September 20, Toronto, Canada

September 21, Montréal, Canada

September 23, Boston, MA—Cliffs of Dooneen

The *Nevermind* album is released on September 23

September 24, Boston, MA

September 25, Providence, RI

September 26, New Haven, CT

September 27, Trenton, NJ

September 28, New York, NY (two performances took place on this date)

September 30, Pittsburgh, PA

October 1, Philadelphia, PA

October 2, Washington, DC

October 4, Chapel Hill, NC

October 5, Athens, GA

October 6, Atlanta, GA

October 7, Memphis, TN

October 9, Columbus, OH

October 10, Cleveland, OH

October 11, Detroit, MI

October 12, Chicago, IL

October 14, Minneapolis, MN (two performances took place on this date)

October 16, St. Louis, MO

October 17, Lawrence, KS—Paw

October 19, Dallas, TX—Sister Double Happiness, Thinking Fellers Union Local 282

October 20, Houston, TX—Sister Double Happiness

October 21, Austin, TX—Sister Double Happiness (two performances took place on this date)

October 23, Tempe, AZ—Sister Double Happiness

October 24, San Diego, CA

October 24, Tijuana, Mexico—Hole, Sister Double Happiness

October 25, Los Angeles, CA—Hole, Sister Double Happiness

October 26, San Francisco, CA—Sister Double Happiness

October 27, Los Angeles, CA—Hole

October 29, Portland—Mudhoney, Sprinkler

October 30, Vancouver, BC—Mudhoney

October 31, Seattle, WA—Mudhoney

November 4, Bristol, UK—Midway Still

November 5, London, UK—Captain America, Television Personalities

November 6, Wolverhampton, UK—Captain America

November 9—Nirvana records a radio session at the BBC Maida Vale Studios, London, UK, for the *Mark Goodier Evening Session*

November 10, Berlin, Germany

November 11, Hamburg, Germany

November 12, Frankfurt, Germany

November 13, Munich, Germany

November 14, Vienna, Austria—Skin Yard

November 16, Muggia, Italy

November 17, Mezzago, Italy

November 19, Rome, Italy

November 20, Baricella, Italy

November 23, Ghent, Belgium—Hole

November 25—Nirvana records their last-ever radio session at the NOB Audio Studio, Hilversum, the Netherlands, for the *Nozems-a-Gogo* and *Twee Meter De Lucht In* shows

November 25, Amsterdam, the Netherlands

November 26, Bradford, UK—Captain America, Shonen Knife

Nirvana appears on the *Top of the Pops* TV show in Borehamwood on December 27

November 27, Birmingham, UK—Captain America, Shonen Knife

November 28, Sheffield, UK—Captain America, Shonen Knife

November 29, Edinburgh, UK—Captain America, Shonen Knife

November 30, Glasgow, UK—Captain America, Shonen Knife

December 1, Edinburgh, UK (as Teen Spirit)—the Joyriders

December 2, Newcastle, UK—Captain America, Shonen Knife

December 3, Nottingham, UK—Captain America, Shonen Knife

December 4, Manchester, UK—Captain America, Shonen Knife

December 5, London, UK—Captain America, Shonen Knife

Nirvana appears on the *Tonight with Jonathan Ross* TV show in London, UK, on December 6

December 7, Rennes, France

December 27, Los Angeles, CA

December 28, Del Mar, CA
December 29, Tempe, AZ
December 31, Daly City, CA

1992

January 2, Salem, OR
Nirvana rehearses on January 9 in New York, ready for their TV appearance on
    Saturday Night Live on January 11
Nirvana records a performance for MTV in New York on January 10
January 24, Sydney, Australia—Tumbleweed
January 25, Sydney, Australia
January 26, Gold Coast, Australia
January 27, Brisbane, Australia
January 30, Adelaide, Australia—Tumbleweed
January 31, Melbourne, Australia—the Guttersnipes, Tumbleweed
February 1, Melbourne, Australia—Tumbleweed
February 2, Melbourne, Australia—Tumbleweed
February 5, Canberra, Australia—Tumbleweed
The *Hormoaning* EP is released in Asia/Pacific on February 5
February 6, Sydney, Australia
February 7, Sydney, Australia—Crow, Nunbait
February 9, Auckland, New Zealand—Second Child
February 14, Osaka, Japan
February 16, Nagoya, Japan
February 17, Kawasaki, Japan
February 19, Tokyo, Japan
February 21, Honolulu, HI
February 22, Honolulu, HI
The "Come as You Are" single is released March 3
The *Bleach* album is reissued in April
April 7 and one unknown date—Nirvana enters the Laundry Room Studio to
    record B-side material
The *Eight Songs for Greg Sage and the Wipers* compilation is released in June,
    featuring Nirvana covering "Return of the Rat" by the Wipers
June 21, Dublin, Ireland—Teenage Fanclub

June 22, Belfast, Ireland—Teenage Fanclub

June 24, Paris, France—Teenage Fanclub

June 26, Roskilde, Denmark—Teenage Fanclub

June 27, Turku, Finland—Teenage Fanclub

June 28, Sandvika, Norway—Teenage Fanclub

June 30, Stockholm, Sweden—Teenage Fanclub

July 2, Valencia, Spain—Teenage Fanclub

July 3, Madrid, Spain—Teenage Fanclub

July 4, Bilbao, Spain—Teenage Fanclub

The "Lithium" single is released on July 13

August 30, Reading, UK—Björn Again, Pele, Shonen Knife, Teenage Fanclub

Nirvana rehearses on September 8 in Los Angeles for their TV appearance at the MTV Video Music Awards ceremony on September 9

September 10, Portland, OR—Calamity Jane, Jello Biafra

September 11, Seattle, WA—Fitz of Depression

October 3, Bellingham, WA—(unannounced guest show) Mudhoney, Medelicious, Saucer

October 4, Seattle, WA—(unannounced guest show) Mudhoney

October 25–26—Nirvana enters the Word of Mouth Productions studio, Seattle, WA (formerly Reciprocal Recording) to record the first demos for their next album

October 29, Buenos Aires, Argentina—Novoselic and Grohl join Pirata Industrial onstage at a nightclub

October 30, Buenos Aires, Argentina—Calamity Jane, Los Brujos

November—Cobain enters the Laundry Room Studio to record the guitar part for a single to feature William S. Burroughs. He also joins Melvins in San Francisco for the *Houdini* sessions

The "In Bloom" single is released on November 30

The *Incesticide* compilation is released on December 14

1993

January 16, São Paulo, Brazil—Biquíni Cavadão, Defalla, Dr. Sin

January 19–21—Nirvana enters the BMG Ariola Ltda Studio in Rio de Janeiro to record further demos for their new album; Cobain also takes part in a demo session for Hole on January 21

January 23, Rio de Janeiro, Brazil—Biquíni Cavadão, Defalla, Dr. Sin

February 12–26—Nirvana enters the Pachyderm Recording Studio near Minneapolis, MN, to record *In Utero*

The "Oh the Guilt"/"Puss" split-single with the Jesus Lizard is released on February 15

April 9, Daly City, CA—Benefit for the Tresnjevka Women's Group

May—Cobain enters the Bad Animals Studio, Seattle, for the remixing of the "Heart-Shaped Box" and "All Apologies" single A-sides

The single "The Priest They Called Him" is released on July 1, featuring Cobain's guitar work backing William S. Burroughs's reading

July 14–15—Nirvana stages their first rehearsal since *In Utero* with cellist Lori Goldston and second guitarist "Big" John Duncan

July 23, New York, NY—the Jesus Lizard

August 6, Seattle—Hell Smells, Kill Sybil, Tad

The "Heart-Shaped Box" single is released on August 30

September 8, New York, NY—Cobain and Courtney Love duet for Rock Against Rape

The *In Utero* album is released on September 13

Nirvana rehearses on September 23 in New York, ready for their TV performance on *Saturday Night Live* on September 25

October—Cobain joins Hole at Triclops Recording in Atlanta, GA, for a demo session

October 14–16—Nirvana enters Hayvenhurst Studios in Van Nuys, CA, to rehearse, ready for the *In Utero* tour

October 18, Phoenix, AZ—Mudhoney

October 19, Albuquerque, NM—Mudhoney

October 21, Kansas City, KS—Mudhoney

October 22, Davenport, IA—Mudhoney

October 23, Chicago, IL—Mudhoney

October 25, Chicago, IL—Mudhoney

October 26, Milwaukee, WI—Mudhoney

Nirvana song "Verse Chorus Verse" (aka "Sappy") released on the *No Alternative* compilation for the Red Hot AIDS Benefit Series on October 26

October 27, Kalamazoo, MI—Boredoms, Meat Puppets

October 29, Detroit, MI—Boredoms, Meat Puppets

October 30, Dayton, OH—Boredoms, Meat Puppets

October 31, Akron, OH—Boredoms, Meat Puppets

November 2, Verdun, Canada—Boredoms, Meat Puppets

The Nirvana song "I Hate Myself and I Want to Die" is released on the *Beavis and Butt-head Experience* compilation on November 3

November 4, Toronto, Canada—Boredoms, Meat Puppets

November 5, Amherst, NY—Boredoms, Meat Puppets

November 7, Williamsburg, VA—Half Japanese

November 8, Philadelphia, PA—Half Japanese

November 9, Bethlehem, PA—Half Japanese

November 10, Springfield, MA—Half Japanese

November 12, Fitchburg, MA—Half Japanese

November 13, Washington, DC—Half Japanese

November 14, New York—Half Japanese

November 15, New York—Half Japanese

Nirvana rehearses on November 16–17 at a studio in Weehawken, NJ, ready for their appearance on *MTV Unplugged* on November 18 in New York; the Meat Puppets accompany them

November 26, Jacksonville, FL—Come

November 27, Miami, FL—Come

November 28, Lakeland, FL—Come

November 29, Atlanta, GA—Come

December 1, Birmingham, AL—Come

December 2, Tallahassee, FL—Come

December 3, New Orleans, LA—Shonen Knife

December 5, Dallas, TX—Shonen Knife

December 6, Houston, TX—Shonen Knife

The "All Apologies"/"Rape Me" single is released on December 6

December 8, Oklahoma, OK—Shonen Knife

December 9, Omaha, NE—Shonen Knife

December 10, Saint Paul, MN—Shonen Knife

Nirvana fails to rehearse on December 12, ready for their TV appearance on December 13 for *MTV Live and Loud*; Cypress Hill accompany them

December 14, Salem, OR

December 15, Boise, ID

December 16, Ogden, UT

December 18, Denver, CO

December 29, San Diego, CA—Butthole Surfers, Chokebore

December 30, Inglewood, CA—Butthole Surfers, Chokebore

December 31, Oakland, CA—Butthole Surfers, Chokebore

1994

January 1, Central Point, OR—Butthole Surfers, Chokebore

January 3, Vancouver, BC—Butthole Surfers, Chokebore

January 4, Vancouver, BC—Butthole Surfers, Chokebore

January 6, Spokane, WA—Butthole Surfers, Chokebore

January 7, Seattle, WA—Butthole Surfers, Chokebore

January 8, Seattle, WA—Butthole Surfers, Chokebore

January 28–30, Seattle—Last ever Nirvana recording session

Nirvana appears on the *Nulle Part Ailleurs* TV show in Paris on February 4

February 6, Cascais, Portugal—Buzzcocks

February 8, Madrid, Spain—Buzzcocks

February 9, Barcelona, Spain—Buzzcocks

February 10, Toulouse, France—Buzzcocks

February 12, Toulon, France—Buzzcocks

February 14, Paris, France—Buzzcocks

Nirvana's last-ever photo session takes place late on February 14/early on February 15 in Paris

February 16, Rennes, France—Buzzcocks

February 18, Grenoble, France—Buzzcocks

February 21, Modena, Italy—Flor de Mal

February 22, Marino, Italy—Flor de Mal

Nirvana makes their last-ever TV appearance on the *Tunnel* TV show in Rome on February 23

February 24, Milan, Italy

February 25, Milan, Italy

February 27, Ljubljana, Slovenia

March 1, Munich, Germany—Nirvana's last-ever show

March 4, Rome, Italy—Cobain hospitalized

March 8, Rome, Italy—Cobain released from hospital

March 12, SeaTac Airport—Cobain returns home

March 25, Seattle—Drug intervention at Cobain's home; Cobain records his last demo session with Pat Smear in the basement of the house

March 30, Los Angeles, CA—Cobain arrives at rehab

April 1, Los Angeles, CA—Cobain leaves rehab

April 5, Seattle, WA—Cobain commits suicide

April 8, Seattle, WA—Cobain's body found

INDEX

A&M Records, 153
Aaron, Tim, 148
Abdul, Paula, 164
AC/DC, 43, 47
Aerosmith, 34, 43
Aigner, Ryan, 4–8, 15–16, 18, 25–26,
    31–32, 62–63, 76–78, 151, 156,
    159–60
Albini, Steve, 270–71
Albright, Sam, 55
Alice in Chains, 81, 95, 153, 187, 263,
    264, 277, 288
ALL, 160
Alletzhauser, Billy, 98, 100, 102–4, 122
Allin, Colin, 317
Allin, GG, 164
Allin, Merle, 165
Alternative Press, 119
Amnesty International, 145–46
Amorphous Head, 61
AMQA, 11
Anderson, Billy, 274
Anderson, Michael, 69, 97
Anderson, Scott, 196
Angkor Wat, 308

Ann Arbor, Mich., 99, 143
Anomie Records, 65
Anxiety Prophets, 36, 189
Apramian, Lisa Rose, 186
Araca, David N., 317
Argentina, 255–61, 269, 287
Arm, 173
Arm, Mark, 60, 68, 186, 234, 246
Aronstamn, Joseph, 175
Atlantic Records, 275
Australia, 217–22, 224–29
Australian National University, 224
Awn, Slater, 317
Axiom, 85–88
Ayers, Scott, 65

B-52's, 255
Babes in Toyland, 184, 186
Babior, Greg, 156
Backbeat, 303
Backlash, 118, 119
Bad Brains, 205, 245
Bad Mutha Goose, 42
Bags, 84
Barnett, Jules, 223, 231

Bartholomew, Marc, 121, 128–32
Bayou Pigs, 65
BBQ Killers, 287
Beat Happening, 55, 134
Beatles, 105, 120, 134, 147, 160, 248, 271
Bed Rock, 10
Beesecker, Marci, 258
Beezer, Leighton, 56–58, 66, 69–70, 134, 245–46
Beezus and Ramona, 47
Bell, Lawrence, 210
Berman, David, 145
Bernstein, Jesse, 70
Bernstein, Nils, 57
Berz, George, 158
Bhang Revival, 84, 184
Biafra, Jello, 180, 243–44
Bible Stud, 38, 118
Bierkeller, 211
Big Black, 13, 33
Big Drill Car, 160
Bikini Kill, 153, 182, 194, 245
Billig, Janet, 286
Binder, Damien, 218, 226, 227, 230–31
Biquini Cavadão, 262, 264
Birch, Steve, 207
Bischoff, Matt, 103, 187
Bishop, Alan, 35, 85–86, 90, 203–4
Björn Again, 240–41
Black, Chris, 12, 14, 41
Black Flag, 15, 32, 73, 141, 178
Black Ice, 2, 4, 44
Black Sabbath, 130, 149, 169
Bland, Danny, 64, 97, 135
Blank Frank and the Tattooed Gods, 188
Blind Pig, 99, 143
Bliss, 13–15, 41
Bloch, Al, 191, 193, 197
Blood, Bliss, 65
Blood Circus, 41, 50, 59, 70
Blue Gallery, 82, 176, 177
Bodenheimer, Duane Lance, 20–21, 118, 138–39, 163–66, 169, 174, 186, 246
Boggan, Scott, 26
Bollen, Andy, 212–15

Bolton, Paul, 109
Bombshells, 133–34, 183–84
Boothby, Hugo, 171, 172
Boothby, Jebb, 171–72
Boredoms, 298
Bowie, David, 164
Boyce, Megan, 252–53
Bratmobile, 194
Brazil, 262–68
B-Real, 294–95, 297
Breeders, 290–91, 293
Brennan, Abe, 23, 58, 59, 67, 118, 233–35
Brennen, Jen, 218
Brewer, Jed, 53–54, 116, 122, 129–31
Brockhoff, Paul, 219–22, 224, 227
Brokaw, Chris, 287–90, 297–99
Buenos Aires, 257–62, 264, 265, 273
Bulging Eye, 103
Burckhard, Aaron, 2, 4, 6, 15, 34, 57, 159, 160
Burdyshaw, James, 36–37, 65–66, 71, 82–84, 97, 195
Burns, Colin, 94, 108, 117–18, 140, 144, 183, 196–97
Burnside, Jonathan, 273–76
Burroughs, William S., 282
Burton, Cliff, 3
Busic, Ivan, 262–64, 266, 269
Butcher, Shaun, 216–17, 219, 222, 223, 225, 226, 228, 229
Butthole Surfers, 137–38, 217, 293
Buzzcocks, 236, 309

Caddyshack, 26, 27, 30, 51
Calamity Jane, 30, 45, 184, 257, 258, 260, 261, 287
Cambodia, 308–9, 314
Camper Van Beethoven, 153
Canada, 133
Canary, Kelly, 186
Canzi, Mike, 11–14
Captain America, 210–12
Carlson, Dylan, 38, 77, 127
Carroll, Ted, 130–31, 271
Cat Butt, 36, 64, 65, 82, 97

Cateran, 109
Caustic Soda, 74
Cave, Nick, 175
Center on Contemporary Art (CoCA), 82–83
Chamberlain, Jimmy, 202
Channing, Chad, 22, 33, 39, 57–59, 76, 87, 103, 112, 125, 130, 134, 139, 141, 143, 151–52, 155, 158, 169, 173, 235
Charmin' Children, 201
Chavez, Dave, 12, 14
Cheater Slicks, 88
Chemical People, 160
Chemistry Set, 26, 277
Chi Pig, 188
Chokebore, 286, 292
Chrome, 275
City Heat, 118
Claw Hammer, 88
Cliffs of Dooneen, 202, 203
Club Lingerie, 191
Cobain, Frances Bean, 257, 267, 274, 298
Cobain, Kurt, 2–4, 6–8, 15, 16, 17–20, 22, 23, 27–28, 31–34, 38–40, 44–47, 50, 51, 55, 57–59, 68–71, 72, 75–80, 82–86, 88–90, 93, 95, 96, 100, 102–4, 111–13, 115, 123–29, 131, 132, 134, 139, 141–43, 145, 148, 149, 150–51, 153–60, 166, 168–69, 171–73, 175, 177, 182, 186, 187, 189, 190, 191, 194–96, 199, 200, 205–10, 212–15, 217, 221, 223–32, 235–42, 244, 245, 253, 254, 256, 257, 259–62, 264–68, 272–76, 279–81, 283, 284, 285–89, 291, 293–301, 302–16
    clothing of, 12–13
    death of, xv, 302, 313–17
    dresses worn by onstage, 164, 165, 244
    drug use of, 173–75, 222–23, 240, 241, 260, 266, 269, 272, 275, 276, 279, 284, 289, 305, 308, 312–13
    eyeliner worn by, 170, 174
    living arrangements of, 7, 194, 235, 302
    Love and, 159, 209, 229, 235, 239, 254, 284, 286, 297
    as music fan, 225–26
    skin problems of, 306–7
    songwriting of, 105, 107, 134, 150, 153, 156–57, 161, 169, 180, 192, 215, 270, 299–301
    stomach problems of, 112, 126, 223
Coffin Break, 19, 40, 41
College Music Journal (CMJ), 91, 92
Columbia Records, 153
Come, 286, 287
Community World Theater (CWT), 1, 7, 9–13, 17, 19, 22, 28, 37, 57
Cordelia's Dad, 53, 146
Corgan, Billy, 202
Cornell, Chris, 26
Cosloy, Gerard, 137
Cosmic Psychos, 220
Cows, 93, 249
Crash Worship, 85, 90
Crawford, Craig, 36, 101–2, 109
Creature Booking, 103
Credo, Rich, 106
Creed, Helios, 275
Creep, 26
Crover, Dale, 2, 3, 17–19, 21–23, 25–26, 33, 57, 160, 170, 275
Crow, 217, 218
Crunchbird, 20, 60, 124
Cruz Records, 160
Crystal Image, 2
Cunsolo, Marcello, 311, 312
Cypress Hill, 294–95
C/Z Records, 55, 199, 235, 247

Dahlia, Blag, xv, 107, 136, 164–66, 174, 271
Damned, 91
Dangermouse, 9, 38
Danielson, Kurt, 64, 111–13, 128–19, 135–37, 251, 284
Dark, Tom, 51, 53, 65, 100, 103, 106, 317
Daudt, Castor, 262, 263, 266–69
Davidson, Kai, 112, 316
Davies, Mark, 162–63, 208
Davis, Peter, 103

Day, Doug, 97
Dead Federation, 106
Dead Kennedys, 219, 248
Death of Samantha, 86
Defalla, 262, 263
Delgardo, J. R., 88
Denenfeld, Renée, 74, 176–78, 184, 185
Derelicts, 20, 165, 186
Desjardins, Chris, 85
Devo, 33
DGC Records, 153, 179–80, 232, 233,
    250, 276, 283
Dharma Bums, 75
Dickless, 54, 187
Didjits, 204
Diggle, Steve, 236–37, 287, 302–5, 307,
    309–10, 314
Dillard, Mike, 3
Dilley, Shelli, 6, 8, 156, 235, 239
Dinosaur Jr., 34, 98, 195, 200, 201, 218
Dischord, 162, 175
Distorted Pony, 130
D.O.A., 40
Dobie, J. M., 317
Doroschuk, Ivan, 188
Doughboys, 109, 188
Dow, Dan, 53
Doyle, Tad, 57–58, 68, 111–12, 129,
    131–32, 143, 200, 234, 281
Dr. Sin, 262, 263
Duet, David Emmanuel, 83
Duran Duran, 265
DUSTdevils, 170
Duvall, Siobhan, 133–34, 183–84
Dwarves, xv, 164–66
Dyer, Tom, 54

Eakin, Scott F., 103, 317
Earth, 127, 157
Echo and the Bunnymen, 47
Eckman, Chris, 66
Eckman, Grant, 66
Edinburgh, 214
Edu K, 262, 263, 265–69
Eickelberg, Anne, 137–38, 208

Ein Abend In Wien, 200
Eleventh Dream Day, 53
Ellis, Timo, 132, 180, 190
Emery, Jill, 161, 210
eMpTy, 55
Endino, Jack, 16, 18, 20–23, 44, 50, 61,
    66, 67, 135, 160, 162
Epic Records, 153
Erlandson, Eric, 162, 209, 276, 313
Erotic Music Law, 242
Europe, 109–11, 134, 224, 233–42
Evergreen State College, 155, 170, 180,
    182
  Greater Evergreen Students'
    Community Cooperation
    Organization, 8–9, 39
Everman, Jason, 78–79, 90, 288
Extreme, 263
Eye, Yamantaka, 298–99

Fair, Jad, 285, 290–92, 294, 298, 300
Fallon, Dennis, 89
Fallout Records, 118
False Prophets, 14
Farnsworth, Ed, 52, 58, 86–87
Farrell, John, 89
Feedtime, 220
Fender's, 118
Fenton, Peter, 217–18, 221, 223, 227
Fisk, Steve, 55
Fitzgerald's, 106
Fitz of Depression, 181
Flaming Lips, 102
Flea, 264, 266, 295
Fleetwood, Mick, 192
Fleming, Don, 161, 162, 179–80,
    199–200, 204, 303
Flesh Eaters, 85
Flipside, 119, 120
Flor de Mal, 311, 312
Floyd, Gary, 205–7, 209, 245
Fluid, 103, 122, 187
Flynn, 203
Flynn, Tom, 63
Flying Nun Records, 217

Forgotten Apostles, 317

Forrest, 100–101, 139–40

Foster, Dave, 17, 25–26, 28, 29, 31–34, 48, 57, 76, 77, 151

Fotheringham, Ed, 26, 246

Franke, Kevin, 131

Franklin, Neil, 195–96

Fraser, Cam, 109, 111

Fredericks, Beau, 37, 108, 161, 167, 245, 252

Freeborn, Tim, 11, 13–15

Frogs, 182

Fugazi, 130, 204–5, 217

Geffen Records, 179–80, 218, 236

Germany, 313

Germs, 288

Gersh, Gary, 278

Giant Henry, 48

Gillard, Doug, 86, 105, 137

Ginoli, Jon, 108, 243–45

Girls School, 184

Girl Trouble, 10, 55, 176

Gits, 55, 279–81, 283

Globo TV, 268

Gobblehoof, 146, 148, 158

God Bullies, 91, 92

God's Acre, 84

Goldenvoice, 118

Goldring, Joe, 61, 79–80

Gorilla Gardens Rock Theater, 11, 40

Go Team, 127

Gouveia, Bruno Castro, 262, 264, 266, 268

Grapmayer, Marcus, 173

Greater Evergreen Students' Community Cooperation Organization (GESCCO), 8–9, 39

Green, Kerry, 158

Green Day, 107

Green River, 41, 47, 84, 121, 180

Grinch, 98

Grind, 73, 82

Grohl, Dave, 58, 130, 141, 168–73, 175, 177, 180, 189, 191, 192, 194–97, 199,
201–2, 207–11, 213, 214, 226, 228–32, 234–35, 237, 239, 241, 253, 254, 257, 260, 261, 264, 266, 282, 283, 288, 289, 292, 293, 295, 297, 298, 301, 302–4, 312

Grunge Years, The, 187

Guerrisi, Gabriel, 255, 256, 258, 260–61, 269

Gumball, 161

Guns N' Roses, 243, 269, 285, 288–89

Guttersnipes, 197, 216, 219

Haden, Josh, 56, 235

Hale, Terry Lee, 66–67, 277

Half Japanese, 285, 300

Hallerman, Stuart, 190

Hampshire College, 145–47

Hampson, Robert, 142, 149

Hanna, Kathleen, 182, 283

Hanner, Gilly Ann, 45–48, 74, 182, 184, 186, 203, 256–61

Hanner, Megan, 258, 259

Hanzek, Chris, 20

Happy Dogs, 89

Harbine, Scott, 47, 253, 254

Hard, Mike, 91, 92, 99, 101, 108, 205

Hard-Ons, 160

Harner, Duke, 3, 44

Harvey, Curtis, 289

Hatch, Dana, 88, 165, 234, 249–50

Hayden, Joseph, 158

Hayden, Josh, 50

Haynes, Gibby, 313

Haywire, 116

Heavy into Jeff, 69

Helbert, Steve, 30

Hell House, 10, 11

Hell's Kitchen, 12

Hell Smells, 70, 281

Helltrout, 20, 25, 32, 33, 76, 79, 154

Hell Yeah Records, 52

Herd of Turtles, 29

He Sluts, 11

Hill, Nathan, 38, 72

Hirst, Damien, 309

Hitting Birth, 42, 157

Hole, 161, 162, 184–86, 210, 276, 286

Holland, Keith, 53

Hollywood Rock Festival, 262–69

Holy Rollers, 175

Home Alive, 282

Homestead, 137

Hootie and the Blowfish, 282

Houdini, 273–76

House, Daniel, 55, 160

HUB Ballroom, 128–29

Hunter, Matt, 117, 140–42, 152, 158

Hurst, Mark, 216, 221, 222, 227, 230

Hüsker Dü, 89, 98, 121, 153

Huston, Paula, 42

Inspector Luv and the Ride Me Babies, 11, 37

International Pop Underground Convention, 198

I Own the Sky, 158

Ireland, Allen, 189

Iron Maiden, 3

Irvine, Peter, 53, 64, 145–47, 248–49

Italy, 311

Jabberjaw, 191–93

Jackson, Michael, 201

Jackson, Theo, 231

Jacob's Mouse, 170–72

Jane's Addiction, 175, 205

Japan, 232

Jasper, Meagan, 186

Jeevers, Eric "Danno," 200–202

Jensen, Rich, 135

Jesus Lizard, 141, 235

Jett, Joan, 283

Johnson, Arthur, 287

Johnson, Calvin, 26, 38, 39, 47, 52, 121, 127, 163, 170, 198

Johnson, Jaime Robert, 20, 21, 60, 73, 95, 99, 119, 120, 125, 277–78

Johnston, Daniel, 314

Johnston, Tom, 286

Joseph, Lee, 52

Joseph, Lori, 84, 119–20, 143–44, 184

Joy Division, 215

Joyriders, 316

Judgment Night, 295

Jury, 127

Kai Kln, 195, 196

KAOS, 10, 19, 120, 121, 168

Kaptain "Scott Gear" Skillit Weasel, 124–25

Kasper, Adam, 300–301, 302

Karren, Billy, 194

Kastner, John, 109–10, 188–89

KCMU, 60, 62, 67, 120, 121

KDVS, 122, 129, 131

Keen, Gordon, 211–13

Keithley, Joe, 40–41, 43, 73–74, 248

Kelly, Dec, 214

Kerr, Tim, 42, 86, 117, 182, 247

Kerslake, Kevin, 237–38, 272–73, 315

Kiedis, Anthony, 295

Kilburn National, 211

Killing Joke, 169

Kill Sybil, 28

Kimball, Paul, 20, 31, 46, 48, 54, 58, 68, 76–79, 169–69, 180, 317–18

King Krab, 38, 72

Kings of Oly, 26

Kirkwood, Cris, 285–86, 292–94, 297–98

Kiss, 43, 160, 193, 251

Knack, 153

Knife Dance, 51, 317

Koenig, Lisa, 30–31, 98, 183

Koretzky, Dan, 53

Kostelnik, Alex, 46–47, 132, 155–56

Kot, Greg, 122

K Records, 20, 47, 52, 54, 55, 109, 130, 163, 170, 314

Kriz, Josh, 36, 189–90

KUSF, 206

L7, 172, 184, 186, 209–10, 269, 279

Lamefest UK, 111

Lanegan, Mark, 38, 127

Lansdat Blister, 20, 46, 76
L.A. Times, 275
Lawlor, Shawn, 29, 32
Lead Belly, 151
Leamy, John, 92, 93, 200, 317
Learned, Brian, 26
Leary, Paul, 283, 297, 299, 313, 314
Leech, Nick, 242
Legends, 123, 126
Lennon, John, 309
Lenquette, Youri, 222, 223, 225–26, 283, 306–8, 311–15
Lewis, Richard, 217–26, 229, 230
Lianos, Lex, 202
Lifticket, 102
Litwin, Peter, 19, 40, 59, 60, 64
Live! Tonight! Sold Out!, 272–73, 314–15
Logan, Glen, 38, 81, 118–21, 204, 316
Loiselle, Ryan, 12, 18–19, 168, 195, 247, 277
Lollapalooza, 295, 301
Lonely Moans, 42, 317
Long Gone John, 137
Loop, 142
Los Brujos, 255–58, 261
Love, Courtney, 161, 162, 172, 174, 185, 186, 210, 229, 253, 254, 257–60, 264, 267, 274, 279–81, 284, 289, 293, 297, 313
 Cobain and, 159, 209, 229, 235, 239, 254, 284, 286, 297
Love, Gerard, 197, 235, 238–40
Love Battery, 26, 49, 121
Lubricated Goat, 220
Lukin, Matt, 83, 123, 217, 234, 253
Lush, 19, 28, 30, 38, 57, 78, 317

Mabra, Maria, 70, 185, 250, 278, 280–82
Machine, 7, 12, 123
Macias, Tony, 131
MacLeod, Murdo, 109–12, 214, 316
Magnet Men, 14
Malakie, Marc, 195
Man Ray, 139, 144
Manson, Charles, 113

Marander, Tracy, 6–8, 105, 150–51, 153, 158–59, 183
Marsh, Sam, 170–71, 175
Mascis, J, 98, 142, 146, 149, 158
Matador, 137–38
Maximum Rocknroll, 119, 120, 245
Maxwell's, 235
May, Jim, 10, 11, 14, 17
Mazzy Star, 210, 313
MC5, 99, 248
McCartney, Paul, 119
McCorkle, Steve, 273
McDonnell, Evelyn, 275
McDonnell, Sean, 317
McDowell, Mike, 27
McKinnon, Ian, 68, 126, 317
McManus, Michael, 197, 218–20, 222, 225, 227–30
Meat Puppets, 285
Medelicious, 108, 252
Meijers, JB, 201
Melody Maker, 284
Melvins, 2, 3, 7, 10, 16, 17, 18, 33, 49, 60, 63, 71, 72, 79, 81, 108, 121, 123, 125, 127, 134, 160, 166, 167, 272–76, 312
Men Without Hats, 188
Mercury Records, 153
Metal Church, 2–3, 16
Metallica, 3, 263, 285, 288
Metropolis, 26
Midway Still, 176
Miller, George, 61
Minor Threat, 140
Mission of Burma, 140
MIT, 140, 144–45, 148
Monkees, 134
Monkeyshines, 87
Montgomery, Craig, 193, 215
Moody, Rod, 41, 135–36, 138
Moon, Slim, 6, 8–10, 14, 19, 25, 30, 32–34, 37–38, 43–44, 55, 59, 68, 82, 94, 135, 150–51, 156, 169, 170, 173, 186–87, 194, 198, 317
Moore, Dale, 317
Moore, Eric, 75, 128, 207

Moore, Thurston, 303

Morales, Jason, 32–34, 68, 154

Morasky, Mike, 41, 63, 81, 101, 102, 103

Moriarty, Steve, 55–57, 95, 124, 126, 169, 187, 194, 250, 279–83

Morris, Paul, 12–15

Mother Love Bone, 153

Motor Sports International Garage, 164–66

Mould, Bob, 121

Mousetrap, 36

MTV, 149, 203–4, 219, 224, 244, 261, 286, 287, 290, 293–97

MTV Brazil, 262–63

MTV Live and Loud, 295–96

MTV Unplugged, 224, 261, 293–94

Mudhoney, 47, 63, 68, 69, 72, 75, 79, 80, 83, 84, 95, 96, 98, 99, 108, 109, 111, 121, 122, 152, 161, 164, 207, 217, 218, 235, 252, 254, 277, 296

Munat, Ben, 73, 75, 82, 169, 247–48

Murphy, Eric Sean, 202

Music 6000, 154

Muzak, 27, 60

Myers, John, 120

Myles-Era, Ronna, 29–30, 52, 52, 79–82, 151–52

My Name, 23, 233, 235

Napalm Sunday, 52

Naubert, Brian, 1

Naz, Dave, 160

Nelson, Monica, 71

Neoboys, 184

New Hope Records, 65

New Music Seminar (NMS), 91, 279

New Radiant Storm King, 117, 142

New Zealand, 220, 223, 230

Nicholls, Mike, 281

Nirvana:

    "About a Girl," 105, 224, 274

    "All Apologies," 215, 271

    Asia/Pacific tour of, 216–32, 233

    "Beans," 156

    "Been a Son," 134

    "Beeswax," 198

    Bleach, 23, 71, 72, 78, 81, 82, 84–85, 87, 88, 94, 97, 98, 104, 105, 107, 134, 154, 169, 172, 187, 200, 201, 216, 217, 218, 223–24, 251, 252, 272, 304

    Blew, 108, 199

    demo recordings of, 17–24, 25

    "Dive," 187–88

    "Downer," 159, 187–88

    "Dumb," 271

    in Europe, 109–11, 134, 224, 233–42

    first performance of, 27–28

    first release of, 61–62

    first tour of, 72–93

    "Floyd the Barber," 159, 190

    gay rights and, 243–45

    "Heart-Shaped Box," 271, 283

    "In Bloom," 135, 161, 244

    Incesticide, 23, 188, 241, 255, 260

    In Utero, 215, 238, 244, 270–84

    In Utero tour of, 181, 261, 284, 285–301, 305

    "Lithium," 135, 155

    "Love Buzz," 61–63, 67–68, 76, 94, 109, 159–60, 190

    "Mexican Seafood," 159, 199

    "Molly's Lips," 274

    "Mr. Moustache," 159

    name of, 28

    Nevermind, 105, 135, 169, 172, 190, 191, 194–97, 198, 202, 204–7, 211, 216, 218–20, 224–25, 233, 236, 237, 243, 245, 249–51, 270, 272, 277, 279, 290, 300, 304

    "On a Plain," 192

    "Pennyroyal Tea," 271

    "Sappy," 116

    "Scentless Apprentice," 271

    second tour of, 94–106

    "Sliver," 172, 176, 237, 274

    "Smells Like Teen Spirit," 70, 190, 196, 201–3, 206, 213, 217–19, 236, 241, 243, 259–62, 264, 265, 272

    social activism of, 180, 182, 183, 186, 242–45

"Something in the Way," 192, 229
in South America, 255–69, 290
"Spank Thru," 217, 274
"Stain," 134
"Stay Away," 105
success and fame of, 181–82, 206, 207,
    209, 212–13, 215, 216, 218–21, 232,
    233, 236, 242, 247–50, 252, 255, 270,
    285–87
in United Kingdom, 169–73, 210–14
women and, 181–84, 186, 279
"You Know You're Right," 301
Nirvana Live Guide, xvi
Nisqually Delta Podunk Nightmare, 6
Nomeansno, 14
No More Wars, 180–81
No On 9, 243–44
Not Bad for a Girl, 186
Novoselic, Krist, 2–8, 10, 15–16, 17–19,
    31, 33, 34, 39, 44, 47, 55, 58–59, 63,
    71, 77–90, 95, 100, 103, 105, 111, 112,
    123–25, 129–31, 134, 141–45,
    147–49, 151, 155–57, 159–60, 166,
    168, 171–73, 176, 177, 180, 181, 187,
    189, 191, 193–96, 199, 200, 206–11,
    213, 226, 228–31, 233–35, 237, 239,
    241, 244, 253, 254, 257, 260, 261,
    265, 268, 279, 281, 286, 289, 292–93,
    295, 297, 298, 301–4, 312–14
Novoselic, Robert, 3, 63
Noxious Fumes, 7, 10, 27
Nubbin, 132, 180
Nunbait, 216

Off Ramp, 162, 175
Oily Bloodmen, 73, 317
OK Hotel, 190
Ong, Dana, 117, 140, 141, 144–45, 148
Orth, Lisa, 135
Osborne, Buzz, 71, 275
Outhouse, 100–101

Palace, 225, 229
Palladium, 193
Pansy Division, 108, 243, 245

Paperclip, 109–10
Paradogs, 200
Pavitt, Bruce, 23, 26, 27, 50, 55–56, 60,
    61, 64–67, 95, 103, 135–37, 163,
    250–52
Pavlovic, Steve, 217, 218, 223, 225
Pearl Jam, 149, 153, 251, 263, 277, 282,
    285, 295
Pele, 242
Pen Cap Chew, 12
Peringer, Robin, 69, 84, 175–76, 246
Perry, Seth, 73, 75, 125
Peters, Dan, 158, 164, 168, 234, 296
Peterson, Charles, 26, 135
Peterson, Cole, 106
Peterson, Ed, 83
Peterson, Erik, 83
Pickerel, Mark, 55, 127, 153, 251
Pinkerton, Peyton, 142, 145, 147–49, 151
Pirata Industrial, 257
Pixies, 157, 164
Plaster, Carl, 128, 289
Poirier, Glenn, 12, 14
Poison Idea, 163, 166
Poison-Tete, Victor, xvi, 145
Polygram, 153
Poneman, Jonathan, 23, 37, 40, 50, 56,
    60, 61, 64, 66–67, 94–96, 103, 124,
    135–37, 163, 250–52
Pop, Iggy, 117, 145, 193
PopLlama, 54–55
Porn Orchard, 14
Posies, 121, 153
Poukkula, Tony, 2–5
Preston, Joe, 194
Primus, 140, 188
Proton Energy Pills, 217
Prowse, Ian, 242
Psychlodds, 4, 76–78
Psycho Samaritan, 25
Public News, 86
Pugh, Chris, 26, 27, 34, 97
Pukkelpop, 261
Purkey, Bruce, 2, 10–11, 13–15, 23–24,
    48, 98

Purkey, John, 7, 10, 17–18, 21–23, 28, 67, 96, 123, 127, 150, 159, 204, 247, 277, 314
Pyramid Club, 93, 145, 152

Quinn, Chris, 18, 33, 46, 49, 51, 94–95, 126, 252, 253, 272

Rainbow Tavern, 26
Raincoats, 172, 177
Ramones, 140
Ranaldo, Lee, 184
Rape Relief, 183
Rat at Rat R, xvi
Rawhead Rex, 75
Razor's Edge Recording, 274
Reading Festival, 238, 240–42
Reagan, Ronald, 205
Reciprocal Recording, 17, 20, 67, 116
Red Hot Chili Peppers, 257, 263–65, 269, 285
Reid, Larry, 82–83
Reko/Muse, 79, 81, 183
REM, 153
Rice, Anne, 274
Rich, Dana, 54
Riddle, Daniel, 42–43, 73, 157, 174, 176–78, 181, 248
Riot Grrrl, 182, 184–86
Rizzo, Rick, 53, 104, 122
Robinson, Geoff, 50, 51, 58–59, 70, 75, 96–97, 136, 138
Robinson, Mark, 53, 163, 170, 288
Rock Against Rape, 186, 279
Rocket, 118, 119
Rock for Choice, 186, 209–10
Rogers, Neil, 164
Rolling Stone, 119, 249
Rolling Stones, 248
Rollins, Henry, 102, 178
Romero, Damon, 19–20, 30, 31, 39–40, 45, 52, 57, 75–76, 78, 80–81, 151–54
Room Nine, 26
Rose, Axl, 244
Rose, Kevin, 188, 197, 205

Roseland, 279
Rosemus, Rich, 317
Rosenfelder, John, 204
Roth, Rob, 71
Rough Trade, 137–38, 274
Roy, Jim, 146, 149
Rubin, Vadim, 116, 118, 120, 126, 130
Rudzitis, Ron "Nine," 26
Rutmanis, Kevin, 93, 249

SABA, 26
St. Thomas, Kurt, 202
Saltpeter, 164
São Paulo, 268
Saturday Night Live (SNL), 165, 234, 244, 283
Satyricon, 74–76, 177
Saucer, 37, 252, 253
Schemel, Larry, 28, 55, 282
Schemel, Patty, 159, 185
Scientists, 220
Scratch Acid, 33, 149
Scrawl, 184
Scream, 168–69, 196, 303
Screaming Trees, 55, 127, 153, 188, 189, 277
Seattle, Wash., 35–48, 49, 73, 74, 107–10, 129, 141, 149, 152, 163, 175, 185, 202, 220, 245–47, 252, 277–78
Sebba, Jardel, 267, 268
Second Child, 218, 223, 226, 231
Seven Year Bitch, 279
Sex Pistols, 266
S.G.M., 106
Shark Sandwich, 52
Shepherd, Ben, 98
Shipman, Charles, 146, 148
Shocking Blue, 61–62
Shonen Knife, 55, 134, 172
Silent Treatment, 11
Silly Killers, 26
Silva, John, 193, 197
Silver, Susan, 26, 153
Silver Jews, 145
Simmons, Tracy, 97

Sims, Rick, 204–5, 248, 251, 270–71, 296
Sinder, Josh, 234, 251–52, 282, 284
Singer, Shambie, 42, 58, 61, 64, 91, 93,
    96, 114–15, 152, 161
Singles, 278
Sin Hipster, 178
Sister Double Happiness, 205, 206
Sister Skelter, 18, 45, 46
Skid Row, 1, 7, 9, 12
Skin Barn, 317
Skin Yard, 16, 81, 73, 160
Slapshot, 183
Slaughter Shack, 94, 140
Smashing Pumpkins, 202, 203
Smear, Pat, 288, 289, 295, 297, 303–4,
    308
Smith, George, 9, 39, 44–45, 51–52, 54,
    62, 117, 126, 132, 150, 154, 157–58,
    233
Smith, Lisa, 54, 158–59, 185–86, 200, 313
SNFU, 188
Snyder, Jon, 155, 156
Social Distortion, 188
Solyan, Tim, 141, 143, 172–73
Sonics, 225
Sonic Youth, 13, 63, 84, 140, 153, 161,
    179–80, 184, 199, 234, 235, 282, 285
Sons of Ishmael, 11, 12
Soria, Jose, 89–90
Soul Asylum, 10
Sound City Studios, 191–92
Soundgarden, 41, 56, 67, 91, 95, 98, 109,
    121, 140, 152, 153, 188, 251, 263,
    278, 282
South America, 255–69, 290
Soylent Green, 2, 11
Spin, 285
Sprinkler, 207
SST Records, 56, 205
Stahl, Franz, 191
Stahl, Pete, 191
Staley, Layne, 264
Steel Pole Bath Tub, 41, 63, 102
Stella, André, 262–63, 266–67
Stephen, Rod, 240–42

Stereolab, 288
Steuben, Fred, 252–54
Stomach Pump, 245–46
Stone by Stone, 85
Stooges, 99, 164, 193
Sub Pop, 20, 22, 23, 33, 40, 42, 44, 54–57,
    60–66, 69, 74, 75, 83, 84, 89, 92,
    94–100, 103, 105, 107–9, 116, 118,
    121, 122, 124, 126, 129, 135–39, 152,
    154, 155, 161–65, 187, 195, 216, 217,
    236, 250–52, 274, 277
Sub Pop Singles Club, 62, 96, 124, 201
Sub Pop 200, 65–67, 69, 70, 71, 84, 217
Subvert, 11, 18
Sugar, 121
Sun City Girls, 35, 85, 90
Surgery, 92, 317
Swallow, 26, 27, 41, 67, 97
Swanson, Dave, 86
Swaziland White Band, 89
Sweek, Brad, 26
Sweet Lickin' Honey Babes, 146
Sympathy for the Record Industry
    (SFTRI), 137
Szankiewicz, Henry, 108, 253, 254

Tad, 60, 62, 64, 68, 95, 99, 108–11, 116,
    122, 128–31, 133–34, 143, 200, 234,
    252, 278, 282, 284
Tafoya, Tim, 31
Takino, Chris, 54
Team Dresch, 245
Teenage Fanclub, 197
Television Personalities, 212
Tennis, Whiting, 59
Terror Bull Ted, 206
Thinking Fellers Union Local 282,
    137, 162
Thomson, Paul, 176, 210–11, 213–14
Thornucopia, 53
Thorstensen, Gary, 60
Thrasher, Lindsey, 62, 80, 105, 121–22,
    203
Three Merry Widows, 146
Thrown Ups, 56, 66, 71, 246

Top of the Pops, 213
Treacherous Jaywalkers, 50, 56
Treacy, Dan, 212–13
Treeclimbers, 60
Tree House, 30
Treehouse, 29, 78
Tremeni, Warren, 100
Tribe 8, 245
Triebwasser, David, 82
Triple J, 217–18
Tropicana, 183
Trosper, Justin, 48, 126, 194
Trower, Jennie, 158–59
True, Everett, 147
Truell, Lynn, 206–10
Truly, 71
Trusnovic, Tom, 87, 89, 91
Tumbleweed, 217
Turner, Steve, 72, 246, 254, 289, 291
24-7 Spyz, 100, 140

U-Men, 13, 47
United Kingdom, 107–9, 169–73, 210–14
University of Washington, 124
Uno, Conrad, 54–55
Unrest, 53
Unwound, 48
Urge Overkill, 191

Vail, Tobi, 127, 153, 182
Vampire Lezbos, 22, 28
van de Geer, Chris, 226, 230
Vanderhoof, Kurdt, 16
Vanderpool, Scott, 26, 27, 37, 39, 50,
    58–62, 66, 95, 120–21, 135, 234
Varnum, Matt, 72
Vaselines, 134, 164
Vedder, Eddie, 295
Vegas Voodoo, 121, 131
Velvetone, 55
Verbal Abuse, 12
Victim's Family, 141, 173
Vig, Butch, 191–92
Vogue, 278
Voivod, 188

Vomit Launch, 62
von Balthazar, Troy, 286–88, 291–93, 300
von Bargen, Ryan, 181–82, 190–93,
    234–35
von Ohlerking, David, 85–86, 88–89,
    106

Wahl, Jon, 88, 137, 235
Walkabouts, 66
Walker, Bill, 188
Walker, Brett, 63
Walsh, Lloyd, 89
Warby, Russell, 109, 171
Warner Bros. Records, 250
Was, Don, 303
Washam, Rey, 149, 159
Waterfront Records, 217
Watson, Pat, 2
WBCN Rock 'n' Roll Rumble, 117–18
Western Washington University, 252–54
WFNX, 202, 203
Whiting, David, 22, 28, 29, 43, 45
Whittaker, Bob, 47
Whitworth, Kevin, 49–50, 67–68, 136,
    299
Wilcox, Kathi, 182
Willman, Ty, 37, 119, 278–79
Wipers, 178
Witchypoo, 156, 194
WNUR, 119–20
Wongs, 188
Wood, Crispin, 84–85, 105, 127–28, 139,
    142–44, 149, 163
Wood, Jeff, 317
Wool, 191
Wright, Blake, 55

X, 282

Yamano, Naoko, 172, 212, 232, 291,
    296–97
Yammer, David, 65, 87–88, 316
Yankovic, "Weird Al," 233
Yellow Snow, 1, 2
Young, Neil, 234, 304, 309

Young Fresh Fellows, 29
Young Pioneers, 26, 27
Your Flesh, 103
Youth of Today, 13
Yow, David, 235–36, 279

Zapata, Mia, 124, 261, 279–83
Zedek, Thalia, 286, 289–91, 293, 294,
    298, 299, 300
Zed Records, 118
Ziede, Elias, 257